ROYAL HISTORICAL SOCIETY

STUDIES IN HISTORY

New Series

POWER AND BORDER LORDSHIP IN MEDIEVAL FRANCE

POWER AND BORDER LORDSHIP
IN MEDIEVAL FRANCE

THE COUNTY OF THE PERCHE,
1000–1226

Kathleen Thompson

THE ROYAL HISTORICAL SOCIETY
THE BOYDELL PRESS

First published 2002

A Royal Historical Society publication
Published by The Boydell Press
an imprint of Boydell & Brewer Ltd
PO Box 9, Woodbridge, Suffolk IP12 3DF, UK
and of Boydell & Brewer Inc.
PO Box 41026, Rochester, NY 14604–4126, USA
website: http://www.boydell.co.uk

ISBN 0 86193 254 4

ISSN 0269–2244

A catalogue record for this book is available
from the British Library

Library of Congress Cataloging-in-Publication Data
Thompson, Kathleen, 1951–
    Power and border lordship in medieval France : the county of
the Perche, 1000–1226 / Kathleen Thompson.
        p. cm. – (Studies in history. New series, ISSN 0269–2244)
    Includes bibliographical references and index.
    ISBN 0–86193–254–4 (alk. paper)
    1. Perche (France) – History.   2. Perche (France) –
Biography.   3. Rotrou family.   I. Title.   II. Royal Historical
Society studies in history. New series.
DC611.P42 T46 2002
944'.2021 – dc21   2001037855

This book is printed on acid-free paper

Printed in Great Britain by
Antony Rowe Ltd, Chippenham, Wiltshire

Contents

In memory of my father,
Herbert Hapgood

List of Maps

List of Figures

Publication of this volume was aided by a grant from the Scouloudi Foundation, in association with the Institute of Historical Research.

Acknowledgements

The preparation of this book has left me with many debts to acknowledge. I am particularly grateful to Edmund King who, assisted by David Crouch, supervised the doctoral research on which the book is based and who has advised and encouraged me over a number of years. Without the support of the University of Sheffield, which enabled me to carry out full-time research at a time of life when such opportunities are seldom available, that doctoral research would not have been undertaken. I would also like to thank the archivists and librarians without whom no historian can work effectively, in particular the staff of the Archives départementales of the Eure-et-Loir at Chartres and of the Orne at Alençon, together with the library staff in the Bibliothèques municipales at Nogent-le-Rotrou and Alençon. In England I have made most demands on the library staff at the University of Sheffield, Sheffield Hallam University and the Brotherton Library of the University of Leeds, and they have always responded courteously and helpfully.

For points of clarification and interpretation, as well as for fellowship and encouragement I am grateful to many scholars, but especially to Julia Barrow, Jean-Michel Bouvris, Marjorie Chibnall, Richard Dace, Véronique Gazeau, Lindy Grant, Judith Green, Katharine Keats-Rohan, the late Tom Keefe, Carlos Laliena Corbera, Graham Loud, Jane Martindale, Alan Murray, Daniel Power, Len Scales, Nicholas Vincent, Simon Walker and Alex Woolf. Although my husband's academic interests lie elsewhere, he too must be thanked for his unfailing support and welcome advice, as well as for the photograph of the Château Saint-Jean at Nogent-le-Rotou which appears on the dust-jacket. I am particularly grateful to John and Eleanor Magilton for organising the maps.

Finally two scholars need special acknowledgement: Richard Fletcher of the University of York who first directed me to read the *Ecclesiastical history* of Orderic Vitalis, and David Bates, who developed that Anglo-Norman interest, fostering and encouraging my research.

Kathleen Thompson,
February 2001

Abbreviations

AD	Archives départementales
AN	Archives nationales
Annales	*Annales: économies, sociétés, civilisations*
ANS	*Anglo-Norman Studies*
BL	British Library
BN	Bibliothèque nationale
BSHAO	*Bulletin de la Société historique et archéologique de l'Orne*
cant.	canton
CCM	*Cahiers de civilisation médiévale*
CDF	*Calendar of documents preserved in France*, ed. J. H. Round, London 1899
ch.-l. du cant.	chef-lieu du canton
Clairets	*Abbaye royale de Notre Dame des Clairets: histoire et cartulaire, 1202–1790*, ed. le vicomte de Souancé, Nogent-le-Rotrou 1894
Cluny	*Recueil des chartes de l'abbaye de Cluny*, ed. A. Bernard and A. Bruel, Paris 1876–1903
CMD	*Cartulaire de Marmoutier pour le Dunois*, ed. E. Mabille, Châteaudun 1874
cme	commune
CMPerche	*Cartulaire de Marmoutier pour le Perche*, ed. P. Barret, Mortagne 1894
CP	*Complete peerage of England, Scotland, Ireland, Great Britain and the United Kingdom*, ed. G. E. Cokayne, London 1910–59
DB	*Liber censualis, seu Domesday Book*, London 1783–1816
EHR	*English Historical Review*
GC	D. Sammarthanus, *Gallia Christiana in provincias ecclesiasticas distributa*, ed. P. Piolin, Paris 1870–7
Gesta	*Gesta regis Henrici secundi*, ed. W. Stubbs (RS xlix, 1867)
HMC	Historical Manuscripts Commission
La Trappe	*Cartulaire de l'abbaye de Notre-Dame de la Trappe*, ed. H. de Charencey, Alençon 1889
LBSMS	MS Livre Blanc de Saint-Martin de Sées (Bibliothèque de l'évêché de Sées)
MGH	Monumenta Germaniae Historica
MGH SS	Monumenta Germaniae Historica, Scriptores
Monasticon	W. Dugdale, *Monasticon anglicanum*, ed. J. Stevens, London 1817, repr. 1846

MSAEL	*Mémoires de la Société archéologique d'Eure-et-Loir*
NDC	*Cartulaire de Notre-Dame de Chartres*, ed. E. de Lépinois and L. Merlet, Chartres 1865
NLR	*Saint-Denis de Nogent-Le-Rotrou, 1031–1789*, ed. Charles Métais, Vannes 1894
OV	Orderic Vitalis, *Ecclesiastical history*, ed. M. Chibnall, Oxford 1969–80
Perseigne	*Cartulaire de l'abbaye cistercienne de Perseigne*, ed. G. Fleury, Mamers 1880
PL	*Patrologia Latina*, ed. J. P. Migne, Paris 1844–64
PR	Pipe roll
PRO	Public Record Office
PRS	Pipe Roll Society
RCVD	Recueil sur la Chartreuse du Val Dieu (Bibliothèque municipale d'Alençon, MS 112)
RHF	*Recueil des historiens des Gaules et de la France*, ed. M. Bouquet and others, Paris 1869–1904
RS	Rolls Series
SPC	*Cartulaire de Saint-Père de Chartres*, ed. B. Guérard, Paris 1840
Tiron	*Cartulaire de l'abbaye de la Sainte-Trinité de Tiron*, ed. L. Merlet, Chartres 1883
VLM	*Cartulaire de Saint-Vincent du Mans*, ed. R. Charles and S. Menjot d'Elbenne, Le Mans 1886

Introduction

In November 1135 the English king, Henry I, lay dying at Lyons-la-Forêt in upper Normandy, surrounded by the nobles, officers and ecclesiastics who made up the royal entourage in a period when the king of England was, more often than not, also duke of Normandy.[1] Among these men was the king's former son-in-law, Rotrou count of Mortagne, a man of mature years, probably well into his middle age and an experienced warrior who had participated in the First Crusade and who had also fought, apparently with some distinction, against the Muslims in Spain. In his account of the death scene and elsewhere in his *Ecclesiastical history* the Anglo-Norman historian, Orderic Vitalis, describes Rotrou as count of Mortagne, but by 1135 men were beginning to call him the Percheron count (*comes perticensis*), and Rotrou and his descendants would themselves adopt that style. This confusion of nomenclature is revealing, for it marks the final stage in the emergence of a new political unit, as the disparate collection of lands belonging to Rotrou's family coalesced into the county of the Perche; it is the formation of that county and its subsequent history which are the subject of this book.

This study illuminates a number of issues that have preoccupied historians of western Europe in the central Middle Ages, the period from around 900 to 1200. Historical analyses of these years have usually been developed in the language of political fragmentation and decline because the successors of the emperor Charlemagne (768–814) were unable to prevent the disintegration of the Carolingian empire and the emergence of territorial principalities that were apparently independent of royal control. For more than two hundred years power was localised until the recovery of the monarchy under King Philip II Augustus of France (1180–1223). It is with his reassertion of royal power over the principalities and the emergence of other centralised monarchies, the forerunners of modern nation states, that the central Middle Ages have been taken to end.

Resistance to the Viking raids on western Europe in the ninth century was most effectively organised at local level by officials, the counts, who ran Charlemagne's empire for his immediate descendants. They sought to secure the services of fighting men by making grants of the royal land under their control in return for military service, and a new military device was introduced, the castle. As time passed the counts secured hereditary control of their offices, together with the royal property that went with them, becoming in effect 'territorial princes'. In this response to the Viking raids the great French historian, Marc Bloch (1886–1944), saw the foundations of the

---

1   OV vi. 448.

1

so-called 'feudal system'.[2] This process need not necessarily undermine royal power as long as the king controlled the distribution of patronage, but, as Janet Nelson pointed out in her biography of Charles the Bald, at the end of the ninth century attendance at the royal court was hardly worthwhile because, by then, the kings had less to give than the princes.[3]

By the year 987, when the Carolingian dynasty was finally supplanted by the Capet family as kings of the Franks, large tracts of territory were controlled by the princes.[4] Territorial fragmentation did not end with the emergence of the major power blocs, however, and as the eleventh century progressed ever-smaller units are revealed by the sources.[5] In 1953 Georges Duby published a study of the Mâconnais in which he argued that continued fragmentation was the result of the seizure of power by local lords, who now controlled the castles that had originally been intended to protect the surrounding population from Viking attack. Duby's studies of the judicial institutions of the Mâconnais suggested to him that up to the tenth century the counts had preserved the forms of Carolingian government and had maintained public order, but that a crucial change had taken place around the year 1000. The old institutions had collapsed and there was no protection for the general populace from the rapacity and demands of the castellans and their mounted troops, the knights.[6]

Duby's observations caught the imagination of a generation of historians and several regional studies produced findings that supported his main conclusions.[7] Attention was thus focused on the year 1000 and historians began to look on it as an important watershed in the history of not only France, but western Europe. Those working on the southern parts of the Frankish kingdom suggested that Roman institutions had survived in the south until they fell prey to the knightly onslaught at the beginning of the eleventh century, and movements such as the Peace of God were perceived as attempted controls on that violence.[8] Although some historians began to

---

[2] M. Bloch, *Feudal society*, 2nd edn, London 1962, trans. by L. Manion of *La Société féodale*, Paris 1939–40, esp. ch. ii.

[3] J. Nelson, *Charles the Bald*, London 1992, 254–64.

[4] J. Dhondt, *Études sur la naissance des principautés territoriales en France (IXe–Xe siècle)*, Bruges 1948, 1.

[5] J.-F. Lemarignier, 'La Dislocation du *pagus* et le problème des *consuetudines*', in *Mélanges d'histoire du moyen âge dédiés à la mémoire de Louis Halphen*, Paris 1951, 401–10.

[6] G. Duby, *La Société aux xie et xiie siècles dans la région mâconnaise*, Paris 1953. Duby's analysis was first published as 'Recherches sur l'evolution des institutions judiciaires pendant le xe et le xie siècle dans le sud de la Bourgogne', *Le Moyen Âge* 4th ser. i (1946), 149–94; ii (1948), 15–38, trans. as 'The evolution of judicial institutions', in his *The chivalrous society*, ed. C. Postan, London 1977, 15–58.

[7] A. Chédeville, *Chartres et ses campagnes (XIe–XIIIe s.)*, Paris 1973; G. Devailly, *Le Berry du Xe siècle au milieu du XIIIe siècle*, Paris 1973; J.-P. Poly, *Le Provence et la société féodale, 879–1166*, Paris 1976.

[8] P. Bonnassie, *La Catalogne du milieu du xe à la fin du xie siècle: croissance et mutation d'une société*, Toulouse 1975–6. For an expression of the dominance of this interpretation see R. Delort (ed.), *La France de l'an mil*, Paris 1990. For a summary of the scholarship on the Peace

voice doubts about these interpretations, it was not until the 1990s that developments of Duby's model were challenged with great conviction. Then the attack was led by Dominique Barthélemy whose work on the Vendômois led him to question what had come to be characterised as 'le mutation de l'an mil'.[9]

In preference to a revolution between the tenth and eleventh centuries Barthélemy proposed a revelation. There was no significant change in the way that society functioned around the year 1000, precipitated by an increase in lordly violence against their social inferiors. In preference to a great division between public order in the tenth century and the privatisation of power in the eleventh century, Barthélemy suggested that there lay a distinction in historians' understanding of the tenth and eleventh centuries. That distinction was a product of the monasteries' preservation of documents, giving details of their legal disputes with lordly neighbours, and these documents provide a much more detailed picture of what was happening in the eleventh century. As details of legal proceedings began to be preserved the vocabulary used to describe them started to evolve, but the processes they describe were subject to evolutionary rather than revolutionary change.[10] Although Thomas Bisson has called attention to the usefulness of the 'feudal revolution' as a concept in 'characterizing and explaining the enormously expanded and energized societies of post-millennial Europe', the prevailing orthodoxy in French historical studies has shifted.[11]

Rather than concentrating on the limitations of the king's position, which has been conventionally described as political weakness, the question has been turned on its head and the more detailed documentation of the eleventh century has been exploited to show that other controls operated to regulate society.[12] It is not necessarily appropriate, therefore, to characterise the period as one of political weakness.[13] It could be seen instead as a period of experimentation when territorial princes operated with less recourse to the king, but his position was always recognised. Eventually the kings of the Franks asserted their traditional powers and exploited new developments in the law

---

of God see T. Head and R. Lander (eds), *The peace of God: social violence and religious response in France around the year 1000*, Ithaca, NY 1992.

[9] D. Barthélemy, *La Société dans le comté de Vendôme de l'an mil au xive siècle*, Paris 1993.

[10] Idem, 'La Mutation féodale a-t-elle eu lieu? (Note critique)', *Annales* xlvii (1992), 767–75.

[11] T. N. Bisson, 'Reply: debate: the "feudal revolution" ', *Past & Present* clv (1997), 209. See also his 'The "feudal revolution" ', ibid. clii (1994), 6–42.

[12] P. Geary, 'Vivre en conflit dans une France sans état: typologie des mécanismes de règlement des conflits (1050–1200)', *Annales* xli (1986), 1107–33. Important studies on dispute resolution include F. Cheyette, '*Suum cuique tribuere*', *French Historical Studies* vi (1970), 287–99, and S. D. White, '*Pactum legem vincit et amor judicium*: the settlement of disputes by compromise in eleventh-century France', *American Journal of Legal History* xxii (1978), 281–308.

[13] For the limitations on royal power see J.-F. Lemarignier, *Le Gouvernement royal aux premiers temps capétiens (987–1108)*, Paris 1965.

and governmental practice to curtail the powers of the princes and to lay the foundations of the new centralised state that would become France.[14]

Before the accomplishment of this transformation in royal power, however, the kings of the Franks had to face down a major challenge. During the eleventh century the difficulties experienced by the kings in dealing with a number of territorial princes were increased when the duke of Normandy greatly enhanced his own position by the conquest of the kingdom of England in 1066. With access to the resources of the English kingdom the dukes of Normandy could more effectively defy Capetian kings and their newly acquired royal title lifted them to the status of rivals.[15] This threat of the over-mighty subject was compounded in the twelfth century by the rise of the so-called Angevin empire, when the challenges presented by the dukes of Normandy, the counts of Anjou and the dukes of Aquitaine were united in the person of Henry II of England, who held all these offices by inheritance and marriage.[16] In the second half of the twelfth century Henry and his sons, Richard and John, controlled more land than the king of the Franks and, with the advantage of their offshore kingdom, were masters of far greater resources.[17] Yet by the death of King Philip Augustus the power of the monarchy had been reasserted, the lands of the dukes of Normandy and counts of Anjou had been recovered by the king and their offices no longer existed, although the titles continued to be claimed by Henry II's descendants.[18]

The history of the Perche can make a significant contribution to the study of this period. Its history is essentially that of a lineage which, in the two hundred years before the failure of the male line in 1226, rose from apparently obscure origins to considerable prestige and a recognised position among the territorial princes of France. The family was renowned for its participation in almost every significant crusading venture and its members formed, through marriage, religious patronage and landholding, an extensive network of relationships across France, England, Spain and Sicily, extending even into the empire.

---

[14] B. Guenée, 'Les Généalogies entre l'histoire et la politique: la fierté d'être capétien en France au moyen âge', *Annales* xxx (1978), 450–74; J. W. Baldwin, *The government of Philip Augustus: foundations of French royal power in the Middle Ages*, Berkeley, CA 1986.

[15] The literature on the Norman Conquest is vast. For an overview see M. Chibnall, *The debate on the Norman Conquest*, Manchester 1999. On the cross-Channel implications see J. Le Patourel, *The Norman empire*, Oxford 1976; C. W. Hollister, 'Normandy, France and the Anglo-Norman *regnum*', *Speculum* li (1976), 202–42; D. Bates, 'Normandy and England after 1066', *EHR* civ (1989), 851–80.

[16] On the use of the term 'empire' see Chibnall, *Debate*, 115ff. On the Angevin realm see J. Boussard, *Le Gouvernement d'Henri II Plantagenêt*, Paris 1956, and J. Gillingham, *The Angevin empire*, London 1984.

[17] F. M. Powicke, *The loss of Normandy*, 2nd edn, Manchester 1960; J. C. Holt, 'The end of the Anglo-Norman realm', *Proceedings of the British Academy* lxi (1973), 3–45, repr. in his *Magna Carta and medieval government*, London 1985, 23–66, and 'The loss of Normandy and royal finance', in J. Gillingham and J. C. Holt (eds), *War and government in the Middle Ages: essays in honour of J. O. Prestwich*, Woodbridge 1984, 92–105.

[18] R.-H. Bautier (ed.), *La France de Philippe Auguste: temps des mutations*, Paris 1982; Baldwin, *Government*, 331ff.

A body of documentary material has survived which makes it possible to observe the Rotrous' powerbase. During the course of the eleventh and the early twelfth centuries a centre of power and influence was created in the Perche that reinforced the family's position through devices such as the count's court, the use of religious patronage and dispute settlement. In analysing territorial rivalries with neighbours, the construction of a clientele and the expression of power and piety through religious patronage it is possible to demonstrate how power and lordship actually worked over a long period when royal power was ineffective.

Yet this lineage does not conform to the specifics of Duby's model. In the years after 1000 members of the family built castles, engaged in warfare against their neighbours and attacked the property of the Church, but they did so within the existing power structures, as agents of their overlords rather than as independent and uncontrollable castellans. In the eleventh century the Rotrou lineage continued to acknowledge the overlordship of the counts of Blois/Chartres, as they had probably done for much of the tenth. The distancing of the Rotrous from their overlords did not take place until the 1100s when an alliance with the dukes of Normandy, first developed at the time of William the Conqueror, was exploited to the full. For the Rotrou counts the crucial factor was their geographical position as border lords and their ability to maintain several alignments.[19]

As the twelfth century progressed the rulers of the Perche were able to play an important part in western European politics as a result of the Perche's strategic position between the lands of the king of the Franks and the major power blocs of Normandy, Anjou and Blois, which had evolved from the territorial principalities of the ninth and tenth centuries. This role was maintained during the period when the power of Henry II of England and his sons eclipsed that of the French kings; the counts' role in the struggle between the kings and the rulers of the Angevin empire illustrates the strengths and weaknesses of the two sides.

As the challenge from the princes was faced down and the French monarchy was strengthened under Philip Augustus, it became much harder for the counts to sustain the position of the Perche. The devices used by the French king at the beginning of the thirteenth century to undermine them give an additional perspective on the nature of the kings' power. For historians, eager to trace the rise of centralised institutions, the emergence of a more prestigious monarchy ended the period of political dislocation that had begun with the collapse of the Carolingian empire. For those interested in the anatomy of power it marks the end of a phase during which kings found it difficult to work effectively with local forces such as the Rotrou lineage and sees the start of the harnessing of localised power to royal purposes.

---

[19] On borders see R. I. Burns, 'The significance of the frontier in the Middle Ages', in R. Bartlett and A. Mackay (eds), *Medieval frontier societies*, Oxford 1989, 307–30; J. A. Green, 'Lords of the Norman Vexin', in Gillingham and Holt, *War and government*, 47–61.

Figure 1
The house of Rotrou, c. 1000–1226

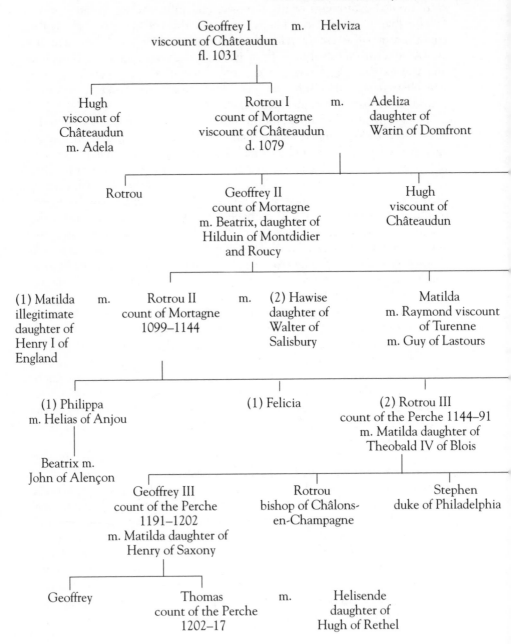

Geoffrey I m. Helviza
viscount of Châteaudun
fl. 1031

Hugh
viscount of
Châteaudun
m. Adela

Rotrou I m. Adeliza
count of Mortagne daughter of
viscount of Châteaudun Warin of Domfront
d. 1079

Rotrou

Geoffrey II
count of Mortagne
m. Beatrix, daughter of
Hilduin of Montdidier
and Roucy

Hugh
viscount of
Châteaudun

(1) Matilda m.
illegitimate
daughter of
Henry I of
England

Rotrou II
count of Mortagne
1099–1144

m. (2) Hawise
daughter of
Walter of
Salisbury

Matilda
m. Raymond viscount
of Turenne
m. Guy of Lastours

(1) Philippa
m. Helias of Anjou

(1) Felicia

(2) Rotrou III
count of the Perche 1144–91
m. Matilda daughter of
Theobald IV of Blois

Beatrix m.
John of Alençon

Geoffrey III
count of the Perche
1191–1202
m. Matilda daughter of
Henry of Saxony

Rotrou
bishop of Châlons-
en-Champagne

Stephen
duke of Philadelphia

Geoffrey

Thomas
count of the Perche
1202–17

m. Helisende
daughter of
Hugh of Rethel

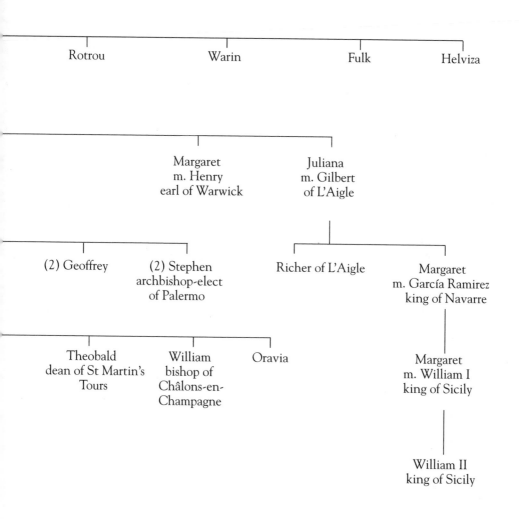

Rotrou   Warin   Fulk   Helviza

Margaret
m. Henry
earl of Warwick

Juliana
m. Gilbert
of L'Aigle

(2) Geoffrey

(2) Stephen
archbishop-elect
of Palermo

Richer of L'Aigle

Margaret
m. García Ramirez
king of Navarre

Theobald
dean of St Martin's
Tours

William
bishop of
Châlons-en-
Champagne

Oravia

Margaret
m. William I
king of Sicily

William II
king of Sicily

1

The Perche and its Counts

The Perche region of France is best-known for its forests and the sturdy Percheron workhorse, but these are not attractions to bring large numbers of visitors to the area and it is not a well-known region of France. For the English it lies off their chosen routes to the holiday destinations of the Dordogne or Provence, yet beyond the weekend break territory of Paris or Normandy. For the French it is a possible, though not highly sought-after, location for a *maison secondaire*. An ill-defined region, its name has been applied within an area, some 150 kilometres west of Paris, that stretches from the borders of Normandy as far south as Vendôme. This widespread use of the placename 'the Perche' reflects its origin in the great forest which once lay to the west of the Seine, but it is with the most northerly reaches of this area that the name came to be most closely associated. Here, in the hilly country between Chartres (Eure-et-Loir) and Alençon (Orne), more or less on the watershed between the Seine and Loire basins, the county of the Perche emerged (*see* map 1).

In common with many of the historic regions of France the Perche has no modern day administrative equivalent and is now distributed between the modern *départements* of Orne, Eure-et-Loir and Sarthe. None the less the area retains a sense of identity that defies modern boundaries and is more than the creation of a late twentieth-century tourist board. There is a self-awareness about the area, which in French renders it a 'pays – un territoire habité par une collectivité et constituant une réalité géographique dénommée'. This sense of internal cohesion found expression as long ago as the sixteenth century in the publication of a *coutume* for the Perche. A *coutume* is a body of customary law accepted and adhered to within a clearly demarcated area, and it is indeed the boundaries of the area where that body of customary law was accepted that define the Perche for the purposes of this study. The *coutume* was, however, a product of the creation of the Perche rather than its cause; for that cause it is necessary to look back beyond the sixteenth century to the beginning of the second millennium.[1]

The origins of the Perche lie in the central Middle Ages, that is in the

---

[1] For a definition of *coutume* and a brief history see A. Colin and H. Capitant, *Traité de droit civil*, ed. L. Julliot de la Morandière, i., Paris 1957, 112–17. For a general description of the *coutume* of the Perche see J. Yver, *Égalité entre héritiers et exclusion des enfants dotés: essai de géographie coutumière*, Paris 1966, 131–3. Details of communes where the *coutume* was accepted are given in G. Bry de la Clergerie, *Histoire des pays et comté du Perche et duché d'Alençon*, Paris 1620, rev. P. Siguret, Paris 1970, at pp. 10–15 of the notes section.

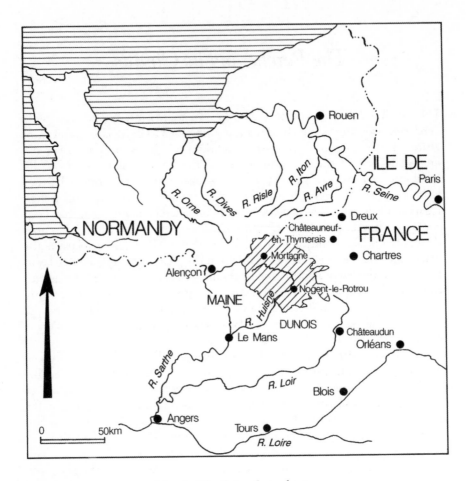

Map 1. The Seine-Loire basin

years around AD 1000, a period when royal power was effective only sporadically and the rulers of many small territories asserted their identity. Unlike most of these territories, however, the Perche was not based on an existing administrative unit, such as its neighbours, the counties of Maine and Chartres, nor was it coterminous with an ecclesiastical jurisdiction. It grew up at the margins of several larger units, and there was no major population focus nor great religious centre such as a cathedral or ancient abbey within it. It owed its existence to the ambition and energy of successive members of a lineage from the warrior elite, several of whom bore the personal name of Rotrou. In the area that would become the Perche there were rivalries between a number of kin-groups from this elite, but an ascendancy was ultimately established by the Rotrous who, on the basis of property and rights accumulated over several generations, succeeded in establishing themselves as counts in an entirely new political unit, the county of the Perche.

The first traceable member of the family is the Viscount Geoffrey who was active in the first third of the eleventh century. Under his son, Rotrou I, a contemporary of William the Conqueror, duke of Normandy (1035–87) and king of England (1066–87), and grandson, another Geoffrey, the position of the lineage was consolidated. In the fourth generation a second Count Rotrou established a formidable reputation as a warrior through his participation in the First Crusade and in the Spanish wars against the Muslims. He was an ally of the English king, Henry I (1100–35), and secured landed interests in England, marrying two English wives in the process. He was succeeded by his son and grandson, Count Rotrou III and Count Geoffrey III, but the lineage effectively ended when Count Geoffrey's son, Count Thomas, was killed at the battle of Lincoln in 1217. Thomas's uncle, Bishop William of Châlons-en-Champagne, ruled the Perche for nearly a decade, but he could leave no direct heirs with the result that on his death in 1226 the comital title became extinct and the family's property was divided between collateral heirs.

From a position of apparent obscurity, then, the Rotrous rose to play an important part in the high politics of France in the eleventh and twelfth centuries through a network of marriage and patronage connections, and their area of influence coalesced into the durable entity of the Perche. That process of coalescence has attracted scholars from the very emergence of history as a modern discipline and forms the subject of this study. A fine work by Gilles Bry de la Clergerie, *Histoire des pays et comté du Perche et duché d'Alençon*, published in 1620 in response to contemporary interest in customary law in the localities, established the chronology and underpins most of the subsequent historical work on the area. In the nineteenth century Marc Oeillet des Murs published a lengthy narrative history specifically on the house of Rotrou, *Histoire des comtes du Perche de la famille des Rotrou de 943 à 1231*, which runs to some 700 pages, and the Vicomte Olivier de Romanet made an important collection of references and texts in his *Géographie du*

Perche et chronologie de ses comtes suivies de pièces justicatives formant le cartulaire de cette province (1890–1902). His reconstruction of the genealogy of the Rotrou family and the numeration he assigned to the counts have found their way into most modern texts and are now more often taken as fact than hypothesis.

The materials on which all these studies have been based are varied. The counts of the Perche are rarely mentioned in contemporary narratives at any time during their ascendancy. Chronicles written in the kingdom of France pay scant attention to their activities and there are little more than passing references to the Rotrous in the English sources such as Roger of Howden and Ralph of Diss. Only Orderic Vitalis showed any sustained interest in the family, largely because they were both near neighbours of his own monastery at Saint-Evroul in southern Normandy and relations of the abbey's patrons, the L'Aigle lineage. A little information on the comital family may be obtained from necrologies, the records used by religious houses to preserve the memory of their patrons, and some light is shed on the activities of the counts by contemporary letter collections. There are, for example, references to the Rotrous among the correspondence of two of the most famous bishops of Chartres, Fulbert (1007–28) and Ivo (1090–1115), and they are mentioned by Abbot Suger of Saint-Denis (1122–51) and Hildebert, successively bishop of Le Mans (1096–1125) and archbishop of Tours (1125–33). The text of a letter written by a member of the comital family survives, together with a memorable pastoral letter directed to the Countess Richenza-Matilda.

Although these sources are not substantial, there is fortunately a large quantity of charter evidence preserved by the religious houses which the Rotrou counts patronised. These records present a necessarily one-sided picture for the house preserved only accounts of the legal proceedings which it won or the gifts made to it, but rarely recorded the property which it lost. None the less they are valuable indications of prevailing political, social and economic conditions and can be used to assess the extent of a donor's landed or other wealth, his social position as indicated by his entourage and indeed the counts' own self-image. In the parlance of medieval historians these records are known as the Rotrou family acts or *acta* and nearly three hundred of them can be identified, ranging in date from the first half of the eleventh century through to the 1220s. Most of this material is to be found in the archives départementales of the Eure-et-Loir and Orne, located respectively in Chartres and Alençon, but there are also important deposits in the Archives nationales and the Bibliothèque nationale in Paris, as well as in the archives of neighbouring *départements*. Sometimes it is even possible to locate material in institutions whose origins lie in this period; valuable records are still owned, for example, by the hospital at Nogent-le-Rotrou, the successor of the Maison-Dieu founded there in the twelfth century.

Somewhat surprisingly, perhaps, much material of this kind has been preserved in England, where the counts accumulated considerable holdings. It ranges from copies of grants, made to religious communities and preserved in their cartularies or record books, to surviving acts in favour of individuals to whom the counts granted or more usually leased land. This material has never been systematically studied from the perspective of the Rotrou counts and is particularly valuable because it can be placed in context and supplemented using the great record series produced by English government, such as the pipe rolls. It is therefore the case that the history of what is now a small and comparatively unknown region of France can in part be written in the British Library Manuscripts Room and the Public Record Office.

This documentary material is at first sight opaque and difficult to interpret. It is often undated and therefore not easily related to the information that can be derived from narrative sources. None the less it is, as it were, a first-hand account of comital power. Even the physical features of these acts can be used to make observations about the nature of comital government and, for example, the degree to which the counts had integrated personnel trained in the newly emerging schools of Paris into their entourages. The counts' benefactions to religious houses indicate the extent and location of their landed resources and their wealth. They are also a commentary on the counts' powers. Exemptions from such powers suggest that they were effective and a waiver was a privilege worth securing, while the grant of a proportion of a toll, for example, demonstrates capacity to levy that toll effectively at a particular point. For much of the period in question comital acts were witnessed by local men of status, demonstrating the counts' prestige. The toponymics, that is the placenames associated with individuals, are particularly valuable as an index of comital power, for they are perhaps the best indication of the area which recognised the authority of the Rotrous and which would eventually coalesce into the Perche.

It was by no means a large area. The boundaries of the *coutume* of the Perche encompass territory that is an irregular lozenge in shape, covering some 250,000 hectares and extending at its greatest width about 60 kilometres in a north/south direction and approximately 70 kilometres in an east/west direction. It is upland, frequently wooded, country traversed by narrow wet valleys, and the physical feature which gives the area its greatest cohesion is its most significant watercourse, the River Huisne, which forms in effect the crooked spine of the region. It rises in an area formerly covered by the forest of Blavou and runs erratically west to east before turning abruptly south near Saint-Germain-des-Grois (Orne, cant. Rémalard) and then running in a south-westerly direction for some 25 kilometres through Nogent-le-Rotrou and out of the county near La Ferté-Bernard (Sarthe). A few streams which run off the northern hills of the Perche flow into the Avre and the Sarthe rivers, the most notable of which is the River Hoëne, but it is remarkable that most of the watercourses which drain the region run into the Huisne. The river divides the area virtually in half; on the left bank to its north and east the country is often wooded, while on its right bank to the

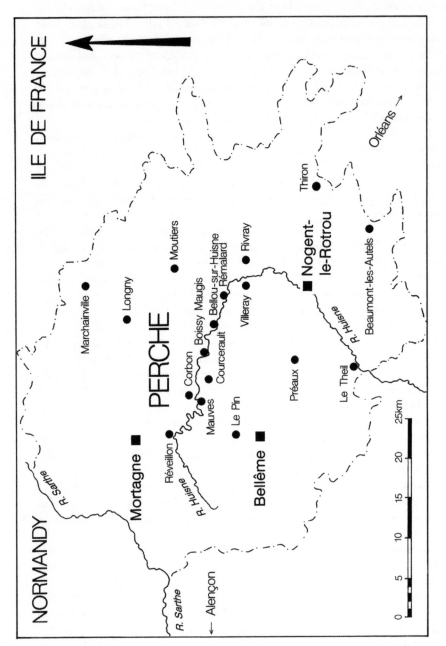

Map 2. The Perche

south and west lies open rolling countryside, which is essentially *pays d'élevage* or livestock-rearing country (*see* map 2).[2]

This division between the wooded areas and agricultural land is a reflection of the soils of the Perche, which indicates its position between two major geological formations.[3] The forested uplands are continuations of the flinty clay plateau of the Beauce, but lack the overlay of silt which gives that region its fertility. As a result it has never been worthwhile to clear the forests, which still run, with little clearance between them, from the forest of the Perche on the borders of Normandy, through the forests of Réno and Longny to the east of Mortagne (Orne, ch.-l. du cant.), towards the Bois de Voré and the forest of Saussay between the valleys of the Huisne and the Corbionne rivers. On small outcrops of the same geological formation, near Nogent-le-Rotrou, lie the Bois de Perchets and the woods of Les Clairets. The lowlands of the Perche, lying within the loop of the River Huisne, are marls whose impermeable nature lend themselves to grassland. This countryside is the classic bocage, cleared from the forest, but with many trees surviving in hedgerows, small woods and copses. None the less even in these areas the forest is not far away since it reappears on the rocky outcrops, which underlie, for example, the forest of Bellême and the Bois de Sublaines.

In the earliest references relating to the area, which date from the sixth century, the Perche is virtually synonymous with forest. These references mostly relate to the careers of holy men who withdrew to the inaccessible wastes of the Perche to practise their asceticism. St Avitus, for example, is described by Gregory of Tours in his 'Liber in gloria confessorum', as an abbot in the Chartres region which is called Pertensis. The cult of Avitus, and of others such as Laumer and Carileph, was later seized upon by ninth-century hagiographers who tell us little about the Perche in the sixth century, but demonstrate the perceptions of their own time concerning the 'vastas loci Perthici solitudines'.[4] An anonymous life of St Bohave of Chartres reinforces this impression of inaccessibility by describing the flight into the Percheron wood in AD 600 of Lothar II king of the Franks after an unsuccessful campaign against a rival.[5]

This is not to suggest, however, that the area was uninhabited in the years before 1000. It is clear that the woodlands, which covered the Perche and much of the rest of northern France in the early Middle Ages, were valuable resources and were exploited by their occupants in a mixed economy which included arable farming as well as the management of woodland products.[6]

---

[2] R. Musset, 'Le Perche – nom du pays', *Annales de géographie* xxviii (1919), 346.
[3] Idem, 'Le Relief du Perche', ibid. xxix (1920), 99–126.
[4] Gregory of Tours, 'Libri octo miraculorum, viii: liber in gloria confessorum', MGH Scriptores rerum merovingicarum i. 810. A. Poncelet, 'Les Saints de Micy', *Analecta Bollandiana* xxiv (1905), 11. For ninth-century hagiographers see T. Head, *Hagiography and the cult of saints: the diocese of Orléans, 800–1200*, Cambridge 1990, passim.
[5] *RHF* iii. 489b.
[6] On woodland economy see C. Wickham, 'European forests in the early Middle Ages:

Timber was the major resource, but pollarded trees were also harvested for stakes and poles, and deadwood and prunings could also be valuable. Pigs foraged among the trees and a payment known as *pasnagium*, which was associated with pig-rearing, could be very lucrative. Other animals such as horses and cattle were pastured in the forest and some sections might be exploited as *haies*, where arable farming was practised under licence. Woodland products, such as honey and wax, are mentioned in documents and the latter was clearly particularly important for ecclesiastical use. Finally there is evidence of metal-working in the region, not least in placenames, such as La Ferrière (Eure-et-Loir, cant. Nogent-le-Rotrou, cme Brunelles), Les Ferrières (Orne, cant. Moulins-la-Marche, cme Saint-Martin-les Pézerits) and Mont Ferré in the forest of Réno or Mézières (Orne, cant. Tourouvre, cme Les Croix Chemins). Indications can also be found in the names of individuals, such as Robert Maschefer (slag, clinker) who held a mortgage on the revenues of the priory at Bellême (Orne) in the twelfth century.[7]

This woodland economy prevailed over much of the area that became the Perche, but the records of religious houses also make it clear that quantities of grain were produced in a locality which is scarcely noted for its arable products today, and horses and cattle were also raised. For these agricultural activities it is necessary to look to the area around Bellême, the upper valley of the River Huisne and the hilly country around Mortagne. Here placename studies indicate that the countryside had been exploited for agricultural purposes since the early Middle Ages and probably since Roman times, as the Roman villa found at Villiers-sous-Mortagne indicates. There is a high incidence of placenames containing the element 'court', such as Courcerault, Courgeon, Courgeoût and Colonard. These compound placenames often contain a Frankish personal name as their second component and suggest an agricultural settlement which became the property of, or at least maintained, a particular Frankish warrior.[8]

This division between the woodlands and the agricultural landscape of the Perche is reflected in the very earliest document which provides detailed information about the area, the polyptych of Irminon. The polyptych is a record of the property of the Parisian abbey of Saint-Germain-des-Prés, which was made for its Abbot Irminon in the first half of the ninth century.[9]

---

landscape and land clearance', in *L'ambiente vegetale nell'alto medioevo* (Settimane di studio del Centro Italiano di Studi sull'alto Medioevo xxxvii, 1990), 523–8.

7   On Roman metal working see P. Siguret, 'Recherches sur la formation du comté du Perche', *BSHAO* lxxix (1961), 27–8. For Robert Maschefer see AD Orne, priory of Bellême, MS H2154.

8   See Siguret, 'Recherches', 29, for the villa, and also J. Adigard de Gautries, 'Étude onomastique ornaise, II: Les toponymes anciens formés à l'aide de l'appellatif *court*', *BSHAO* lxxviii (1960), 3–17.

9   *Polyptique de l'abbaye de Saint-Germain-des-Prés*, ed. A. Longnon, Paris 1895; J. J. François, 'Les Domaines de l'abbaye de Saint-Germain au IXe siècle', *MSAEL* xxvii (1974/7), 41–77.

The property held by the abbey in the Perche region falls into two groups, that in and around Corbon (Orne, cant. Mortagne) on the River Huisne (section XII within the polyptych) and a rather more widespread set of holdings which were administered from Boissy-Maugis (Orne, cant. Rémalard) (section XIII). The Boissy-Maugis property, much of which lies to the south-west of Dreux (Eure-et-Loir), that is outside the boundary of the later *coutume* of the Perche, is diverse in forms of tenure, size and location.[10] The products of the area, however, as indicated by the renders which had to be made to the abbey, suggest the mixed woodland economy. Barrel hoops, metal ores, such as iron, shingling, torches, wax and soap were owed, while arable and pasture land is also recorded. In contrast the Corbon property consisted of forty-seven smallish agricultural units, made up of an area of arable, meadow and an allotment of woodland.

Woodlands, arable and pastures, then, were the mainstays of the Perche and exchanges of their products were the economic foundations of the Rotrou lineage's power. It is significant therefore that the focal point of the Rotrous' power was Nogent-le-Rotrou (Eure-et-Loir, ch.-l. du cant.), a trading centre which by the late twelfth century had adopted the family's characteristic personal name as part of its own name. Nogent lies in the south of the county, where the valley of the River Huisne is broad and the river meanders through good quality pasture land. The very name of Nogent implies that it had been consciously founded as a new market (*Novum mercatum*) and it was well-placed as a local trading centre. It lies at the junction of two of the three major road crossings of the Perche, where the road from Chartres to Le Mans (Sarthe) crosses a road passing through Nogent on its way from Alençon and the southern reaches of Normandy to Orléans (Loiret). The route of the Roman road from Le Mans to Chartres and ultimately to Paris probably ran across the hills to the south of Nogent, but by the eleventh century it was a *via calciata* (foot way) and most traffic probably took the road along the lower valley of the Huisne. Nogent could therefore benefit from the traffic between urban centres, the seats of bishoprics, where urban life had continued unbroken from Roman times, but more particularly from exchanges of livestock and woodland products derived from its own uplands and the grains of the Beauce region, where cereal production was already well-established in Carolingian times.[11]

It is here in Nogent during the eleventh century that the Rotrou lineage can first be detected; the castle, which still dominates the town, together with the remains of the priory church of Saint-Denis in the valley below it,

---

[10] The original editor of the polptych, Benjamin Guérard, identified *Buxido* with Boissy-en-Drouais precisely because much of the property lay in that region, but Auguste Longnon makes a convincing case for Boissy-Maugis in his edition: *Polyptique*, ii. 175 n. 2. The question is still debated: Siguret, 'Recherches', 34 n. 47.

[11] K. Randsborg, *The first millennium AD in Europe and the mediterranean: an archaeological essay*, Cambridge 1991, 179.

are visible manifestations of the family's power. The records of the Rotrous' religious benefactions indicate that the centre of their family property lay in and around Nogent-le-Rotrou and there is evidence that the family made every effort to exploit it with efficiency. During the course of the twelfth century various developments were undertaken. Vineyards were established around the town, for example, and new mills were built, while in the wooded hills to the south and east of the town *medietaria* or share cropping holdings were in operation. The counts controlled the commercial life of the town and it was not uncommon for them to grant an urban tenement to a particular individual or religious house as a sign of favour.

While the core of the Rotrous' property lay around Nogent, they derived their comital title from Mortagne. The town lies in the hills above the upper reaches of the River Huisne, on a site that appears chosen for defensive reasons and there is an early thirteenth-century reference to land tenure in return for a month's castle-guard at the count's summons.[12] Beyond Mortagne the hills of the Perche reach their greatest height, often over 200 metres above sea level, before levelling off to the flatter countryside of the Norman marches towards Moulins-la-Marche (Orne, ch.-l. du cant.) and Bonsmoulins (Orne, cant. Moulins-la-Marche) and it is in the dense woodlands of this area that the River Avre, traditionally the southern border of Normandy, takes its source. Placename evidence suggests that, in the central Middle Ages, this was an area of economic expansion and that many of the settlements to the north of Mortagne were recent colonies in the woodland.[13] It was here, in the twelfth century, that the most famous of the Percheron religious houses, La Grande Trappe, was founded and patronised by the Rotrou dynasty. The records of the Rotrou family's religious patronage indicate, however, that the Rotrous did not directly control much landed property around Mortagne. Their resources in the area seem to have involved access to ready cash, which they later assigned to individuals and religious foundations. Since the town commands the third major road crossing of the Perche, which runs across the Seine/Loire watershed, linking Alençon in southern Normandy with Verneuil-sur-Avre (Eure), Evreux (Eure) and Dreux, the implication is that the family's control in this area derived less from the profits of the direct exploitation of land, than from the market tolls and customs dues which were payable to them as counts. In the eleventh and twelfth centuries the counts of the Perche were to possess two other sources of income which were situated on roads into the country at Longpont (Orne, cant. Bazoches-sur-Hoëne, cme La Ménière) and Montisambert (Orne, cant. la Bazoches-sur-Hoëne, cme La Ménière) and an act in favour of the abbey of

---

[12] RCVD, fo. 11.

[13] Hagiotoponyms, that is placenames derived from saints' names, which are common in this area of the Perche, are related to colonisation in the forest around the year 1000 by E. Le Roy Ladurie and Z. Zysberg: 'Géographie des hagiotoponyms en France', *Annales* xxxviii (1983), 1312.

Perseigne gives an indication of the range of payments which might be exacted – tolls and bridge taxes, ferry fees and entry and exit charges.[14] The masters of Mortagne were therefore in a position to tax all commercial activity, as well as to benefit from forest revenues, and they also possessed the right to requisition on behalf of the fighting forces which they might call out in the king's name.[15]

In addition to these two centres of power the counts directly controlled other assets, distributed around the area that would become the Perche. These parcels of rights and revenues were usually designated *prepositurae*, a word derived from the *prepositus*, the bailiff or steward placed in charge of them. It is possible to detect such property at various sites in the county, including Le Theil (Orne, ch.-l. du cant.), where the counts are known to have had a residence, Mauves (Orne, cant. Mortagne) and Maisonmaugis (Orne, cant. Rémalard), where they had land and agricultural rights at their disposal, La Ferrière (Eure-et-Loir, cant, Nogent-le-Rotrou, cme Brunelles), La Perrière (Orne, cant. Pervenchères), Montlandon (Eure-et-Loir, cant. La Loupe), Nonvilliers (Eure-et-Loir, cant. Thiron-Gardais) and Montigny-le-Chartif (Eure-et-Loir, cant. Thiron-Gardais).[16] The nature and extent of the demesne resources at each of these places cannot be determined with any precision, although we do know that the count-bishop William anticipated an annual return of about £100 from Montigny-le-Chartif, which he left to his cousin in 1221.[17] A particularly important collection of resources was centred on Rivray (Orne, cant. Rémalard, cme Condé-sur-Huisne) and the bailiff or *prepositus* of Rivray often appears in comital acts. Rivray was the site of a comital residence. A motte and a Romanesque chapel, dedicated to St John the Baptist, have been excavated, revealing traces of a wooden castle, succeeded by a stone keep.[18] These properties were to remain with the comital family throughout its existence and form the bulk of the comital property divided among the collateral heirs in thirteenth century.[19]

Finally, the family was associated with Bellême, the third major settlement in the Perche, which lies more or less midway between Mortagne and Nogent within the loop of the River Huisne. Although it first appears in written

---

[14] For Longpont and Montisambert see BN, MS Duchesne 54, p. 460; for Perseigne see AD Sarthe, abbey of Perseigne, MS H927.

[15] An eleventh-century grant conveyed exemption from military exactions 'liberi ab omni servicio et tallia et seculari consuetudine et exercitu et equitatu': *La Trappe*, 16.

[16] BN, MS Duchesne 54, p. 460.

[17] O. de Romanet, *Géographie du Perche et chronologie de ses comtes suivies de pièces justificatives formant le cartulaire de cette province*, Mortagne 1890–1902, ii, no. 6.

[18] 'in arce comitis': BN, MS franc. 24133, p. 310; J. Decaëns, 'La Motte de Rivray, chronique des fouilles médiévales', *Archéologie médiévale* xxii (1992), 489–90. For 'pretor de Rivere' see AD Orne, priory of the Madeleine, Chartrage, MS H5441; for 'preposito de Rivereio' see AD Eure-et-Loir, priory of Belhomert, MS H5211.

[19] *Layettes de trésor de chartes*, ed. A. Teulet, H.-F. Delaborde and E. Berger, Paris 1863–1909, ii, no. 2064.

sources in the tenth century the fact that it is the focal point of a network of secondary routes which probably had their origins in the Roman period suggests that Bellême was an ancient settlement.[20] In the tenth and eleventh centuries Bellême had been in the hands of a rival but related kin-group and it was not until the Rotrous acquired it in the early twelfth century that the county of the Perche can truly be said to have formed. Again the family had a residence in the town, but there is little evidence of direct control over the landed resources of the area for no tracts of land or agricultural undertakings there were granted to religious houses.

Before the formation of the county the early history of the area which became the Perche is that of a region at the margins of several units of power. The prevalence of the placename element 'marche' within the area – Marchemaisons (Orne, cant. Le Mêle-sur-Sarthe), Marchainville (Orne, cant. Longny), Marcheville (Eure-et-Loir, cant. Illiers-Combray), Marchemigny (Eure-et-Loir, cant. La Loupe, cme Vaupillon), Moulins-la-Marche – demonstrates this border quality and the placename Feigns (Orne, cant. Mortagne) (from the Latin *fines*) suggests that this had been the case in the Gallo-Roman period as well. Indeed, if, as is generally supposed, the diocesan boundaries in northern France reflect the late Roman provincial administration, then the Perche was bisected by the boundary between two Roman provinces. The western part of the Perche is in the diocese of Sées (Orne), which took the boundaries of the *civitas Saiorum*, while the eastern area is in the diocese of Chartres, which was based on the *civitas Carnotum*. These two *civitates* lay in separate Roman provinces, respectively *Lugdunensis secunda* and *Lugdunensis Senonia*.[21] That provincial divide had probably ceased to matter by the time the polyptych of Irminon was compiled in the ninth century but a boundary still ran through the area, for the polyptych is quite specific that Saint-Germain's property in the upper Huisne valley was located in the *centena Corbonensi* within the *pago Oximense*, while the property administered from Boissy Maugis was not. No administrative affiliation is given for the Boissy property, but it is clear, simply from the fact that it is recorded in a separate section, that it was distinct from Saint-Germain's property in the Huisne valley, which lay in the *centena* centred on Corbon and looked to a count operating from Exmes (Orne, ch.-l. du cant.).

By the ninth century much land in the area which would become the Perche was controlled by monastic houses. Saint-Germain's resources there were considerable, as the polyptych indicates, and the survival of the element

---

[20] Siguret, 'Recherches', 20–7. Rather older roads have been detected by J. Pelatan, 'Les Chemins finéraux: leur rôle dans le maintien des structures rurales: l'exemple des confins bocage-openfield dans l'ouest du bassin parisien', *Revue géographique de l'est* xxiii (1983), 359–67.

[21] E. James, *The origins of France: from Clovis to the Capetians, 500–1000*, London 1982, 45–6. The detailed implications for the Perche are considered in de Romanet, *Géographie*, i. 15–21.

'Saint-Germain' in placenames such as Saint-Germain-de-la-Coudre (Orne, cant. Le Theil), Saint-Germain-des-Grois (Orne, cant. Rémalard) and Saint-Germain-de-Martigny (Orne, cant. Bazoches), as well as the dedication of churches in, for example, Préaux-au-Perche (Orne, cant. Nocé) and Bizou (Orne, cant. Longny), suggests that the abbey's influence was widespread. Perhaps not as extensive, but none the less considerable were the lands of the religious community which had been established at Corbion, near present-day Moutiers-au-Perche (Orne, cant. Rémalard). The site had been associated with the sixth-century holy man, St Laumer, who had established a community there, dedicated to St Martin; in the early years of the ninth century it had been taken over by the abbot of Micy, Heriricus, as part of the monastic reforms inaugurated by the Carolingian emperor, Louis the Pious. The emperor gave property to the community and his son, Charles the Bald, added to the endowment.[22] Finally, the great Merovingian foundation of Saint-Denis, north of Paris, may also have held lands in the locality. In the later Middle Ages its property in the Perche was controlled from a priory at Sainte-Gauburge (Orne, cant. Nocé, orne Saint-Cyr-de-la-Rosière and, although it is uncertain when that property was first obtained, it is quite possible that the land had been given to the abbey in the Carolingian period.[23] Most of these monastic endowments had probably reached religious foundations as a result of royal benefactions and the placename Rémalard (Orne, ch.-l. du cant.) (*Regis Malastro*) seems to preserve a memory of royal possessions within the area.

In the middle years of the ninth century there was a major change which detached the area (*centena*) directed from Corbon from its dependence on the county of Exmes and turned it into a separate unit. A capitulary or decree, issued by the Frankish king, Charles the Bald, in 853, describes the circuit to be visited by the king's *missi* or agents working from Le Mans, and equates the Corbon area with other *pagi* or counties, such as Maine, Anjou, the Touraine and the Sées region.[24] The rationale behind this new relationship with Le Mans cannot be recovered, although it may reflect existing economic links with Anjou and the Loire valley, for the tenants of Saint-Germain were involved in elaborate arrangements that enabled the transport of Loire valley wine to Paris.[25] It is possible too that the new arrangements were a restoration of an earlier situation when the area had been ruled from Le Mans, since a gold coin minted at Corbon under the Merovingian kings bears the letters CE for Cenomannis.[26] One modern authority has suggested that the new assem-

---

[22] GC viii. 1350–4; *Recueil des actes de Charles II le chauve, roi de France*, ed. G. Tessier, Paris 1948–55, nos 6, 21, 27.

[23] AN, MS LL1158, Livre blanc de l'abbaye de Saint-Denis, 401–19.

[24] MGH *Legum sectio II: Capitularia regum francorum*, ed. A. Boretius and V. Krause, ii, Hanover 1897, no. 260.

[25] J. Devroey, 'Un Monastère dans l'économie d'échanges: les services de transport à l'abbaye de Saint-Germain des Prés au IXe siècle', *Annales* xxxix (1984), 570–89.

[26] P. Grierson and M. Blackburn, *Medieval European coinage with a catalogue of the coins in the*

blage of territory was intended to support military action to the west to contain the Bretons, who had never been properly integrated into the Frankish *regnum*, but it is also possible that the king had intended it to consolidate the position of Robert the Strong in his task of combating the Viking raids on the Loire and its hinterland.[27]

The reassignment of territory under the command of a particular aristocrat was by no means unusual. It was in such ways that kings co-opted and rewarded their nobility for their service in running the kingdom.[28] An entirely new situation, however, was precipitated by the activities of the Vikings. From the early years of the ninth century effective resistance to their raids proved difficult to organise and constituted the major challenge to the Carolingian kings of the Franks. At first sight it appears that the area that would become the Perche escaped the worst aspects of the devastation, because the waterways did not permit navigation even by Viking shipping and the forested nature of the countryside gave some protection. Indeed, the chronicle of the monastery of Saint-Wandrille explicitly states that the depredations of the Viking Berno were halted by the forests of the Perche, and peaceful conditions are suggested by the choice of Coursessin (Orne, cant. Nocé, cme Courcerault) as one of the sites for the minting of the new coinage which from 864 onwards was probably intended to facilitate the payment of subsidies to the Vikings.[29]

None the less it is clear that the Northmen did have an impact on the area. Serious and prolonged Viking activity is specifically blamed for the removal from Corbion in 872 of the relics of St Laumer, after eighteen years of continuous harassment from the Northmen, while the monks of Glanfeuil, who had taken sanctuary from the raids at their property at Le Mêle-sur-Sarthe (Orne, ch.-l. du cant.) were also driven away by pagan attack.[30] Given the geographical position of the Perche the implication is that this particular harassment was not the result of sea- and river-borne raids, but of the use of

Fitzwilliam Museum Cambridge, I: *Early Middle Ages (5th–10th centuries)*, Cambridge 1986, coin no. 454.

[27] J. Brunterc'h, 'Le Duché du Maine et la marche de Bretagne', in H. Atsma (ed.), *La Neustrie: les pays au nord de la Loire de 650–850* (Beihefte der *Francia* xvi, 1989), i. 80.

[28] Nelson, *Charles the Bald*, 69–71.

[29] Grierson and Blackburn, *Medieval European coinage*, 635–7.

[30] 'Berno nortmannus cum valida classe ingressus est. Deinde junctis viribus usque Particum saltum plurimam stragem et depopulationem fecerunt: 'Chronicle of Saint-Wandrille', in *RHF* vii. 43. See also 'Translatio Sancti Launomari', ibid. vii. 365. The 'Translatio' is a difficult text which has not received a great deal of scholarly attention. It was probably composed at the abbey of Saint-Laumer at Blois, the eventual resting place of the relics, at a much later date when the reasons for the removal of the relics were not fully understood. See also F. Lifshitz, 'The migration of Neustrian relics in the Viking Age: the myth of voluntary exodus, the reality of coercion and theft', *Early Medieval Europe* iv (1995), 175–92. For the monks of Glanfeuil, who were carrying the relics of St Maur, see 'Sermo de mirabilibus gestis sive de translatione corporis sanctissimi Mauri abbatis', BN, MS lat. 3778, fos 165–73, quoted in R. Gazeau, 'Glanfeuil', in *Dictionnaire d'histoire et de géographie écclesiastiques*, xxi, ed. R. Aubert, Paris 1986, 142.

Viking troops as mercenaries in conflicts whose nature and cause are now irrecoverable. Unfortunately no documentation relating to this crucial period of the Perche's prehistory survives, but it is clear that important social change took place, for the lands which the Parisian abbey of Saint-Germain-des- Prés held around Corbon and Boissy-Maugis slipped out of its control, leaving the parish churches dedicated to St Germain as the only traces of its former involvement there.[31]

Although the nature of the evidence makes a precise chronology of events impossible, this secularisation of Saint-Germain's property demonstrates in broad terms the effect on Frankish society of the chronic instability brought about by the Vikings' presence, which was more significant in its outcome than all the regroupings of territory that had created new marches, duchies and even kingdoms under the earlier Carolingians. Effective defence of the locality could only be organised locally, and castles were particularly useful as places of refuge and centres of resistance. In the area that would become the Perche the unsettled conditions must have led to the fortification of easily-defended sites such as Mortagne and Bellême in preference to the former focal point of the *pagus*, Corbon, which lay in the valley of the River Huisne. This response to the Viking threat was repeated throughout the Frankish realm and brought about a localisation of power which was to have profound implications during the central Middle Ages. Historians during the twentieth century have debated the origins of this experiment in local power and there has been great emphasis in the last thirty years on the year 1000 as a pivotal point when the old Carolingian institutions were swept away by local potentates who exercised their power with arbitrary violence. An examination of the development of local power within the Perche, however, tends to support the analysis of Marc Bloch, reiterated recently with some force by Dominique Barthélemy, that it was the military crisis of the ninth century which stimulated the localisation of power.[32]

The polyptych of Irminon hints at the identity of those who, by organising local defence, were to benefit from the localisation of power. The holding of Adlevertus, for example, is described as being held of the favour (*de beneficio*) of Gerald and the holding of Walateus was held of the favour of Rotmundus. Rotmundus seems in fact to have been of some importance for there are three references to his benefice, and the implication is that he and others like him derived profits from the abbey's lands.[33] These were the men who performed the abbey's obligations for military service and the military crisis of the mid ninth century gave them an opportunity to take on a new role as protectors of

---

[31] *Polyptique*, ii. 172, for example, shows the abbey with a holding at Loisé (Orne, cant. Mortagne), but by the eleventh century the church there, dedicated to St Germain, was in the hands of a knight, Gerald: *NLR*, no. xxi.

[32] For a summary of the debate see D. Barthélemy, 'Encore le débat sur l'an mil', *Revue historique du droit* lxxiii (1995), 353–4.

[33] *Polyptique*, ii. 171, 181, 186, 190.

their communities as well as a powerful tool, the castle, to exploit that opportunity. The annals of Saint-Bertin add valuable evidence that self-help was being practised in the area between the Seine and Loire in the late 850s, for sworn associations had been formed to promote resistance to the Northmen.[34] These associations had been founded by the common people and were promptly suppressed by the more powerful, which suggests that the warrior elite were well aware of the potential of their own position and did not want it undermined.

During the tenth century these professional warriors were able to maintain and consolidate their role, remaining on a war footing in the face of a new threat from the highly successful Viking settlement that would develop into the Perche's mighty northern neighbour, Normandy.[35] In the opening years of the century a group of Northmen under their leader Rollo had received from King Charles the Simple (898–922) control of the apparatus of Carolingian power in the Rouen area and within a generation they had taken over not only other Viking settlements on the northern seaboard, but possibly neighbouring Frankish lands as well. Our evidence for the latter occurs in the writings of the historian Flodoard of Rheims (d. 966) who composed a well-informed account of his own times.[36] Flodoard indicates that in 924 King Ralph (923–36) made a second grant to the Northmen, extending their influence westwards and southwards towards Bayeux and Maine. While historians have been ready to accept Flodoard's narrative in relation to Bayeux, the grant of Maine is broadly discredited. When considered, however, in the light of the changes of the mid ninth century, which placed both the Corbonnais and the area managed from Sées under the authority of Le Mans and thus effectively made them part of Maine, Flodoard's assertion is more plausible. The king might well have granted Maine or that part of it now covered by the diocese of Sées to the Northmen.

The king's grant probably had little practical effect, but it did give the Normans claims which might lead to protracted conflict with their southern neighbours. Such claims would clearly have been resisted in the area that would become the Perche by the sons and grandsons of the professional warriors who had fought the Northmen, and the likelihood of such conflict between the Normans and the Franks settled in the Corbonnais opens up the possibility that Mortagne was held by the Normans or their allies at some stage in the tenth century. This may go some way towards explaining a number of indications of Breton activity in Mortagne. The church founded within the earliest fortification at Mortagne, was dedicated to the Breton saint, St Malo, as was the church of nearby Randonnai (Orne, cant. Tourouvre) and there is a Breton presence in the locality, not least that of Abbo the Breton, the ancestor of the Giroie family, which figures promi-

---

34 *Annals of St-Bertin: ninth century histories,* i, trans. J. L. Nelson, Manchester 1991, 89.
35 D. Bates, *Normandy before 1066,* London 1982, 2–24.
36 Flodoard, *Annales,* ed. P. Lauer, Paris 1906, 24.

nently in the Ecclesiastical history of Orderic Vitalis.[37] Local lords, such as Solomon of Courcerault, bore personal names which were popular among the Bretons, and the Breton survivals might be used to suggest a Breton settlement under Norman auspices at this strategic point in the Corbonnais. A possible date for such Normanno-Breton co-operation might be the time of Duke William Longsword (c. 928–42), when Breton settlements in the Avranchin and Cotentin were integrated into Normandy and the duke's heir, Richard I, was the son of his Breton partner, Sprota.[38]

During the tenth century, then, the warrior elite of the Corbonnais and the Percheron forest were probably engaged in a struggle with the Normans for the northern parts of the area controlled from Le Mans, a struggle which enabled them to consolidate their position as masters of their locality. Agricultural change, which promoted the development of communities, including the clearing of forest and the laying out of common fields, would also have required the protection of a fighting elite, particularly in the face of pressure from the Normans to the north.[39] In the early years of the century Hugh the Great, duke of the Franks, possessed substantial influence to the west of Paris which was often described by the name of one of the old Frankish sub-kingdoms, Neustria. Hugh may well have organised these warriors, perhaps setting up a count in the Corbonnais to command them just as the southern parts of his duchy were commanded by the counts of Anjou and Blois.[40] Two references to the existence of a count in the area suggest that there was such an official. A twelfth-century work extolling the virtues of the counts of Anjou mentions a Geoffrey count of the Corbonnais, and an act dated 954 in the cartulary of Saint-Père of Chartres, which was probably compiled in the late eleventh century, is attested by one Hervey count of Mortagne. Admittedly both documents are of a much later date and there is a possibility that the comital toponymic in the latter is an interpolation, yet, taken together, the two references do suggest a lively tradition that such a count existed.[41]

The conjecture that Hugh the Great strengthened the defences of the area that would become the Perche against the Normans is not new, for the distinguished French historian, Jacques Boussard, suggested that the lordships which begin to be visible along the southern border of Normandy in the middle years of the tenth century were established by Hugh as a means of containing the early Normans.[42] M. Boussard focused on Bellême, where by the second half of the tenth century a man called Ivo was master. He

---

[37] De Romanet, Géographie, i. 112, for St Malo; OV ii. 22.

[38] Bates, Normandy, 10.

[39] R. Fossier, 'La Naissance du village', in Delort, La France de l'an mil, 162–8.

[40] J. Dunbabin, France in the making, 843–1180, 2nd edn, Oxford 2000, 67.

[41] Hugh de Cleeris, 'De majoratu et senescalcia', in Chroniques d'Anjou, ed. P. Marchegay and A. Salmon, Paris 1856, 387ff; SPC, 198–9.

[42] J. Boussard, 'Les Destinées de la Neustria du IXe au XIe siècle', CCM xi (1968), 25–6.

possessed a fortified site, or *castrum*, on the spur of hills where the modern town of Bellême is located, and he controlled resources in the settlement called by the locals Vieux-Bellême which lies on the opposite side of the small river valley of the Même.[43] Ivo's *castrum* was the focal point of his property, however, for he built there a new church, dedicated to Notre Dame, devoting considerable resources to its upkeep, and the nature of those resources tells us much about his power. It was clearly substantial, extending from control of churches, like that of Vieux-Bellême, whose revenues he was able to assign to the new foundation, to the outright mastery of two settlements, Courthioust and Corubert (both Orne, cant. Nocé), where lands, meadows, woods, revenues and renders were granted to the new church.

It is not clear when Ivo's fortified site was founded but by the second half of the tenth century when he endowed his church it was well-established. The *castrum* had probably begun as a refuge from Viking attack for the inhabitants of local communities, which placename evidence suggests had been successfully exploiting the land since Roman times.[44] So powerful was the castle's domination of the landscape to become that when describing a particular piece of property at Le Pin-la-Garenne (Orne, cant. Pervenchères) in the middle years of the eleventh century a monastic scribe recorded its location as in the county of the fortification of Bellême.[45] We do not know how Ivo secured control of the castle. Boussard's reconstruction of events suggests that Hugh the Great had entrusted the lordship to him to resist the Normans, but Ivo's act acknowledges no power but his own and there is no reason why he and his ancestors should not have been in possession of Bellême since the previous century. As early as 864, in the Edict of Pîtres, Charles the Bald had encouraged the creation of fortified places as refuges for the populace, although he was careful to insist that those built without royal authorisation should be dismantled.[46] Ivo may well therefore have been the descendant of a member of the warrior elite who had commanded the fortification when it was erected to protect local farming communities. This is not to deny the role in mobilising the defence of the locality against the continuing Norman threat that Boussard assigned to Hugh the Great, but rather to suggest that Hugh's method was to work in partnership with men like Ivo whose hold on the locality was already established.

Our picture of the Perche in the first millennium, then, reflects the nature of the surviving sources. In the sixth and seventh centuries the saints' *Lives* suggest wilderness. In the eighth and ninth century the wilderness has apparently been tamed in some measure by the great monastic estates and we are dimly aware of the apparatus of Carolingian rule. By the tenth century,

---

[43] 'Nuncupatur a circummanentibus Vetus Belismo': CMPerche, no. 1.

[44] Adigard de Gautries, 'Étude onomastique ornaise, II: Les toponymes anciens formés à l'aide de l'appellatif *court*', 3–17.

[45] 'In castri Bellissimi pago': CMPerche, no. 7, p. 19.

[46] Nelson, *Charles the Bald*, 207.

however, a local potentate can be discerned because his benefactions were recorded by the religious community he chose to patronise. Significant social change had taken place in the previous two centuries. Society had been militarised and a warrior elite had emerged as a result of the Viking intervention in Frankish politics. The localities were controlled by the members of that elite who held the castles. The sources for the history of the Perche enable us to deduce these events and infer a working relationship between that elite, particularly the castellans, and the duke of the Franks, but it is also possible to detect the potential for that relationship not to function and for the masters of the localities to slip from the power of dukes and counts just as dukes and counts were slipping from the king's power. After the year 1000 other local potentates become visible as the monastic houses they founded and encouraged began to preserve records of their benefactions. Such records survived in increasing numbers as the eleventh century progressed; it is to them that we are indebted for the history of the Rotrou lineage and its creation of the county of the Perche.

2

The Perche in the Making, 1000–1100

The earliest references to the Rotrou family occur in documents describing events in the early eleventh century. They record the family's religious patronage but in so doing reveal much about its powerbase and its place in the political order. The Rotrous were one lineage among many and there were opportunities for all of them within that political order. Property might be accumulated through inheritance, marriage or appropriation. It could also be secured through association with a more powerful figure, just as local influence might be extended over lesser mortals by manipulation of personal patronage. As the century progressed, the Rotrou lineage was able, despite occasional setbacks, to exploit the range of these opportunities and to consolidate its gains in successive generations, becoming the most successful in the area and precipitating the emergence of its own lands as a new political entity, the Perche.

The localisation of power in response to the Viking raids had made the king a more remote figure for lineages such as the Rotrous and they looked instead for patronage to the successors of the men who had organised the defences against the Vikings. Historians have described these men as the territorial princes. In the area that would become the Perche by far the most powerful local figures were the counts of Blois/Chartres.[1] The Theobalds and Odos who exercised power from Blois and Chartres are often known as the Thibaudian family from the lead name, Theobald, which was used in almost every generation of the dynasty. During the tenth century the Thibaudians had laid the foundations of their own power through a similar association, by acting as agents of the duke of the Franks, Hugh the Great, and when Hugh's son, Hugh Capet, was elected king of the Franks in 987, the Thibaudians were left as the most important magnates in the lands to the west of Paris. In the early eleventh century they added lands in Champagne to their interests in Blois, Chartres, Châteaudun and Tours.[2] Throughout the eleventh century

---

[1] Dhondt, *Études sur la naissance des principautés territoriales*.

[2] There is no adequate modern study of the counts of Blois. There is much useful material in Chédeville, *Chartres*, but it is still necessary to use H. d'Arbois de Jubainville, *Histoire des ducs et des comtes de Champagne*, Paris 1859–66. Important work by K. F. Werner appeared in 'Untersuchungen zur Frühzeit des französischen Furstentums (9.–10. Jahrhundert)', *Welt als Geschichte* xviii (1958), 256–89; xix (1959), 146–93; xx (1960), 87–119; and 'L'Acquisition par la maison de Blois des comtes de Chartres et de Châteaudun', in *Mélanges de numismatique, d'archéologie et d'histoire offerts à Jean Lafaurie*, Paris 1980, 265–74. For a summary see Dunbabin, *France in the making*, 190–5, 310–12.

the Rotrou family would acknowledge the Thibaudians as their superiors and, just as the Thibaudians' fortunes had been founded on service to the dukes of France, so the rise of the Rotrous would begin as agents of the counts of Blois/Chartres. In addition, but slightly further afield, two other territorial princes were potential sources of patronage for the Rotrous: the dukes of Normandy to the north and the counts of Anjou to the south-west.

Within the area that would become the Perche, however, there were also potential rivals. To the south the presence of the Gouet lineage would prevent the emergence of a Rotrou powerbase in the area between Nogent-le-Rotrou and Châteaudun in the Dunois, the original focal points of the Rotrous' interests. Competition with the descendants of the Ivo who had founded Notre Dame of Bellême in the mid tenth century would lead to violent conflict during the eleventh century that would continue into the twelfth. Territorial expansion in a northerly direction would open up rivalries between the Rotrous and other kin-groups, notably the lords of Châteauneuf-en-Thymerais to the east of their lands and the lords of L'Aigle in southern Normandy. Of all these lineages, however, it was the Rotrous that would emerge as the most successful. Promoting themselves as princes, they deployed their material resources to bolster their position and their courts became focal points for dispute resolution. They took a lead in religious matters, supporting monastic communities and expressing their commitment in the conspicuous consumption of lavish architectural patronage. Above all they were mighty warriors and on these foundations the dynasty established a prestige that would stand it in good stead for more than a century.

Family origins

The origins of the Rotrou family have been the subject of much speculation by historians, who, relying on the leading personal names of the family, such as Rotrou, Geoffrey and Hugh, have proposed lines of descent from tenth-century figures of the same name. It is a risky business which can lead to misleading conclusions, particularly where the names are common. The approach can be helpful, however, in the case of the characteristic family name, Rotrou, which is a compound name following Germanic naming patterns. It contains the elements Rot, meaning red or glorious, which also appears in Rotbert and Rotger, and Trou, meaning promise. Many such compound names can be found in the description of the Perche preserved in the polyptych of Irminon, including Rotberga, Rotveus, Rotcaus, Rotgildis and Rotmundus.[3] The family's attachment to this name well into the period when such compounds were falling from favour can be coupled with the coin-

---

[3]   A. Dauzat, *Dictionnaire étymologique des noms de famille et prénoms de France*, 3rd edn, Paris 1951, 528.

cidence of a number of other pieces of evidence to suggest a possible origin for the lineage.

At the turn of the ninth century the Emperor Charlemagne's daughter Rotrudis had been the acknowledged lover of Count Rorgo of Maine, by whom she had a son, Louis. This illegitimate grandson of the emperor was excluded from the succession, but was well-placed to pursue a career in the service of his royal cousins. He became Charles the Bald's archchancellor and also acquired the office of abbot of Saint-Denis, a religious community which from the eleventh century had property in the Perche at Sainte-Gauburge.[4] The origins of that property are unknown but it could have been in the possession of Saint-Denis since Merovingian or Carolingian times, just as Saint-Germain-des-Prés had held the property that is described in the polyptych of Irminon. It is a not unreasonable speculation that Abbot Louis established a brother or a married sister in the area that would become the Perche in a *beneficium* similar to those occurring in the polyptych of Irminon, but held of Saint-Denis. Throughout the early and high Middle Ages settlement of warriors on ecclesiastical property was an effective means of ensuring that the military obligations attached to that property would be fulfilled, although there was always the risk that the property might slip from the control of the Church.[5] If such a brother or sister were to name their offspring Rotrou in honour of their high-born mother, then this personal name might well become the distinguishing symbol of the family. In the eleventh century the Rotrou family were to establish a monastery at Nogent dedicated to Saint-Denis which may recall the family debt.[6] Devotion to this saint was by no means common in the Perche and few parish churches within the Perche are dedicated to him, so it is perhaps all the more significant that the Rotrou dynasty also possessed extensive property at Saint-Denis d'Authou (Eure-et-Loir, cant. Thiron-Gardais).[7]

The Rotrou lineage would in these circumstances have had its origins among the warrior elite that had benefitted from the localisation of power under Viking pressure. They would have taken on the responsibility of protecting the local population when the old royal host, raised by summons, proved too cumbersome to combat the Vikings, and the origins of their *castrum* at Nogent-le-Rotrou would have lain in a refuge for the inhabitants of the valley of the Huisne. Another important focus of the Rotrous' power

---

[4] Nelson, *Charles the Bald*, 110. For Saint-Denis's property in the Perche see AN, MS LL1158 (Livre blanc de l'abbaye de Saint-Denis), 401–19. In the early eleventh century the Bellême family had attempted unsuccessfully to found other religious communities there: *SPC*, 155–6.

[5] M. de la Motte-Callas, 'Les Possessions territoriales de l'abbaye de Saint-Germain des Prés du début du IXe au début du XIIe siècle', in *Mémorial du XIVe centenaire de l'abbaye de Saint-Germain-des-Prés*, Paris 1957, 49–80.

[6] *NLR*, no. v.

[7] For dedications to St Denis (Saint-Denis-sur-Huisne, Bubertré, Condeau and Moulicent) see De Romanet, *Géographie*, i. 112–15. For Authou see *NDC* i. 221.

lay at Rivray, where as late as the twelfth century the local populace was obliged to undertake three days work a year to repair the defences, and that fortification was probably the next place of refuge.[8] The family would have worked in partnership with those who commanded the local forces. In the early tenth century this would have meant working with Hugh the Great when his power extended over much of the area to the west of Paris, and later it would have meant recognising the leadership of his lieutenants, the counts of Blois/Chartres.

In his influential study of the Chartrain André Chédeville suggests that at the end of the tenth century, Theobald the Trickster (d. c. 974) or his son, Odo I (d. 996), counts of Blois/Chartres, gave responsibility for guarding the forested frontier of the Chartrain to a vassal, Rotrou, who dominated the valley of the River Huisne and the approaches from Normandy and Maine.[9] Chédeville's thumbnail sketch of the Rotrous presents a self-made lineage owing its origins to the count's patronage, but there is no direct evidence for his basic premise that Rotrou was deployed at Nogent by the count. It has to be said, in fact, that there is no direct evidence showing this tenth-century Rotrou in possession of Nogent at all. He is known to have been a regular attestor of comital acts and he gave property at Thivars (Eure-et-Loir, cant. Chartres), just outside Chartres, to the abbey of Saint-Père in Chartres, but these references indicate only an association between Rotrou and the counts of Blois/Chartres.[10] They do not demonstrate that he owed control of Nogent to the count and there is no reason why Rotrou and his forbears should not have been established at Nogent and its locality for some considerable time before the late tenth century. Association with the Thibaudian counts would, none the less, have been to the family's advantage, giving access to comital patronage, including opportunities to exercise power as the counts' agents, and rewards in which may lie the origins of the family's property in and around Chartres.

In the closing years of the tenth century the Rotrou lineage apparently made a marital alliance with another family which was closely linked to the Thibaudian counts. Throughout the ninth and tenth century there are references to viscounts in the Chartrain and Dunois, several of whom bore the personal names of Hugh or Geoffrey, and who came to control Châteaudun for the counts.[11] The exact genealogy of these viscounts has never been estab-

---

8   A. Gouverneur, *Essais historiques sur le Perche*, Nogent-le-Rotrou 1882, 215–16.

9   Chédeville, *Chartres*, 39–40. For an example of the influence of Chédeville's thesis see J. Decaëns, 'Les Châteaux de la vallée de l'Huisne dans le Perche (R. Allen Brown Memorial lecture 1994)', *ANS* xvii (1994), 3–5.

10 'Rotrocus seculari miliciae deditus et Odonis comitis fidelitati devotus': *SPC*, 65, 72, 74, 79, 87.

11 For references to the viscounts, Geoffrey and his wife Hermengarde (c. 970) and their son Hugh (c. 980), see 'Petite Chronique de l'abbaye de Bonneval', ed. R. Merlet, *MSAEL* x (1896), 33. The only study specifically devoted to them is C. Cuissard, 'Chronologie des vicomtes de Châteaudun, 960–1395', *Bulletin de la Société dunoise* viii (1894/6), 25–120. It

lished and the nature of the marital alliance between them and the Rotrous is difficult to recover. The most convincing reconstruction is that a daughter of this lineage named Milesindis married the lord of Nogent-le-Rotrou and, when her family's male heirs failed, her son, Geoffrey, who was probably named for her illustrious ancestors, took over as the counts' agent in Châteaudun.[12]

The evidence for the origins of the Rotrou family is, then, fragmentary and speculative, but it is better than for many other such lineages. It is possible to discern some links with an earlier period which suggest that the family had a long-standing association with the area to the west of Chartres and that it had its origins in the warrior elite that had defended the locality during the period of instability associated with the Viking raids. The family enjoyed a tradition of power in the area between the rivers Eure, Huisne and Loir that it was to exploit during the eleventh and twelfth centuries and it is on that tradition and on an association with the counts of Chartres/Blois that the county of the Perche would be created.

Foundations of power: Geoffrey I (*fl.* 1031)

The securely recorded history of the Rotrou family begins with Viscount Geoffrey, the son of Milesindis, whose activities can be dated to the first third of the eleventh century. Geoffrey was closely associated with Count Odo II of Blois, one of the most active magnates in the Frankish kingdom in the early eleventh century. Odo had inherited from a cousin lands in Champagne and had ambitions in the kingdom of Burgundy through his mother, a Burgundian princess. For much of his life, therefore, the count was preoccupied with high politics, creating a need for able servants, and Viscount Geoffrey was among those who satisfied that need.

Geoffrey's immediate powerbase lay at Nogent-le-Rotrou, where in 1031 he founded a monastery dedicated to Saint-Denis. The property which he assigned to it gives us our earliest insight into the nature of the family's power. As well as agricultural resources such as meadows and woodlands, Viscount Geoffrey gave the churches of Saint-Hilaire at Nogent-le-Rotrou and Saint-Aubin at Champrond-en-Perchet. The trading settlement (*vicus*) near the church was also his to bestow. In fact, just like Ivo of Bellême at Bellême,

has been argued that they were descended from the Rorgonid counts, rulers of Maine until around the year 900: J. Boussard, 'L'Origine des familles seigneuriales dans la région de la Loire moyenne', CCM v (1962), 303–22, 311–14. See, however, reservations expressed in Werner, 'L'Acquisition', 270.

[12] The location of Milesindis's dower at Nogent and at Cossonville (Eure-et-Loir, cant. Auneau) suggests that her husband's family controlled Nogent rather than her own: *NLR*, no. v. De Romanet favoured the opposite hypothesis, that Milesindis was the daughter of the lord of Nogent: *Géographie*, i. 44/45. The issue is discussed further in appendix 1.

Geoffrey appears to have been a local potentate with a firm grip on his area and a *castrum* which protected his interests, but the area which he controlled in this way may not have been very large for no territory assigned to the new community was more than ten kilometres from Nogent.[13]

Geoffrey also had interests in Châteaudun (Eure-et-Loir, ch.-l. du cant.) and in the act of foundation for the monastery at Nogent-le-Rotrou he is described as its viscount (*Castridunensium vicecomes*).[14] Châteaudun had been an important centre since Merovingian times and a mint continued to function there throughout the central Middle Ages. A castle had been built and a viscount exercised powers on behalf of the Thibaudian family from the mid tenth century. It is not known for certain whether this office had become hereditary among Geoffrey's ancestors but it is clear from surviving records that it was a powerful position and few activities escaped Viscount Geoffrey's grasp. He received rent from dwellings, together with customary payments from vineyards and winepresses, and he also had rights over the sale of salt and meat which he had assigned to the community at Nogent-le-Rotrou. In the 1030s his rights to tax the inhabitants were revealed when the abbot of Marmoutier went to law to seek exemption for the dyers who were living on the abbey's property just outside the town.[15]

Finally, Geoffrey had interests in the Chartrain. These included plots of land in the city of Chartres whose rents he assigned to the newly-founded religious community, but he also exercised a coercive power around that city which brought him into conflict with its bishop. In the 1020s Fulbert, bishop of Chartres, complained to the king, Robert II (996–1031), of the 'evil-doer' Geoffrey's lawlessness and he repeated his allegations to the abbot of Cluny. His complaints relate to injuries to church property, the burning of farms and the building of castles. According to the bishop Geoffrey had rebuilt the castle at Gallardon (Eure-et-Loir, cant. Maintenon) and established a new fortification at Illiers-Combray (Eure-et-Loir, ch.-l. du cant.).[16]

Geoffrey's power, then, can be traced in three distinct areas: Nogent-le-Rotrou, Châteaudun and the Chartrain. Its nature seems to have varied in each area. In the Chartrain his power was coercive, but he held little property. In Nogent, on the other hand, he had considerable property at his disposal and made his monastic foundation there. In Châteaudun there is less evidence of landed property, but he exercised lucrative rights and was able to found a church there, dedicated to the Holy Sepulchre, which may indicate that he, like many others of his generation, such as Count Fulk Nerra of Anjou or Duke Robert I of Normandy, had undertaken a pilgrimage to the

---

13 *NLR*, no. v.
14 Werner, 'L'Acquisition', 270.
15 *SPC*, 400–1; *NLR*, no. v; *CMD*, no. i.
16 Fulbert of Chartres, *Letters and poems*, ed. F. Behrends, Oxford 1976, letters 59, 98, 99, 100.

Holy Land.[17] His power, however, was not absolute as the abbot of Marmoutier's action in the court of the count of Chartres indicates. The abbot expected, and was able to secure, a settlement of his grievance at the instigation of Count Odo ('per suggestionem et ordinationem Odonis comitis'), just as Bishop Fulbert anticipated royal redress for his complaints. It is therefore clear that Odo was Geoffrey's superior at Châteaudun and the same relationship of overlord (*senior*) is recorded in the act of foundation for Nogent-le-Rotrou.

Geoffrey's acknowledgement of his association with the count can be further demonstrated by his presence at important ceremonial occasions with his lord. On 16 April 1034, for example, he was at Tours when Count Odo made various benefactions to the abbey of Saint-Julien of Tours and was with the count again in July 1035 when Odo, his wife Ermengarde and sons, Theobald and Stephen, witnessed the act of foundation for the abbey of Pontlevoy.[18] Like Geoffrey's own monastery at Nogent-le-Rotrou, Pontlevoy was founded by the lord of its locality, Gilduin of Saumur, and these acts of lordly piety were in both instances acknowledged by the approval of the count and the local bishop. Thus while there were clearly those like Bishop Fulbert and Abbot Albert of Marmoutier who found some of Geoffrey's activities oppressive, redress was possible since he operated within an accepted framework of power. Geoffrey's activities in the Chartrain which had provoked Bishop Fulbert's condemnation of lawlessness may well have been a legitimate exercise of power. In the early 1020s Count Odo had inherited lands east of Paris that were to preoccupy him for much of the rest of his life and to lead to the prolonged absences from the Chartrain which Bishop Fulbert's letters describe.[19] It is quite possible that the count had empowered Viscount Geoffrey, his agent in the Dunois, to act on his behalf in the Chartrain.

It would be an opportunity which few men like Geoffrey would decline. In addition to his family property at Nogent Geoffrey already had access to the profits of comital power in Châteaudun because he was viscount. Fulbert describes Geoffrey leading knights who burned down farms belonging to the bishopric, but these actions could be those of a zealous lieutenant, enforcing all the rights of his master to secure secular taxes from church property. The construction of castles at Gallardon and Illiers-Combray, which lie on the extremities of the Chartrain plain, even if detrimental to the interests of the Church, would be entirely explicable as the work of a man intent on preserving a hold on the Chartrain that had been entrusted to him by the

---

17 *NLR*, no. v; R. W. Southern, *The making of the Middle Ages*, London 1953, 50–3.
18 *Chartes de Saint-Julien de Tours, 1002–1227*, ed. L.-J. Denis (Archives historiques du Maine xii, 1912), no. 12; *Recueil des actes de Philippe 1er, roi de France*, ed. M. Prou, Paris 1908, no. lxxv.
19 For Odo's inheritance see Ralph Glaber, *The five books of the histories*, ed. and trans. J. France, Oxford 1989, 105. For his absences see Fulbert, *Letters and poems*, letter 61.

count. In one letter to the king Fulbert has to admit that he is unsure whether Geoffrey had permission for the construction of the castles and has sent to Count Odo to find out, while in another he concedes that the count is able to control Geoffrey: 'Entreat Count Odo and earnestly command him in the name of your royal authority to order in all honesty that those hell-inspired devices be destroyed.'[20] The language is colourful, but it is significant that, despite the bishop's complaints, Geoffrey remained in favour. In 1027/8 he was in Paris, where he witnessed the act of foundation for the abbey of Coulombs in the presence of the king and Count Odo, and in the mid 1030s he was with the count on the two important ceremonial occasions at Tours and Pontlevoy.[21]

The date of Geoffrey's death is unknown. Although it is often assigned to the late 1030s, it might have been as early as 1035 or as late as the 1040s. The event is reported in an act preserved in the Cluny archive which mentions the assassination of the heavily-guarded Geoffrey as he left the cathedral at Chartres.[22] The circumstances are not recorded but the location and Geoffrey's unsuccessful precautions suggest that he had enemies in the cathedral city and that his period of power there had led to dissatisfaction among others besides Bishop Fulbert. In an act issued some forty years later Geoffrey's son described him as 'comes . . . atque vicecomes', so it is possible that Geoffrey provoked his rivals or his overlord by adopting a comital title.[23] Geoffrey was clearly an energetic and able man who seized all the opportunities available to him. Building on his paternal inheritance at Nogent-le-Rotrou and on a tradition of working with the counts of Blois/Chartres, he took over the responsibilities of the viscounts of Châteaudun and his effectiveness in that role probably convinced Count Odo to empower him further in the Chartrain. As a comital agent Geoffrey must have been all too successful, but like all effective men of power he provoked complaints and made enemies, and his life was ended by assassination.

The expansion of the lordship: Rotrou I, c. 1040–c. 1066

The violent death of Viscount Geoffrey did not initially challenge the family's position and Geoffrey's son, Hugh, became viscount in his father's place.[24] The new viscount apparently attempted to recover some of his father's concessions to the Church, for the abbot of Marmoutier alleged that

[20] Ibid. letters 99, 100.
[21] RHF x. 619; *Chartes de Saint-Julien de Tours*, no. 12; *Recueil des actes de Philippe 1er*, no. lxxv.
[22] 'inprovisa mors in Carnotina urbe eum ab ecclesia Matris Domini redeuntem atque suorum militum longo ordine circumdatum furtivis anticipavit gladiis': *Cluny*, no. 3517.
[23] *NLR*, no. vi.
[24] 'Post mortem vero vicecomitis Gausfredi cum filius eius Hugo patris successisset in honorem': *CMD*, no. i.

Hugh's officials were harassing the abbey's tenants at Chamars with unjust impositions, and he is known to have authorised a sale of property to the abbey of Marmoutier for which he received £3 and his wife an ounce of gold.[25] It is evident, however, from the records of the 1040s and 1050s that he did not maintain his father's dominant role in the Dunois and it seems likely that he died young.

It is hard not to associate this disruption with the major upheaval which occurred in 1044 when Count Geoffrey Martel of Anjou took the city of Tours from his great rival the count of Blois/Chartres, Theobald III. It was a major act of appropriation by one territorial prince against another and a significant loss for Theobald, for the city, with its links with St Martin, was an important ecclesiastical centre as well as the major settlement on the Loire. The counts of Anjou had had designs on it for more than fifty years and had patiently built up support in the locality.[26] Viscount Hugh may have lost his life in the conflict with the Angevins and his overlord, Count Theobald, having suffered the setback of losing a substantial part of his interests in the Loire valley, may have chosen to retain Châteaudun and its resources in his own hands as he consolidated his more northerly interests.

The sole representative of the Rotrou lineage to remain was, therefore, Viscount Geoffrey's second son, Rotrou. It is unusual for anything to be known of the youth of medieval figures, but we know that Rotrou must have been born before the foundation of the monastery at Nogent-le-Rotrou in 1031 since he is mentioned in the account of that ceremony, and there is some information about his early years in an act of confirmation that Rotrou issued near the end of his life. He ignores the existence of his elder brother, describing how he succeeded his father as a 'lad' (*juvenculus*) and had to 'endure many dangers on the stormy sea of life'.[27] Rotrou's statement that he had succeeded his father directly suggests that Geoffrey had divided his inheritance, leaving Hugh the grander responsibilities as viscount at Châteaudun and Rotrou the family interests around Nogent-le-Rotrou.[28] On the evidence of Geoffrey's act of foundation for the monastery at Nogent, it was a fairly limited inheritance and on Rotrou's own testimony insecure, yet by 1058, when he witnessed two charters given by King Henry I of France, Rotrou had extended his sphere of influence and adopted the title of count, a title that was recognised by the royal chancery.[29]

---

[25] *CMD*, no. xlix.

[26] The most accessible account of early medieval Tours in English is S. Farmer, *Communities of St Martin: legend and ritual in medieval Tours*, Ithaca, NY 1991, 13–37. On the repercussions of Geoffrey's success see J. Boussard, 'L'Éviction des tenants de Thibaut de Blois par Geoffroy Martel, comte d'Anjou en 1044', *Le Moyen Âge* lxix (1963), 141–9.

[27] 'cum inter hujus pelagi procellas multa pertulissem pericula': *Cluny*, no. 3517. The wording varies slightly in *NLR*, no. vi.

[28] *NLR*, nos v, vi.

[29] *Catalogue des actes d'Henri Ier roi de France (1031–1060)*, ed. F. Soehnée, Paris 1907, nos 112 (sealed original preserved in the AN), 114.

This remarkable advance in family influence was based on a northerly shift in the family's interests, for Rotrou's comital title was associated with Mortagne (Orne), which lies some thirty-eight kilometres north of Nogent.[30] By the late 1050s the upper reaches of the River Huisne and the land around Mortagne had come into the possession of Rotrou of Nogent, and his acts are witnessed by men whose toponymics link them with the region such as Salomon and Hubert of Courcerault (Orne, cant. Nocé), Fulbert son of Ralph of Réveillon (Orne, cant. Mortagne), Hugh of Courtoulin (Orne, cant. Bazoches) and Aylmer of Condeau (Orne, Rémalard).[31] In the 1050s, when Rotrou made a benefaction to the abbey of Saint-Vincent of Le Mans, he did so at Mortagne in the house of Roger the dean and his act was witnessed by the local bishop, Ivo of Sées, who also witnessed a grant to the Rotrou family foundation of Saint-Denis of Nogent-le-Rotrou.[32]

It is uncertain how Rotrou established himself in this second centre of power. He may have owed the extension of his influence to inheritance, marriage to an heiress or to simple appropriation.[33] Since there is no evidence to associate Viscount Geoffrey with the area, a combination of the second two factors is most likely. Rotrou's marriage linked him with an important neighbouring lineage. His wife was Adeliza of Domfront, the great-grand-daughter of the Ivo who had controlled Bellême in the mid tenth century. Her grandfather, William of Bellême, had extensive interests stretching from Bellême through Alençon to Domfront in the Passais more than ninety kilo-metres to the west. By the time of Adeliza's marriage, however, the kin-group was seriously depleted. The power which they had accumulated brought them into conflict with both the dukes of Normandy and the counts of Maine and the sons of the lineage on occasion met violent ends. Bellême came into the possession of Adeliza's uncle, Bishop Ivo of Sées, and only two legitimate heirs survived from her father and five uncles: Adeliza and her cousin Mabel, daughter of William Talvas of Alençon. Subsequent events have all the neat-ness of a settlement. By the early 1050s Mabel was married to the Norman, Roger of Montgommery, who can later be found in possession of all the Bellême family's westernmost possessions: Domfront, Alençon, Sées and the northern Manceau interests. Adeliza meanwhile married Rotrou of Nogent-le-Rotrou, son of the Viscount Geoffrey, and by the late 1050s he was styled

---

[30] OV ii. 360; VLM, no. 609.

[31] Respectively VLM, nos 609, 589, 589, 609; NLR, no. xxxviii.

[32] See NLR, no. xxxviii for attestation.

[33] In the absence of direct information most modern commentators have been content to follow the suggestion that Rotrou acquired the county by inheritance through his mother Helviza from a line of counts of Mortagne, which included her father, Fulcuich: De Romanet, Géographie, i. 40–1. This reconstruction has remained unchallenged by historians because it illustrates how a lineage could benefit from the uncertainties of life in the eleventh century, securing additional interests – in this case the right to a comital title – through marriage to a woman who became her family's sole heir when her brother died. The evidence, however, is by no means conclusive. The issue is further discussed in appendix 2.

count of Mortagne, suggesting that Adeliza's portion was the easterly interests of her family. It seems not unreasonable to suggest, therefore, that matters had been negotiated by Adeliza's surviving uncle Bishop Ivo.[34]

With the extension of power northwards Rotrou adopted the title of count and took a vital step in the formation of the county of the Perche, but family claims in Châteaudun were not forgotten. In his great act of confirmation to his father's monastic foundation at Nogent-le-Rotrou Count Rotrou is described as both count of Mortagne and viscount of Châteaudun, and there is evidence that from the late 1050s he was able to reassert his father's influence in the Dunois.[35] The timing of that reassertion of power is significant, for it coincides with the death of an important neighbour, William Gouet I, whose lands were centred on the valley of the river Ozanne to the south of Nogent-le-Rotrou. The Gouet family probably originated from Château-du-Loir (Sarthe, ch.-l. du cant), midway between Le Mans and Tours, but in the middle years of the eleventh century interests in the Dunois were acquired when William Gouet I married the heiress of Alluyes (Eure-et-Loir, cant. Bonneval). In addition to this powerbase between Chartres and Châteaudun, he also controlled castles at Brou (Eure-et-Loir, ch.-l. du cant) and Montmirail (Sarthe, ch.-l. du cant.), and as a result emerged as an important figure in the 1050s.

Like Rotrou's father, Viscount Geoffrey, in the previous generation, William Gouet I probably owed some of his power to an association with the count of Blois/Chartres. Count Theobald III's fortunes were at a low ebb. He had already lost Tours to his rival, Count Geoffrey of Anjou, in 1044 and in the early 1050s the count of Anjou was to become even more powerful by extending his influence over Maine.[36] As a result Count Theobald may well have encouraged William Gouet's ambitions to control the territory centred on the River Ozanne, since that territory and the castle at Montmirail might offer some resistance to further expansion by Geoffrey of Anjou.[37] The death of William Gouet in the late 1050s forced Count Theobald to look for a new associate and the sudden appearance of Rotrou in his father's old role as viscount of Châteaudun suggests that Theobald had decided to revive the

---

34 K. Thompson, 'Family and influence to the south of Normandy in the eleventh century: the lordship of Bellême', *Journal of Medieval History* xi (1985), 215–26.

35 Rotrou refers to himself as *vicecomes* of Châteaudun only in *NLR*, no. vii (c. 1078). A record of a plea in the court of the Countess Adela of Blois/Chartres, dating from 1097/8, describes property at Châtenay (Eure-et-Loir, cant./cme Châteaudun) being in the hands of the Rotrou family for the previous forty years, twenty years 'tempore Rotrochi' and twenty years in the time of the next *vicecomes* of Châteaudun: *CMD*, no. clvi. This would place Rotrou's resumption of the title of *vicecomes* in 1057/8.

36 For Geoffrey Martel see L. Halphen, *Le Comté d'Anjou au xie siècle*, Paris 1906, 48–9.

37 K. Thompson, 'The formation of the county of Perche: the rise and fall of the house of Gouet', in K. S. B. Keats-Rohan (ed.), *Family trees and the roots of politics: the prosopography of Britain and France from the tenth to the twelfth century*, Woodbridge 1997, 299–314. See *Tiron*, no. xii for a tithe of travellers' tolls at Montmirail; *CMD*, no. xliv for woodland property.

long-standing relationship between his own family and the Rotrou lineage. It was a recovery of the family fortunes as they had existed in Rotrou's childhood and presented him with the opportunity for further expansion.

At this point Rotrou's accumulation of power was checked. Although he recovered influence in Châteaudun, the concentration of power which William Gouet I established to the south of Nogent-le-Rotrou proved remarkably durable. William's widow, Matilda, remarried and the survival of that Gouet family territory, which later became known as the Perche-Gouet, must largely be attributable to the efforts of her second husband, Geoffrey of Mayenne.[38] Rotrou is known to have waged at least two campaigns in Gouet territory, involving assaults on the castles of Dangeau (Eure-et-Loir, cant. Brou) and Brou (Eure-et-Loir, ch.-l. du cant.), but he was never able to impose his power throughout the area from the Huisne to the Loir.[39]

Rotrou was joined in the assault on Brou by Roger of Montgommery, the viscount of the Hiémois in Normandy and husband of his wife's cousin, Mabel. Roger, a close associate of the Norman duke, William the Bastard, who was later to conquer England, had successfully enforced his claim to his wife's share of the Bellême inheritance, taking control of Alençon and asserting his power beyond the River Sarthe in northern Maine.[40] In doing so Roger would have become aware of the Gouet castle of Montmirail that dominated northern Maine and he may well have developed ambitions towards it that encouraged him to make common cause with Rotrou. Relations between Roger and Rotrou might have been strained because of their wives' claims to the Bellême inheritance, but seem to have remained cordial for the rest of Rotrou's life and it is not unreasonable to speculate that the unknown Helviza, who was the second abbess of Roger's nunnery at Almenêches, was Rotrou's daughter of the same name.[41] Their alliance to attack the Gouet lands reveals the opportunities and the uncertainties of their political situation. Both men had been successful in accumulating interests and, in alliance, sought further gain at the expense of a neighbouring family. They were thwarted, however, by the widow Matilda's shrewd judge-

---

[38] William Gouet I was dead by 1059 when his widow and son approved (*SPC*, 163) and shortly thereafter she married Geoffrey of Mayenne (*SPC*, 192–3). Details of her marital history are given in the *Cartulaire Manceau de Marmoutier*, ed. E. Laurain, Laval 1911–45, 126: 'dominee mee Mahildis filie Galterii de Aloia, filiorumque ac filiarum ejusdem quibus patres fuere Guillelmus cognomento Gugetus et Gauffredus de Meduana'. See also OV ii. 26–8, 118.

[39] '. . . cum domino suo Rotroco Mauritaniensi comite ad bellum pergens ad Domionem castrum': *NLR*, no. xix. See also LBSMS, fo. 28, for his military expeditions: 'In anno quo Rogerius vicecomes de Montegomerici et Rotrocus comes de Mortania assalierunt Braiou . . .'.

[40] Roger's control of the Talvas lands in the Sées/Alençon region is demonstrated by his restoration of the abbey of Saint-Martin of Sées in the late 1050s: LBSMS, fo. 2. For exercises of power in northern Maine by Roger of Montgommery see VLM, nos 587, 589, 765.

[41] For the abbesses of Almenêches see *Rouleaux des morts de IXe au XVe siècle*, ed. L. Delisle, Paris 1866, 325; *NLR*, no. vi.

ment in choosing a second husband who protected her children's inheritance and ultimately preserved the powerbase her first husband had created.

Although Rotrou never succeeded in imposing himself on the Gouet territory, he can be shown to have recovered some of his father's influence in the rest of the Dunois. The family foundation at Nogent-le-Rotrou received endowments there from local men of influence who began to be attracted to Rotrou's entourage and Rotrou himself gave vineyards at Fréteval. Men whose toponymics link them with the Dunois, such as Fulchard of Arrou or Ivo of Courville, can be found among Rotrou's entourage, and when a new priory was established at Chuisnes (Eure-et-Loir, cant. Courville-sur-Eure), Rotrou attended the dedication of the church, attesting the act of endowment first among the laity.[42] According to Orderic Vitalis, Rotrou even emulated his father in his harassment of episcopal lands. Orderic gives no details but indicates that Rotrou had been excommunicated after repeated warnings from the bishop and he attributes Rotrou's chronic deafness to divine displeasure.[43]

Rotrou I and the Normans, c. 1066–79

The formidable powerbase that Count Rotrou was establishing just beyond the southern frontiers of Normandy cannot have escaped the attention of the duke of Normandy, who was from 1066 also the king of England: William the Conqueror would have been well-aware of the potential threat it might present. In the intermittent warfare across the southern Norman border Rotrou might easily support the duke's opponents, if he did not actually take part, and it is known, for example, that in 1058 he was in attendance on King Henry of France when the king besieged the Norman outpost of Thimert. There is sound evidence too of further risks to Norman security when the Perche was used as a base by rebels. In the 1050s and early 1060s the Norman exile, Arnold of Échauffour, had assembled men from Rotrou's lands of Mortagne and the Corbonnais to attack the duchy.[44] It is clear, however, that Rotrou's relations with Normandy subsequently improved, perhaps as a result of his links with William the Conqueror's friend and supporter, Roger of Montgommery, and in 1066 Rotrou's son, Geoffrey, took part in the Hastings campaign. The extent of the realignment and the significance of the change become apparent in the late 1070s when Robert Curthose, the Conqueror's eldest son, entered upon the first of his rebellions.

When the king's quarrel with his eldest son came to a head, William had been preparing to embark upon an expedition against the men of the Corbonnais. There is no indication in contemporary sources that Rotrou was the king's potential adversary, so William was probably planning a general

---

42 *NLR*, nos xix, xxxviii; *CMD*, no. cix.
43 OV ii. 360.
44 OV ii. 124.

show of strength on the southern borders of Normandy to discourage raiding from the Corbonnais.[45] Subsequent events, however, involved a campaign of altogether different kind, for the king needed to pursue his son, Robert, to the bases from which he and his supporters were harassing Normandy. One of those bases was Rémalard, which lies on the River Huisne, some thirteen kilometres due north of Nogent-le-Rotrou. In the late 1070s, Orderic tells us, it lay in the fee (*de feudo*) of Count Rotrou, but the castle belonged to Hugh of Châteauneuf-en-Thymerais, who had placed it at the disposal of Robert Curthose and his associates.

William's military intervention at Rémalard in 1078 marks an important development in relations between the Normans and the Rotrou lineage. For the first time a ruler of Normandy found it necessary to secure the co-operation of the Rotrou family, and William seems to have adopted this course quite deliberately. Faced with a number of crises, William selected Rotrou as his ally, making peace with him and paying a subsidy, before joining forces with Rotrou against his son's supporters in Rémalard. It is the first known occasion when a Norman duke paid for the support of the ruler of the Perche, and it set a pattern of events which was to recur for more than a hundred years. Rotrou's gain from the association with Normandy was more than simply the king-duke's subsidy, however. It was recognition and reinforcement of his power, and perhaps more significantly, it also clarified the relationship between the Rotrou lineage and other lordly lineages.

The presence of the young bloods of Normandy who had followed Robert Curthose to Rémalard presented two dangers to Count Rotrou. First they brought disorder to the area, compromising the count's ability to maintain the peace, but a second subtler challenge to Rotrou's position is detectable in the support given to the Rémalard garrison by one of the local lords of the Huisne valley, Aylmer of Villeray. Orderic indicates this support by expressly stating that the 'king's enemies' were lodged in Aylmer's castle as well as at Rémalard. From his base at Villeray (Orne, cant. Rémalard, cme Condeau), a bluff above the River Huisne, some eleven kilometres from Nogent-le-Rotrou, Aylmer of Villeray dominated a bloc of territory extending from the village of Condeau on the valley floor up into the hills behind Villeray itself. Like the Rotrous' own territory around Nogent, it was a fairly compact area, and, also like the Rotrous, he had interests further afield, from the church at Vieuvicq (Eure-et-Loir, cant. Brou) to the woods of Monceaux (Orne, cant. Longny).[46] Aylmer was representative of the lineages that dominated the localities in the eleventh century and Rotrou himself was from a similar

---

[45] 'Quondam dum rex contra Corbonienses expeditionem facere praepararet . . .': OV ii. 356. 'Bellis itaque passim insurgentibus cordatus rex exercitum aggregauit, et in hostes pergens cum Rotrone Mauritaniensi comite pacem fecit': OV ii. 360.

[46] *CMD*, no. cxiii; *SPC*, 206. The date of the act is deduced from the fact that in 1086 a dispute concerning the woods refers to the monks' tenure having lasted fifteen years: *SPC*, 206.

stock. Yet the Rotrous now aspired to a comital title and if they were to retain the title that Rotrou had assumed it was vital that the support of men such as Aylmer should be retained.[47]

The Rotrous were not the only lineage that had begun to edge away from their neigbours such as the lords of Villeray, however. There was an alternative power not far away in the lords of Châteauneuf-en-Thymerais (Eure-et-Loir, ch.-l. du cant.). Like many of the important lineages of the eleventh century, the origins of the lords of Châteauneuf-en-Thymerais are obscure. They took their name from a fortification, first mentioned in the 1060s, which was built at the point where the road between Dreux and Le Mans met the road from Chartres to southern Normandy. There was another castle nearby at Thimert, which in the late 1050s had been garrisoned briefly by the Normans, and it is possible that the new castle was erected as part of the campaign of King Henry of France against the Normans in the late 1050s. At some point the new castle came into the possession of one Guaszo, who was besieged therein during the course of a long war with his brother-in-law, Albert Ribaud, but by the late 1070s the castle and Albert's property had been inherited by Guaszo's son, Hugh.[48]

Hugh's interests stretched from Dreux to Rémalard as the castles he placed at the disposal of Robert Curthose demonstrated, and he had made his own connection with the Normans by marrying Mabel, daughter of Rotrou's ally, Roger of Montgommery. The major alignment of Hugh's family seems to have been with the Capetian kings of France, however, and it is likely that the family had gained prominence from a role as the king's warriors in the hostilities that were conducted along the southern Norman border for much of the eleventh century. When Hugh's uncle, Albert Ribaud, gave the church of Brezolles (Eure-et-Loir, cant. Dreux) to the monastery of Saint-Père of Chartres, he secured royal confirmation because the property was held by the king's favour ('ex nostro beneficio') and property he held in Dreux was similarly of the king's gift. None of the family's members aspired to the title of count, but the powers as described in Albert's grant to Saint-Père were little different from those of Count Rotrou.[49] Here then was another potential rival for the Rotrou lineage, occupying a similar position and eager to secure influence, and the castle at Rémalard brought this rival's influence well into Rotrou's territory.

Both the lords of Châteauneuf and the Rotrous had links with the lords of Villeray in the 1050s and 1060s, but when it came to the Rémalard campaign

---

[47] CMD no. cix; NLR, no. xxxviii. Two toponymics, Condeau and Villeray, are used to describe Aylmer. See SPC, 206, 337, both of which describe a single benefaction by the Villeray family, but use the toponymics interchangeably.

[48] For Thimert see Recueil des actes des ducs de Normandie, 911–1066, ed. M. Fauroux (Mémoires de la Société des antiquaires de Normandie xxxvi, 1961), no. 147. For Châteauneuf-en-Thymerais see De Romanet, Géographie, i. 143–8; SPC, 133–7.

[49] SPC, 127.

of 1078 Aylmer followed Hugh of Châteauneuf, siding with Robert Curthose, rather than supporting Count Rotrou and his ally, William the Conqueror. Shortly before his death in 1078 Aylmer had received a visit from the man who was or would soon become Hugh of Châteauneuf's son-in-law, the king of France's steward, Gervase.[50] With the defection of Aylmer Rotrou had lost control of the central part of the Huisne valley and thus the heart of the area over which he exercised his comital power. It is quite possible, too, that other lords from the forested areas to the north and east of the River Huisne looked to Châteauneuf-en-Thymerais for leadership as much as to Count Rotrou. Perhaps Aylmer had become uncomfortable with the comital power that Rotrou had assumed and the realignment with the Normans that the new count had been developing since 1066. Orderic is emphatic that Aylmer had a history of conflict with the Normans, for he had been a thorn in the side of the Norman lord, Roger of Montgommery, and he may have fought with the Châteauneuf lineage against the Normans.[51]

The alliance between William and Rotrou in 1078 was, therefore, a significant development for both parties. William was enabled to pursue his rebellious son and his accomplices, while developing friendly relations with a neighbour whose continuing support could strengthen the security of the Norman border. Rotrou received the king's subsidy and was assisted in the restoration of order. He regained control of the central Huisne valley which had been lost when the two castles at Villeray and Rémalard were garrisoned against him. Most significantly, however, his connection with his mightier neighbour enhanced his power, giving him the edge over potential rivals such as the lords of Châteauneuf and reinforcing his ascendancy over his neighbours. The Norman alliance was therefore the factor which singled the Rotrou lineage out from its rivals, facilitating the continuance of its comital status.

By the end of the 1070s Rotrou could feel that he had achieved much and his wealth seems to have been considerable. He was, for example, able to make one religious benefaction of ninety-two ounces of gold, four silver cups and £40 in Poitevin and Manceau coin.[52] While it is difficult to be precise about values in a society where exchange did not always rely on money, comparisons indicate that this was a substantial sum. The 300 monks of Cluny, for example, could be clothed for £120, and in the complex of transactions surrounding the foundation of the priory of Saint-Gabriel, the monks of Fécamp valued seven horses at £39 6s. 6d.[53] Some of this largesse may have

---

[50] For the visit see OV ii. 360. For Gervase as the steward see SPC, 245–6.
[51] CMPerche, no. 5; OV ii. 360: 'Rogerii comitis contra quem diu hostiliter seruierat'.
[52] Cluny, no. 3517.
[53] G. Duby, 'Le Budget de l'abbaye de Cluny entre 1080 et 1155', Annales vii (1952), 159; R. H. C. Davis, The medieval warhorse: origin, development and redevelopment, London 1989, 57.

been King William's subsidy, but Rotrou's access to large amounts of coin of varying origin suggests that a proportion of his income was derived from his capacity to levy tolls and customs on trade that was taking place over considerable distances in western France. Perhaps most significant as an indicator of his wealth, however, was his disposition of gold, the most obvious item of conspicuous consumption and in the mid eleventh century still as powerful a symbol of the giver's status and wealth as it had been to the barbarian chieftains of the early Middle Ages.[54]

Rotrou chose to proclaim his success by enhancing his father's foundation of Saint-Denis of Nogent-le-Rotrou. Some time previously, in the years before 1069, he had sent to the abbey of Saint-Père of Chartres to secure monks for his father's foundation and a small community existed there throughout the 1070s, probably supervising the completion of the new church.[55] There had apparently been some misunderstanding about the precise status of the community and it was claimed as a priory by Saint-Père, but Rotrou asserted in the court of the bishop of Chartres that the foundation was independent. In December 1078 a ceremony was held to dedicate the church that had been begun by Viscount Geoffrey.[56] It had been completed in some style by Rotrou, but by that date his health was probably failing and some weeks later in January 1079 he sent his son, Geoffrey, to Chartres to secure an abbot for the community. Rotrou's confirmation of the monastery's endowment was enacted again at Chartres in the presence of Count Theobald, and the new abbot, Hubert, arrived at Nogent in time to be invested with his staff of office a few days before Rotrou's death on 1 March 1079.[57]

Rotrou then did much to establish the county of the Perche. His inheritance appears to have been little more than the immediate vicinity of Nogent, but he was able to promote his position over that of his neighbours. He assumed the title of count, extending his power over the Corbonnais and Mortagne and overtaking other lineages that had been similarly successful in accumulating power. Subsequently he re-established his family's traditional position in Châteaudun, but the durability of the Gouet territory made it impossible for him to link the two areas of his interest. He retained the traditional affiliation of his family to the counts of Blois/Chartres, declaring the count's approval of his confirmation to Nogent-le-Rotrou, but he also developed important new links with the dukes of Normandy and other Norman

---

[54] On the effect of gold-giving see Jane Martindale, 'The French aristocracy in the early Middle Ages: a reappraisal', *Past & Present* lxxv (1977), 26–7.

[55] For the history of the house in the 1060s see *NLR*, nos xxv, xxvi, lxiv.

[56] *NLR*, no. vi; *Cluny*, no. 3517.

[57] *Cluny*, no. 3517, is a version of Rotrou's confirmation to Saint-Denis, witnessed by Count Theobald of Blois/Chartres in Chartres on 11 Jan. 1079 (n.s.). For Rotrou's obit see *Obituaires de la province de Sens*, ii, ed. A. Molinier and A. Longnon, Paris 1906, 184.

lords. Although he was unable to exercise power throughout the area from the Norman border to the River Loir, his achievement was to form the basis of the new county.

Widening horizons: Geoffrey II, 1079–99

Although Count Rotrou's achievement was considerable, it did not survive in its entirety. On his death his lands were partitioned between two of his sons, Geoffrey and Hugh. Geoffrey received the northernmost portion, including Mortagne and Nogent-le-Rotrou, while the family's interests around Châteaudun were taken by Hugh Capellus – a by-name presumably referring, like Robert's Curthose, to a physical characteristic. There are no contemporary accounts of this division, but we know that the partition had taken place by 1080. Three other brothers, Warin, Rotrou and Fulk, were left without an interest. The younger Rotrou was provided for by marriage to the heiress of Gennes (Sarthe, cant. Montfort-le-Rotrou – also known as Montfort-le-Gesnois), while the two other brothers probably did not survive their father. Warin's last dateable appearance took place in 1076 and he did not attest his father's act in favour of Saint-Denis of Nogent-le-Rotrou in December 1078, although Fulk was still alive at that point.[58]

At first sight the division appears to have been something of a setback for the lineage and the rationale for the split is not apparent. There may have been an attachment to partible inheritance, indicated by Viscount Geoffrey's similar division between his two sons, which gave Châteaudun to Hugh and Nogent to Rotrou. It is difficult, however, to reconcile the division with any pattern of inheritance by which the eldest son received the patrimony and the younger the acquisitions, since it is almost impossible to determine whether Châteaudun or Nogent-le-Rotrou was the original family holding. It may be that Hugh Capellus was the eldest surviving brother: he approved with his father a grant made to Saint-Vincent of Le Mans in 1076 and he appears the senior family figure in approving the grant of Saint-Léonard of Bellême to Marmoutier.[59] It is even possible that a three-way division had been envisaged whereby Hugh would receive Châteaudun, Geoffrey Nogent

---

[58] CMPerche, no. 16 (1092); CMD, no. cxl (1080). For Warin see VLM, no. 589; NLR, no. xxvi. For Fulk and Rotrou see NLR, no. vi. For Rotrou and the lineage he established at Montfort-le-Gesnois (Sarthe, ch.-l. du cant.), later known as Montfort-le-Rotrou, see NLR, nos xviii, xlix; AD Eure-et-Loir, abbaye of Saint-Avit de Chateaudun, MS H4611; AD Sarthe, priory of Gué de Launay, MSS H84, H85; priory of Torcé, MS H375; priory of Bersay, MS H1113. Rotrou survived until at least 1108: NLR, no. xx bis.

[59] VLM, no. 589; '. . . Hugo vicecomes de Castroduno auctorisavit ecclesiam sancti Leonardi sancto Martino Majoris Monasterii cum omnibus possessionibus seu rebus ad eamdem ecclesiam pertinentibus . . . annuentibus istis: Gausfredo comite fratre ejus. . . . Isti sunt fidejussores quod Hugo vicecomes dedit monachis Sancti Martini pro fratribus suis Gausfredo et Rotroco': CMPerche, no. 16.

and Warin Mortagne. Warin approved two of his father's acts with the otherwise inexplicable soubriquet Warin Brito, which may imply a link with Mortagne and its Breton connections.[60] The unknown factor in events is the role of the count of Blois/Chartres. It may be that Count Theobald had had misgivings about the Norman connections which Count Rotrou had developed and insisted that Rotrou's legacy should be divided between his sons. Initially the brothers may have attempted to preserve their father's influence by working together since documents surviving from the period immediately after Count Rotrou's death suggest that they maintained an interest in each other's lands, but it becomes increasingly difficult to detect these links and the conclusion that the brothers began to pursue independent policies is inescapable.[61]

At the very outset of his rule Count Geoffrey took a step that consolidated the position attained by his family. When Geoffrey succeeded his father in 1079 the status of the monastery at Nogent-le-Rotrou had recently been clarified in the court of the bishop of Chartres. The claims put forward by the abbey of Saint-Père of Chartres that Nogent was one of its many priories scattered around the Chartrain and Norman borders had been refuted. A new abbot, Hubert, had been invested with his office by Count Rotrou on his deathbed and the establishment of the monastic community at Nogent appeared complete. Shortly after the death of his father, however, the new count took the family foundation in an entirely new direction. Expressing concern at both the standard of monastic life and the credentials of the abbot, Geoffrey engineered the deposition of Abbot Hubert and the house was handed over to the Cluniacs.[62]

In the second half of the eleventh century the Burgundian abbey of Cluny was at the height of its power, promoting monastic reform under St Hugh. In looking to Cluny for advice on the improvement of his family foundation Geoffrey followed the example of many of his contemporaries, but in giving the house to Cluny he was in the forefront of a new institutionalisation of reform. Nogent-le-Rotrou was one of the earliest northern French houses to formally become part of the Cluniac network, preceded only by the king's grant of Saint-Martin des Champs in Paris and the foundation of Longpont.[63] Geoffrey's imaginative act of monastic patronage gave Nogent powerful protection against the claims of Saint-Père, loosening the dynasty's ties with the counts of Blois/Chartres, and associated him with the most up-to-date expression of the monastic ideal.

This deployment of monastic patronage also had the effect of enhancing the role of the count's court, for subsequently disputes about the endowment

---

60 VLM, nos 587, 589.
61 CMD, no. cxl; NLR, nos xlix, xxxvii.
62 NLR, no. xx; BN, MS de Bourgogne 78, item 144, published as Cluny, no. 3563.
63 H. E. J. Cowdrey, The Cluniacs and the Gregorian reform, Oxford 1970.

could and did come to the count's court for resolution. The deathbed grant of property at Fontaine-Raoul (Loir-et-Cher, cant. Droué) by Robert Metsasella, for example, began a series of disputes which continued over a number of years. An unlawful seizure of the property was rectified in the count's court after the perpetrators were forced to come to judgement ('ad judicium venire compulsi') by Count Geoffrey. A claim on the property by a knight Salierus was also settled in the court after an impressive proceeding involving judgement under the leadership of Count Geoffrey. Similarly a lawsuit concerning the priory's property at Flacey (Eure-et-Loir, cant. Bonneval) came to Geoffrey's court. After the division of Count Rotrou's territory both these localities lay well to the south of Geoffrey's interests and might more naturally look to the court of his brother, Hugh, for the settlement of their disputes.[64]

The records of the community at Nogent provide, in fact, our only evidence of the court of Count Geoffrey, but it was clearly an important element in reinforcing the prestige and power of the dynasty. It was a gathering dependent on the count that offered the opportunity for dispute resolution and a means of making public a settlement or a property transaction.[65] Its proceedings appear to have been essentially oral, although the written evidence of a charter admitted in a plea between Joscelin Malaterra and the monks of Saint-Denis suggests that towards the end of the eleventh century the use of the written word was becoming more important. The ceremonial and the activities of the court, however, revolved around the count, who acted as its president and received its proceeds from fees and fines. Its effect was to promote the count as guardian of an ordered society, and Geoffrey was thus able to maintain much of the prestige of his father's position, becoming a figure of some stature to whom disputes might be referred for arbitration.

In the closing years of the eleventh century an increasing self-confidence can be detected among the Rotrous as the reputation of the lineage continued to grow, enhanced by the formidable Geoffrey. Although the territory controlled by the Rotrou family was small and had been fragmented by the division with Geoffrey's brother, it was strategically important and when the conflict between William the Conqueror and the French king entered a new phase towards the end of the Conqueror's life, it cannot be without significance that King Philip met Geoffrey of Mortagne at Dreux in 1086.[66] Perhaps the most telling indicator of the enhanced standing of the dynasty, however, was Geoffrey's marriage to Beatrix, daughter of Count Hilduin of Roucy.

[64] NLR, nos xix, xlix.

[65] For dispute resolution see NLR, nos lxxxiv (the case of Joscelin Malaterra), xix (the case of Robert Metsasella). For transactions see no. xxxiv. Compare the comments on dispute settlement in S. D. White, 'Inheritances and legal arguments in western France, 1050–1150', Traditio xliii (1987), 55–103.

[66] For the final months of William's life see D. C. Douglas, William the Conqueror, London 1964, 356–7; SPC, 245–6.

Where Geoffrey's father had married the daughter of a neighbouring lineage, Adeliza of Bellême, and his brothers, Hugh and Rotrou, were both to marry local women, Geoffrey took a wife from a family whose centre of influence lay some 200 kilometres away to the north-east of Paris.

Beatrix was descended from the Carolingian kings of the Franks, the early Capetian kings and the first Saxon emperor, Henry I, and her family made marriages of some consequence. Her youngest sister, Felicia became the wife of King Sancho Ramirez of Aragon, while her brother, Ebles of Roucy, had fought in the Iberian peninsula in the 1070s and had married the daughter of Robert Guiscard.[67] Geoffrey's countess therefore brought important contacts which expanded the family horizons beyond the confines of western France and introduced a new element of prestige into Geoffrey's court as well as a powerful personality. According to an account preserved at the abbey of Saint-Père, for example, Countess Beatrix was responsible for the invitation to Cluny and this is by no means an unreasonable suggestion. The centre of her family's power in Roucy lay less than fifty kilometres from the Cluniac foundation at Longpont and Beatrix features in many of the acts relating to Nogent in her husband and son's lifetimes. She took considerable interest in its well-being, apparently dissuading her son from establishing another monastic community at Arcisses (Eure-et-Loir, cant. Nogent-le-Rotrou, cme Brunelles) in the early 1100s.[68]

According to the Saint-Père account old Count Rotrou had made a considerable bequest of his gold, silver, wine and wheat to the community at Nogent, but after his death the wine and wheat were seized and used as collateral for loans by Rotrou's sons, while Beatrix took possession of the gold and silver. When asked to restore it by the monks, she drove them out and substituted the monks from Cluny. It is a scandalous story, recorded by a house which had made an unsuccessful attempt to secure control of Nogent, but it highlights the important role of the countess.[69] It is clear that Beatrix was a woman of some ability who made an important contribution to the development of the dynasty, and in her religious patronage as well as in her commandeering of the family treasure, was emulating the role of her queenly ancestors, for whom spiritual concerns and control of the treasury were important duties.[70]

Despite the increasing self-confidence of the family, however, the resources available to sustain the comital title had declined. Geoffrey could find substantial sums, such as the 300s. *dunois* and £35 11s. *dunois* that he gave to buy the church of Saint-Germain of Loisé for the priory at

---

[67] Guenée, 'La Fierté d'être capetien', 450–77.

[68] *SPC*, 156–8; N. Hunt, *Cluny under St Hugh, 1049–1109*, London 1967, 126ff; Geoffrey Grossus, 'Vita Beati Bernardi Tironiensis', PL clxxii. 1406.

[69] *SPC*, 156–8.

[70] P. Stafford, *Queens, concubines and dowagers: the king's wife in the early Middle Ages*, Leicester 1998, 108, 120.

Nogent-le-Rotrou, but he no longer had access to the lucrative vicecomital powers at Châteaudun possessed by his father.[71] The polarisation of the lineage into northern and southern branches may therefore account for the resolution with which he pursued a quarrel with his neighbour and second cousin, Robert of Bellême. Geoffrey's father, Rotrou, had worked in co-opera-tion with Robert's father, Roger of Montgommery, but in this next generation relations broke down. Geoffrey disputed the distribution of the Bellême inheritance between the two heiresses: his own mother Adeliza and Mabel, mother of Robert of Bellême. Orderic Vitalis asserts that Geoffrey claimed the castle at Domfront and other property, presumably on the grounds that it was the legacy of his maternal grandfather, Warin of Domfront, and in the early 1090s he attacked Robert's property at Échauffour in southern Normandy. Orderic is clear that the struggle between the two men was protracted and that Count Geoffrey seized much booty from Robert's estates.[72]

The destination of much of the Rotrous' wealth is known to us from the records of the religious houses they patronised, but the maintenance of the comital dignity also required military strength and the resources to reward followers. Bishop Fulbert writes of Viscount Geoffrey gathering knights together and leading them against the lands of the Church, while Count Rotrou required warriors to wage his campaigns in the Gouet lands. A regular flow of booty was, of course, one means to sustain such a following and the quest for such booty would have been one of the reasons for Count Geoffrey's participation in the conquest of England as a young man. It is even possible that he had fought in the Iberian peninsula as his brother-in-law, Ebles of Roucy, had done in the 1070s and this might account for the substantial amounts of gold with which the priory at Nogent was endowed at the dedica-tion of its church. Geoffrey's conflict with his cousin therefore may well have been a response to declining resources. This renewed border raiding by followers of the count of Mortagne is revealed in another incident from the early 1090s. As he rode unarmed near the castle of Moulins-la-Marche on the southern Norman borders, a famous Norman knight, Gilbert of L'Aigle, was set upon and killed in an apparently unprovoked attack launched by Count Geoffrey's men, Gerald Capreolus, Roger of Ferrières and others. Their moti-vation is unknown, but it is likely that they intended to hold the Norman lord to ransom.

Despite lacking the full range of resources available to his father, Geoffrey none the less successfully maintained the comital dignity that Rotrou had assumed. The Anglo-Norman historian Orderic Vitalis, writing a generation later, reflected on the elements which contributed to Geoffrey's prestige. He tells us that Geoffrey

---

[71] *NLR*, nos xxii, xxiii.
[72] OV vi. 396–8.

was a distinguished count, handsome and brave, God-fearing and devoted to the church, a staunch defender of the clergy and God's poor; in time of peace he was gentle and lovable and conspicuous for his good manners; in time of war, harsh and successful, formidable to the rulers who were his neighbours and an enemy to all. He stood out among the highest in the land because of the high birth of his parents and his wife, Beatrice, and kept valiant barons and warlike castellans in firm subjection to his government . . . Count Geoffrey . . . supported by arms and men, wealth and friends, and, most important of all, filled with the fear of the Lord, feared no man.[73]

As the eleventh century drew to a close, Geoffrey reinforced that prestige with a series of matrimonial alliances. Acknowledging the fault of his followers in the murder of Gilbert of L'Aigle, Geoffrey used a traditional expedient of conflict resolution and arranged a marriage alliance between his daughter, Juliana, and the man who might otherwise have pursued a feud, Gilbert's nephew.[74] The marriage had the effect of again directing the dynasty's attention northwards. Another daughter, Margaret, further strengthened the family's links with Normandy by marrying Henry, younger son of the Conqueror's associate, Roger of Beaumont. Although Henry had spent much of his youth in the duchy, he was able to secure extensive lands in England in the late 1080s through his support for William Rufus and subsequently became earl of Warwick.[75] The marriage of a third daughter, Matilda, is largely unremarked by modern commentators because Orderic Vitalis makes no reference to it. It is however the most revealing of the family's place in a wider political community, for Matilda went south of the Loire to marry Raymond, viscount of Turenne, and after his death, Guy of Lastours.[76]

It was however the participation of Geoffrey's son, Rotrou, in the First Crusade which established definitively the reputation of the dynasty. The impact of Pope Urban's call to western Christendom is well illustrated by the response of the Rotrou lineage, for the young Rotrou was his father's only son and his presence on the journey to the east is an indication of the commitment of the family and others like it. Accompanied by a local man, Geoffrey of Rivray, Rotrou probably journeyed first northwards to the ducal court at Rouen, for Orderic Vitalis suggests that Rotrou departed in the entourage of Robert Curthose, duke of Normandy, which left in September 1096.[77] In doing so Rotrou followed the example of his father who had served in the Conqueror's forces in 1066 and his presence in this contingent with other

---

73 OV iv. 160.
74 OV iv. 200–2.
75 D. Crouch, 'The local influence of the earls of Warwick, 1088–1242: a study in decline and resourcefulness', *Midland History* xxi (1996), 3–5, and 'Oddities in the early history of the marcher lordship of Gower, 1107–1166', *Bulletin of the Board of Celtic Studies* xxxi (1984), 133–41.
76 Geoffrey of Vigeois, 'Chronicon lemovicense', in *RHF* xii. 424.
77 OV v. 34. For Geoffrey of Rivray see *NLR*, no. x.

associates of the Norman dukes, such as the lords of Saint-Pol and Saint-Valéry, rather than in that of Stephen of Blois, is further evidence for the weakening of ties with the Thibaudian counts of Blois and Chartres.

As part of Robert of Normandy's forces he presumably followed the route of his leader across the Alps, wintering in southern Italy before embarking from Brindisi and journeying to Constantinople. Rotrou next appears in Albert of Aachen's list of those who fought at the siege of Nicaea in mid 1097. He is placed in this list with the same members of the Norman duke's entourage mentioned by Orderic, indicating the survival of the military groupings with which the expedition had begun. It may be that Rotrou was already beginning to make a name for himself for he is described in the list as an outstanding young man: 'Ruthardus filius Godefridi juvenis clarissimus'. His reputation was further enhanced when he commanded one of the divisions which broke out of Antioch in late June 1098; Rotrou himself may have considered his role in this engagement as the high point of his crusading career.[78] An indication that the incident had a special place in family tradition is given by the reference to it, made more than a century later, by Rotrou's grandson William.[79]

As a result of those exploits Rotrou became an important figure in the corpus of old French epic poems set during the First Crusade. Among these literary sources the 'Chanson d'Antioche', which commentators generally agree is the earliest and most reliable of the epics, provides additional information about his crusading career.[80] It links Rotrou with Norman troops, locating him among Bohemond's forces in the battle of Dorylaeum and describing him as a close comrade of Tancred, nephew of Bohemond. There are some improbabilities and inaccuracies in the Chanson's account of Rotrou's activities. He is unlikely, for example, to have influenced the strategy of the crusading army before Antioch as the Chanson suggests and he was certainly not 'li quens . . . del Perche', the count of the Perche, at this period, but only the son of the count of Mortagne.[81] None the less the information it provides is on the whole plausible. Rotrou would have made contact with the Normans when wintering in southern Italy with Robert of Normandy and a fighting comradeship would have been established when Bohemond fought alongside Robert of Normandy's forces at Dorylaeum. The Chanson's picture of Rotrou bivouacked with Olivier of Jussy, Ralph of Beaugency, Richard of Dijon, Raimbaud of Cameli and other not easily iden-

---

[78] Albert of Aachen, 'Historia Hierosolymitana', in *Recueil des historiens des croisades*, iv. 316, 421–2.

[79] De Romanet, *Geographie*, ii. 9; BN, MS lat. 5993A, fo. 145v.

[80] G. R. Myers, 'The manuscripts of the old French crusade cycle', in J. A. Nelson and E. J. Mickel (eds), *The old French crusade cycle*, i, Birmingham, AL 1977, p. xv; *La Conquête de Jérusalem*, ed. C. Hippeau, Paris 1868, lines 1585, 1829, 4236, 7349, 7368, 7916, 7929, 8596.

[81] *Chanson d'Antioche*, ed. S. Duparc-Quioc, Paris 1977–8, lines 70, 114, 160, 166, 194, 199, 244, 307, 441.

tifiable figures before the walls of Antioch suggests that he had by then become detached from Robert of Normandy's troops. Some time later he joined a foraging expedition led by Bohemond and is then portrayed as a comrade of Tancred in an engagement against a Turkish sortie. In the final assault on the city, which was made possible through Bohemond's intrigues with the defenders, Rotrou was the fifth man on the ladder, below Bohemond and Tancred.[82]

He must then have followed the campaign to its culmination with the capture of Jerusalem, though he is not mentioned again in contemporary narratives. Meanwhile, some three years after the departure of his only son, Count Geoffrey fell ill. The old count's preparations for death are described by Orderic Vitalis, who recounts that Geoffrey summoned the nobles of the Perche and the Corbonnais and 'put his affairs in order with great care', instructing the nobles and his wife, Beatrix, to keep the peace until Rotrou's return. Presumably aware that his son had survived the campaign and would return home Geoffrey then retired to the house at Nogent where he took the Cluniac habit and died in mid October. Orderic is not explicit about the year, but these events must have occurred in 1099, for he later implies that Rotrou travelled back to western Europe with Robert of Normandy, who did not arrive until September 1100. Geoffrey was buried in the monastery at Nogent in a ceremony of some consequence, attended by his brother, Hugh of Châteaudun, his son-in-law, Gilbert of L'Aigle, Bishop Ivo of Chartres and his archdeacon, William. Two of his followers, Giroie of Orme and Gouffier of Villeray, made benefactions to the house in his memory.[83]

When the young Rotrou arrived home in 1100, bearing his souvenir palms from the Holy Land, he found his inheritance intact and waiting for him under the watchful eye of his mother. Six days after his arrival he made a ceremonial entry into the precincts of the priory of Saint-Denis and confirmed the grant of the house to Cluny.[84] His family had come a long way since his great-grandfather had laid the foundations of the community in the early 1030s. Instead of a title of viscount which implied subordination to a higher authority, Rotrou was now acknowledged as a count. His territory was not extensive, but it occupied a strategically significant position and was recognised as an identifiable unit. His father and grandfather had forged links with their Norman neighbours, which had begun to distance them from the counts of Blois/Chartres, and Rotrou had enhanced those links through crusading

---

82 On the siege of Antioch as portrayed in the 'Chanson' see L. A. M. Sumberg, *La Chanson d'Antioche: étude historique et littéraire*, Paris 1968, 228–75. Rotrou's crusading career is discussed in K. Thompson, 'Family tradition and the crusading impulse', *Medieval Prosopography* xix (1998), 1–33, esp. pp. 5–10, and J. Riley-Smith, *The first crusaders (1095–1131)*, Cambridge 1997, 144–5.

83 OV vi. 394; *NLR*, nos li, xxxvii.

84 *NLR*, no. x.

cameraderie with Duke Robert Curthose of Normandy. By the turn of the twelfth century both the comital status of the Rotrou lineage and their power from the lands around Mortagne to the upper reaches of the River Huisne were undisputed.

3

Rotrou the Great (1099–1144)

The twelfth century presented new challenges and opportunities for the Rotrou dynasty. In France a new political situation offered potential for gain as successive French kings struggled to contain the growing power of the dukes of Normandy who were often also kings of England and became ultimately rulers of the so-called Angevin empire. In the Holy Land and the Iberian peninsula conflict with the Muslims opened up new horizons for the warrior elite of western Europe. Against this background the most conspicuous of his lineage, Count Rotrou II, ruled the Perche. With his heroic status in the crusading epic tradition and his long service against the Muslims in the Iberian peninsula, Rotrou has a larger-than-life quality which sets him apart from his contemporaries. He dominates the history of his family, leading one modern commentator to dignify him with the epithet, 'the Great'.[1] In his lifetime, and thanks in part to the personal reputation he acquired in Christian warfare, the Perche was consolidated among the principalities of northern France, developing its own relations with the rival French and English kings and distancing itself from the counts of Blois/Chartres.

The completion of the Perche: the years before 1120

On his return from the First Crusade in the autumn of 1100 the young Count Rotrou II found a well-managed and largely peaceful inheritance waiting for him. Charter references which can be dated to the period immediately after his return indicate that the instruction to keep the peace given by his father to the nobles of the Perche and to his mother, the Countess Beatrix, had been followed and Rotrou had simply to ratify the acts made in his absence.[2] Shortly after his return from the east Rotrou visited Chartres where he attested a concession to the cathedral made by Count Stephen-Henry and his wife, Countess Adela.[3] Rotrou's family had traditionally acknowledged the counts of Blois/Chartres as their overlords, but Rotrou had not seen the count for more than two years since Stephen-Henry had left the Christian army in June 1098 during the siege of Antioch and had returned to France. Stephen-Henry was about to depart again for the Holy Land and his benefac-

---

1 De Romanet, *Géographie*, i. 48.
2 *NLR*, nos li, lviii.
3 For Rotrou at Chartres see *NDC* i. 104–8.

tion to the cathedral at Chartres was also witnessed by Ralph of Beaugency, whom the 'Chanson d'Antioche' epic portrays as one of Rotrou's comrades at the siege of Antioch, so it may be that Rotrou and Ralph were providing the most up-to-date information on conditions in the east.[4]

While Rotrou preserved cordial relations with the count of Blois, he appears not to have maintained his links with his crusading comrade, Duke Robert II (Curthose) of Normandy (1087–1106), and in preference associated himself with the duke's brother, King Henry I of England (1100–35). In the opening years of the twelfth century Henry was developing the strategy which would enable him to depose his elder brother, Duke Robert, and reunite Normandy with the English kingdom won by their father, William the Conqueror. Henry's initial tactics were to seek supporters among the Norman baronage and to cultivate those who might foster disorder in the duchy. During this period Duke Robert's most consistent supporter was Robert of Bellême, who had been forced to concentrate his attention on his Norman lands when King Henry had dispossessed him of his English property in 1102. Rotrou's father, Count Geoffrey II of Mortagne, had quarrelled with Robert over the partition of the Bellême inheritance and taken up arms against him. It was a grievance which Robert Curthose was unlikely to settle in Rotrou's favour, so it was perhaps natural that Henry should try to exploit it and win Rotrou to his side. In 1104, when Henry visited his only continental possession at Domfront (Orne), he entertained Rotrou there and at around the same time he gave Rotrou his illegitimate daughter, Matilda, in marriage.[5] Henry thus secured another well-placed supporter and Rotrou a consort, but the alliance is also an indication of the political judgement of the young Rotrou. He had had an opportunity to observe Robert Curthose on the scene of his greatest triumphs in the Holy Land, yet he had made the decision to support Henry. Admittedly this gave him *carte blanche* to continue his father's attacks against Curthose's most prominent supporter, Robert of Bellême, but it was still a gamble and might have committed Rotrou to a lifetime of conflict with the Norman duke and Robert of Bellême if Henry had been unsuccessful.

In the event Rotrou supported the winning side: King Henry defeated his brother at the battle of Tinchebrai in 1106 and took possession of the duchy. Rotrou was henceforth to be closely connected to the ruler who had reconstituted the Anglo-Norman realm. His wife was the king's daughter and one of his brothers-in-law, Gilbert of L'Aigle, was the king's agent in Normandy while another, Henry earl of Warwick, was among Henry's closest allies in

---

[4] On Stephen-Henry's career see J. A. Brundage, 'An errant crusader: Stephen of Blois', *Traditio* xvi (1960), 380–95.
[5] OV iv. 160. For Geoffrey's dispute see OV vi. 396–8, discussed in K. Thompson, 'Robert of Bellême reconsidered', ANS xiii (1990), 263–86. For Rotrou at Domfront see OV vi. 56; for the marriage see OV vi. 40.

England.[6] Rotrou had also acquired interests in England for himself, since Matilda brought her husband two valuable manors in England, Aldbourne and Wanborough in Wiltshire. Although there is some evidence that Matilda was of English descent on her mother's side, it was not her origins which dictated the location of her dowry. King Henry's intention was to give her husband a stake in the continuance of the Anglo-Norman realm, since the English property, a significant increase to the family's resources, ensured that Rotrou had an interest in maintaining the union of Normandy and England. It was an interest which he had earlier lacked, for, despite Orderic's assertion that Rotrou's father had received rich rewards for his participation in the Hastings campaign, there is no record of Rotrou family land in Domesday Book.[7]

Rotrou and his wife were to use some of their English resources to continue the patronage of the Cluniac order which had been practised by both their fathers. Matilda gave land at Wanborough to the Cluniac priory at Lewes while Rotrou donated a hide at Broom in Wiltshire to the Cluniac nunnery at Marcigny, but the count also interested himself in the new, more ascetic orders, which had emerged in the closing years of the eleventh century.[8] Charismatic leaders such as Vitalis of Mortain and Robert of Arbrissel attracted followers who were organised into communities with new approaches to monastic life. These new communities laid greater emphasis on manual labour in a harsh physical environment, and they settled in waste-lands and forests as far as possible from human habitation. Vitalis founded a house at Savigny with the support of the nobleman, Ralph of Fougères, while Robert of Arbrissel, whose followers included many women penitents, estab-lished a community at Fontevraud under a nobly-born abbess, Petronilla of Chemillé, and was soon receiving the patronage of the count of Anjou.[9]

Among these charismatic leaders was Bernard of Abbeville, who settled some thirteen kilometres to the east of Nogent, at Thiron (-Gardais, Eure-et-Loir, ch.-l. du cant.). Like the other leaders Bernard was a great preacher but, unlike them, he had experience of monastic life and had been an abbot. The community he founded was probably therefore more organised and able to act as a focus for reform more promptly. Only a few years after its foundation it

6   For Gilbert see K. Thompson, 'The lords of Laigle: ambition and insecurity on the borders of Normandy', ANS xviii (1995), 184–6. For Henry see Crouch, 'The local influence'.
7   For Henry's policy see K. Thompson, 'Dowry and inheritance patterns: some examples from the descendants of King Henry I of England', Medieval Prosopography xvii/2 (1996), 45–61. For a full discussion of the English estates of the counts of the Perche see ch. 7.
8   BL, MS Cotton Vespasian F xv (Cartulary of Lewes priory), fo. 171v. The Book of fees, London 1921–31, 738, provides the information that the abbess of Marcigny held the vill of Brome by the gift of Rotrou, a gift which must have been made by 1120 when it was confirmed by Pope Calixtus II: Le Cartulaire de Marcigny-sur-Loire (1045–1144): essai de reconstruction d'un manuscrit disparu, ed. J. Richard, Dijon 1957, no. 270.
9   H. Leyser, Hermits and the new monasticism, London 1984, 19.

was able to establish daughter houses, including communities in England, and attracted patronage from both the king of France and the king of England.[10] Count Rotrou's association with the abbey of Tiron was both to increase the prestige of his dynasty and enhance its power at the very fringes of the area that would become the Perche.[11]

Accounts of the early history of the community at Thiron vary. Orderic Vitalis, writing in the mid 1130s, suggests that Bernard settled in the locality under the auspices of Bishop Ivo of Chartres. A *Life* of Bernard, however, written at the abbey of Tiron itself a few years later by Geoffrey Grossus, preserves traditions about its early days which assign a rather fuller role to Rotrou.[12] Geoffrey's version suggests that there had been an initial period of negotiation between Bernard and Count Rotrou over the location of the house. Rotrou had apparently offered Bernard and his followers property at Arcisses (Eure-et-Loir, cant. Nogent-le-Rotrou, cme Brunelles), but had withdrawn the offer on the advice of his mother because it might conflict with the interests of the Cluniacs who had been established at Nogent since the 1080s and with whom Bernard had pursued a bitter dispute when he was abbot of Saint-Cyprien in Poitiers.

There has been a lively debate about the composition of Geoffrey Grossus' *Life* of Bernard. While its modern editor places it firmly in the context of hagiography, the German scholar, Johannes von Walter, writing in the early twentieth century, suggested that Geoffrey had compiled the *Life* from two earlier sources, one of which had probably been available to Orderic, while the other was a later account containing material related to the Rotrou family.[13] A 'Rotrou source' is a distinct possibility for the *Life* is quite emphatic that the community at Thiron received its land from Rotrou ('accepta itaque a consule hac possessiuncula, vir Domini Bernardus . . .') and it may therefore have been a *Life* of the saint written for and even at the request of the Rotrou family, which would naturally stress the assistance given to the founder by them. A likely reconstruction of events is therefore that Bernard, having failed at the papal court in his dispute with the Cluniacs, spent some time travelling and came eventually to Chartres, attracted

---

[10] *Tiron*, nos xiii, xxv, vi, viii.

[11] The modern placename is spelt Thiron on Institut géographique nationale maps, but the order of Tiron is usually spelt without the 'h'.

[12] OV iv. 328–30; Geoffrey Grossus, 'Vita Beati Bernardi Tironiensis', cols 1367–446.

[13] For a modern edition and French translation see B. Beck, *Saint Bernard de Tiron, l'ermite, le moine et le monde*, Caen 1998, 303–461, and on the background to its composition idem, 'Bernard de Tiron ou l'impossible sainteté d'après la *Vita Beati Bernardi* de Geoffroy le Gros', in P. Bouet and F. Neveux (eds), *Les Saints dans la Normandie médiévale: colloque Cérisy-la-Salle (26–29 septembre 1996)*, Caen 2000, 285–301. For the debate see J. von Walter, 'Bernard de Thiron', *Bulletin de la Commission historique et archéologique de la Mayenne* 2nd sér. xxiv (1908), 385–410; J. de Bascher, 'La *Vita* de saint Bernard d'Abbeville, abbé de Saint-Cyprien de Poitiers et de Tiron', *Revue Mabillon* lix (1976/80), 411–50. See *Tiron*, no. i, for the cartulary account.

perhaps by Bishop Ivo's reputation for legal acumen. The bishop then gave him permission to settle within the diocese at Thiron.

Orderic's account contrasts the undeveloped natural site 'where robbers had normally lain hidden' waiting to fall on unwary travellers' with the monastery which Bernard and his followers would build there. According to Orderic all manner of men were attracted to Bernard's settlement and soon a thriving economic community developed: 'among the men who hastened to share his life were joiners and blacksmiths, sculptors and goldsmiths, painters and masons, vine-dressers and husbandmen and skilled artificers of many kinds'. Count Rotrou, impressed by the discipline of the community and perhaps by its economic success, initially offered Bernard the rather better accommodation at Arcisses, but subsequently withdrew his offer on his mother's advice.

The count then perhaps offered his protection to Bernard in return for Bernard's acknowledgement that the land where the community was situated had been received from Rotrou, and he supplemented the offer with additional endowments. Bernard and the monks of Tiron welcomed a patron and an association was forged. It was therefore Rotrou who, in the conventional role of lay protector, approached Bishop Ivo, asking him to consecrate the cemetery at Tiron, and Ivo agreed on the understanding that no secular taxes were to be levied on the property. The chronicle of Saint-Maxient of Poitiers, whose compilers would have had good cause to remain interested in the career of Bernard, the former abbot of Saint-Cyprien in Poitiers, indicates that Bernard's community was established in 1107 and in 1109 the first mass was celebrated within wooden buildings.[14]

By the second half of the 1100s, then, Rotrou was securely established and able to indulge an interest in the newly emerging monastic orders. He had entered an alliance with King Henry I of England which had secured his northern border and given him access to additional property in England. His family connection with the Thibaudian counts of Blois/Chartres did not lapse, but the departure of Count Stephen-Henry to a crusader's death at the Battle of Ramleh in 1102 probably meant it was less actively promoted. The assumption of power by Stephen-Henry's widow, Countess Adela, on behalf of her sons may even have had the effect of drawing Rotrou more closely into alignment with King Henry, for the countess was Henry's sister. Rotrou none the less remained content to acknowledge the comital courts as an incident dating from 1106/7 reveals. Our information is derived from four letters, written by Bishop Ivo of Chartres (1090–1115), which describe a dispute between Count Rotrou and Ivo, the lord of Courville.[15]

---

14 For the cemetery see *Tiron*, no. ii. For the consecration see Geoffrey Grossus, 'Vita Beati Bernardi Tironiensis', cols 1408–9. The chronicle of St Maxient of Poitiers is published in *Chroniques des églises d'Anjou*, ed. P. Marchegay and E. Mabille, Paris 1869, 423.

15 Ivo of Chartres, 'Letters', PL clxii, epp. clxviii–clxx, clxxiii. In the context of comital control of castle-building see Chédeville, *Chartres*, 278.

The disagreement centred on property purchased by Rotrou where he was erecting a fortification (*munitionem*). The lord of Courville took exception to Rotrou's action and enlisted the help of the viscount of Chartres who brought a lawsuit against Rotrou at the court of Bishop Ivo, asserting that Rotrou's conduct was unacceptable because the castle was being constructed in the jurisdiction of Viscount Hugh, who was about to depart for the Holy Land. Since crusaders' property was protected by the Church, Rotrou's act was unlawful. It was a neat piece of litigious argument, but Rotrou was having none of it. He replied that the castle lay in his jurisdiction and the dispute was referred from Bishop Ivo's court to that of Countess Adela of Chartres because such a conflict of opinion could only be resolved by trial by combat (*monomachia*). At the countess's court Viscount Hugh capitulated and shortly thereafter left for the Holy Land.

In the course of his journey the viscount laid the case, or rather his version of it, before the pope who instructed Bishop Ivo to convene a special court consisting of himself, the archbishop of Sens, and the bishops of Paris and Orléans to judge the issue. In the meanwhile Rotrou and Ivo of Courville had finally come to blows and Ivo had been captured by Rotrou's forces. Rotrou and his opponents' advocates duly appeared at the specially convened court, but the advocates refused to take part because Rotrou was continuing to work on the castle and had not restored Ivo's ransom. By the time that Bishop Ivo drafted his last surviving letter on the subject Rotrou lay under threat of excommunication and the case had proved beyond the competence of the court set up to decide it, with the result that the parties had been referred to the pope himself for judgement. The outcome of the case is unknown. Although Pope Paschal II (1099–1118) had pronounced in favour of the Rotrou family foundation at Nogent-le-Rotrou when its donation to Cluny had been challenged by the abbot of Saint-Père of Chartres at the Council of Trier in 1107, it is possible that the pope found against Rotrou in this case.[16] The papal threat of excommunication certainly suggests that Paschal viewed Rotrou's offence seriously and it may be that the incident contributed to Rotrou's decision to spend time in Aragon in conflict with the Muslims.

It was rare for those who had participated in the First Crusade to take any further part in holy warfare, but some of those who did so were to continue the struggle against Islam in the Iberian peninsula.[17] The closer proximity of the war zone may have influenced them, but another motive may have been family connection. The sole evidence for Rotrou's Spanish campaign is the account given by Orderic Vitalis and that account lays emphasis on an appeal by Rotrou's cousin, King Alphonso I (the Battler) of Aragon (1104–34). Alphonso was the son of Felicia, the sister of Rotrou's mother Beatrix, and the strength of the ties between the two branches of the family is suggested by

[16] *NLR*, no. xx bis.
[17] Riley-Smith, *First crusaders*, 166.

the use of Queen Felicia's name for Rotrou's second daughter.[18] Since Rotrou is unlikely to have left his territory before his father-in-law was securely established in Normandy, and Alphonso is known to have campaigned in the Segra valley in 1108, it seems probable that Rotrou's assistance had been sought for that particular purpose.

It was by no means an unusual activity since northern French soldiers had fought in the Iberian peninsula throughout the eleventh century and Rotrou's uncle, Ebles of Roucy, had been involved there in the 1070s.[19] There was ample opportunity for reward and their involvement can be compared to the Norman interventions in southern Italy. After the success of the expedition to Jerusalem, however, the conflict in Spain could be linked to more religious motives and Rotrou's response to his cousin's appeal may have been part of the developing ideology of crusading, particularly if it was linked with the Courville incident and provided an opportunity for a penitential act by Rotrou.[20] Orderic is certain that the count had been promised generous rewards, and it may be that Rotrou saw the expedition as a source of booty for his followers when the imposition of King Henry's peace in Normandy after 1106 meant that he was no longer able to plunder Robert of Bellême's property in the Bellêmois.[21] It is clear, however, that he could confidently absent himself from the family's territory, leaving it presumably in the hands of his mother Beatrix. The expedition ended on a sour note with plots against the French combatants and Rotrou's withdrawal without 'adequate reward'. In 1109 Alphonso had taken on responsibility for the kingdom of Castille when he married its queen, Urraca, and as a result there may have been tensions at his court that were not fully understood by the northerners.[22] None the less contacts had been made that Rotrou was later to exploit.[23]

Shortly after the unsatisfactory conclusion of his adventure in Aragon

---

18 Herman of Laon, 'De miraculis S. Mariae Laudunensis', PL clvi. 965–6; S. de Vajay, 'Ramire II le moine roi d'Aragon et Agnès de Poitou dans l'histoire et dans la légende', in P. Gallais and Y.-J. Riou (eds), *Mélanges offertes à René Crozet*, Poitiers 1966, 730. For Rotrou's daughter see *Tiron*, no. cxlix.

19 For Ebles see Suger, *The deeds of Louis the Fat*, ed. R. C. Cusimano and J. Moorhead, Washington, DC 1992, 34.

20 A. Ferreiro, 'The siege of Barbastro, 1064–5: a reassessment', *Journal of Medieval History* ix (1983), 129–44. See R. A. Fletcher, 'Reconquest and crusade in Spain, c. 1050–1150', *TRHS* 5th ser. xxxvii (1987), 42–3, on papal perception of the Spanish conflict.

21 'strenuosque barones et in armis acres oppidanos': OV iv. 160. For raids see OV iv. 200; ii. 124.

22 OV vi. 396. See J. F. O'Callaghan, *A history of medieval Spain*, Ithaca, NY 1975, 216–17. C. Laliena Corbera, '*Larga stipendia et optima praedia*: les nobles francos en Aragon au service d'Alphonse le batailleur', *Annales du midi* cxii (2000), 159, expresses doubt about Rotrou's first expedition but, although Orderic is the only source, he was well-informed about the Rotrou family.

23 Henry I's Spanish doctor, Peter Alphonsus, may have found his way to Henry's court through this link: C. H. Haskins, 'The introduction of Arabic science into England', in his *Studies in the history of mediaeval science*, New York 1924, 119.

conflict again arose on the southern borders of Normandy. In July 1110 the king of England's ally, Count Helias of Maine, died and his county of Maine, which lay to the south of Normandy, came into the hands of his son-in-law, the new count of Anjou, Fulk the Young (1109–28). The counts of Anjou were among the few territorial princes who came near to rivalling the dukes of Normandy and there was a history of conflict between them. Fulk, moreover, had family connections through his mother with the lords of the Norman border region and, urged on by his uncle, Amaury of Montfort, he seized the opportunity to make raids on southern Normandy. Before long a number of Norman magnates who had never been reconciled to Henry's rule, including Rotrou's cousin, Robert of Bellême, rose in rebellion against the king.[24] Both as Henry's son-in-law, and on account of his lands in England, Rotrou's interests lay with the king, but more than strategic considerations governed the conflict in the Bellêmois where there was clearly a personal edge to the violence.

During the course of the fighting Rotrou was captured by the count of Anjou and imprisoned at Le Mans.[25] In normal twelfth-century circumstances he would have been ransomed and released, but Robert of Bellême personally sought him as a prisoner and was prepared to pay a high price. Rotrou apparently despaired for his life, and he sent the bishop of Le Mans, Hildebert of Lavardin, back to his mother Beatrix with details of his last will and testament. It was only the timely intervention of King Henry who seized and imprisoned Robert in November 1112 that saved Rotrou. It is not surprising, therefore, to find Rotrou in May 1113 in the very forefront of King Henry's forces which besieged and took Bellême from lords loyal to Robert of Bellême's son.[26] Robert of Bellême and his predecessors had acknowledged the king of France as their overlords for the Bellêmois, but in late March 1113 King Louis VI formally conceded it to Henry at a meeting at Gisors.[27] Shortly thereafter the Rotrou lineage reaped its most significant reward for its link with the Normans, for Henry granted Bellême to his son-in-law.

It was an impressive reward for the support Rotrou had given to Henry, although initially Rotrou would have received little more than a burnt-out shell, since the town had been deliberately fired and burned to the ground during the siege in 1113. The Norman chronicler, Robert of Torigni, writing more than twenty years after the event, mentions only the town (*oppidum*) of

---

[24] OV vi. 176–8; C. W. Hollister, 'War and diplomacy in the Anglo-Norman world: the reign of Henry I', ANS vi (1983), 79–81, repr. in his *Monarchy, magnates and institutions*, 280–2.

[25] Geoffrey Grossus, 'Vita Beati Bernardi Tironiensis', col. 1414, recounts the capture, and the *Actus pontificum cenomannis in urbe degentium*, ed. G. Busson and A. Ledru, Le Mans 1901, 406–7, indicates that the count was being held at Le Mans. Bishop Hildebert's own account is given in PL clxxi. 225–8.

[26] For the seizure of Robert see OV vi. 178, 256; for the fall of Bellême see OV vi. 180–2.

[27] For the overlordship of the king of France see SPC, 155; CMPerche, no. 13. For Gisors see also OV vi. 180.

Bellême, although it is apparent from the archives of the priory at Bellême that it had become the focal point of the locality to such an extent that the surrounding area was described as lying 'in castri Bellissimi pago'.[28] The grant of the lordship of Bellême therefore implies that the Rotrou lineage would henceforth possess powers over the locality similar to those they enjoyed in the Corbonnais, including the imposition of tolls and customs, the right to the profits of justice and control of the forest. Surviving acts of the Rotrou lineage show the exercise of precisely those rights, although the 'Rotrou' sections of the *Life* of Bernard of Tiron suggest that some effort was required for Rotrou to impose himself on the area: 'tam sibi quam suis haeredibus deinceps possidenda subjugavit'.[29] Robert of Torigni's use of the word *oppidum* also suggests that King Henry was careful to retain an important element of control: custody of the castle. The castle, founded by the ancestors of Robert of Bellême, was at this period an earthwork surmounted by a citadel (*arx*), and it was probably easily reconstructed for garrison by Henry's soldiers. In line with the king's policy in the duchy of Normandy a royal garrison would remain in Bellême, and the Rotrou lineage would not secure the castle definitively until the 1150s.[30]

The territory around Bellême provided the final component of the new county of the Perche and complemented the arc of territory from Mortagne to Nogent-le-Rotrou which had been in the hands of the Rotrou family for two generations. Henceforward Rotrou would assume the patronage of the priory of Saint-Léonard at Bellême which had been founded by the rival Bellême lineage and the toponymics of the men who attested his acts in its favour demonstrate the extension of his power into the Bellêmois: Geoffrey of Courthioust (Orne, cant. Nocé, cme. Colonard-Corubert), Hugh of Nocé (Orne, ch.-l. du cant.), Hugh of Cicé (Orne, cant. Bellême, cme La Gué-de-la-Chaine), William of Le Pin (Orne, cant. Pervenchères) and William of Préaux (Orne, cant. Nocé).[31] In the years which followed Rotrou increasingly adopted the title the Percheron count 'comes perticensis' or count of the Percherons 'comes perticensium' in preference to the count of Mortagne 'comes de Mauritania'. It is impossible to be precise about the point at which the new title became the preferred usage. Our major narrative source, Orderic Vitalis, who was writing up to the early 1140s, consistently refers to Rotrou as the count of Mortagne, perhaps because Mortagne was close to Saint-Évroul.

---

28 *CMPerche*, no. 7.

29 Geoffrey Grossus, 'Vita Beati Bernardi Tironiensis', col. 1415.

30 'Rex Henricus nobilissimum oppidum ejusdem, nomine Belismum, cepit et illud Rotroco, comiti Perticensi, genero suo dedit': Robert of Torigni, interpolations in *The* Gesta normannorum ducum *of William of Jumièges, Orderic Vitalis and Robert of Torigni*, ed. E. M. C. van Houts, Oxford 1992–5, ii. 264. For the later cession of the castle see Robert of Torigni, *Chronique*, ed. L. Delisle, Rouen 1872, i. 315: 'Rex autem Henricus concessit eidem Rotroco Bellismum castrum'. For the castle see A. Renoux, 'Les Fortifications de terre en Europe occidentale du Xe au XIIe siècles: rapport', *Archéologie médiévale* xi (1981), 31–2.

31 *CMPerche*, nos 22, 63, 21, 22 (for William of Le Pin and William of Préaux).

Rotrou's surviving acts and attestations suggest, however, that he had begun to use a different style from the early part of the century, reflecting an aspiration towards a new identity more broadly defined than the town of Mortagne. In his charter of confirmation to the priory of Saint-Léonard at Bellême Rotrou used the title 'count of the Perche and lord of Bellême' and Spanish sources refer to him as the count of the Perche in the 1120s.[32] Unfortunately most of Rotrou's acts survive only in cartulary copies, which may have been amended to conform to contemporary usage when recopied, and a high proportion, particularly from the cartulary of Saint-Denis of Nogent-le-Rotrou, are undated. The Nogent material which can be dated to the period immediately after his return from the Holy Land describes him as count of Mortagne, but his attestation of an act by Count Stephen-Henry of Blois as 'comes de Pertico' which probably dates from 1100/1 supports a gradual adoption of the new title by Count Rotrou.

While Rotrou pursued the enlargement of his territory there is some evidence that the women of the lineage were contributing to the enhancement of its prestige by fostering links with the Church, a 'permissible even obligatory arena for female action' according to one modern authority.[33] After her initial anxiety about the relationship between the abbey of Tiron and the family's primary foundation of Saint-Denis at Nogent-le-Rotrou, the Countess Beatrix overcame her reservations. She took up residence near the new abbey, to which Bishop Ivo of Chartres conceded a formal charter in 1114, and was responsible for the building of a great stone church there. Her daughter, Juliana, inherited her interest in the house and both women are mentioned in Rotrou's benefactions to the house while several donations were made in the presence of Juliana. So strong are the links between the two women and the community that it seems not unreasonable to suggest that the 'Rotrou source' which Geoffrey Grossus used in the compilation of the *Life* of Bernard was compiled at the request of Beatrix or Juliana to enhance Rotrou II's role in the foundation of the abbey. It was not uncommon for noblewomen to commission narrative works describing the achievements of their families and Juliana is known to have possessed a library which she bequeathed to the Fontevraudine priory of La Chaise-Dieu- du-Theil in the mid twelfth century.[34] By the end of the 1110s the community at Thiron had established a considerable reputation, attracting benefactions from all over western France and in England and contributing to the prestige of the Perche. Rotrou and his mother witnessed a gift by Count Guy of Rochefort, whose

---

[32] *Tiron*, no. vi (before 1112); *NDC* i. 104–8 (1100/1); BN, MS lat. 17139 (Extraits relatifs à Bonneval par Gaignières), p. 56 (1118); *CMPerche*, no. 21.

[33] Stafford, *Queens, concubines and dowagers*, 120.

[34] Geoffrey Grossus, 'Vita Beati Bernardi Tironiensis, col. 1416; *Tiron*, nos vi, lxiv, cvi, xi, xxii, xxxiii, cxx. For Juliana's library see AD Eure, priory of La Chaise de Thiel, MS H1438 (inventaire du prieuré de Chaise-Dieu, cartulaire de Laigle), 1. For women's patronage see J. M. Ferrante, 'Women's role in Latin letters from the fourth to the early twelfth century', in J. H. McCash (ed.), *The cultural patronage of medieval women*, Athens, Ga 1996, 86ff.

family were close associates of King Louis VI and in 1115 the king himself made a benefaction which Rotrou witnessed.[35]

As Rotrou began to deal with kings and his position was enhanced his relations with the Thibaudian counts of Blois/Chartres, whom his father and grandfather had acknowledged as their 'seniores', remained cordial, if rather remote. Rotrou visited Chartres, but there is little evidence to suggest subordination to the Thibaudians.[36] None of his acts were confirmed by the counts of Blois and he is not mentioned among the *optimates* who gave Count Theobald counsel in 1114, nor did he play any recorded part in the Thibaudians' struggle against the lords of Le Puiset or the Capetian kings.[37] Rotrou fought alongside the young Count Theobald IV at Bellême in 1113, but as an ally of King Henry, and his only other known association with the count is his presence at Theobald's court in Chartres in 1118 where he witnessed a judgement in favour of the abbey of Bonneval.[38]

It was in fact his alliance with his father-in-law, Henry I, which dominated Rotrou's relations with the Thibaudian family, as it determined much of his policy. The counts of Blois/Chartres were, like Rotrou, allied to King Henry. Countess Adela, the mother of Theobald IV, was Henry's sister and Theobald found it convenient to continue the close association with his uncle which his mother had developed during his minority.[39] While Rotrou remained within the Anglo-Norman alignment, therefore, his position was unlikely to be challenged by the Thibaudian counts and there are indications of partners within the alliance working together. The Countess Adela had, for example, found in Rotrou's favour in his dispute with the lords of Le Puiset and Courville, and the sympathetic hearing which Rotrou received from Bishop Ivo of Chartres, who worked closely with the countess, may also be a reflection of the political and family ties which bound them.[40] Certainly the presence of Rotrou among Norman troops at the battle of Alençon in 1118, when Count Fulk of Anjou again attacked southern Normandy, suggests that Rotrou never flagged in his support for Henry.[41]

It was an arrangement which suited all its participants. Henry's continental borders were rendered more secure; Count Theobald received his

---

35 *Tiron*, nos vi, vii.

36 For Rotrou at the Thibaudian court see *NDC* i. 24ff, and Ivo of Chartres, 'Letters', PL clxii, epp. clxviii–clxx, clxxiii.

37 *CMD*, no. xciv; Suger, *Louis the Fat*, 84–90, 94–103.

38 BN, MS lat. 17139, p. 56.

39 The countess's role is discussed in Hollister, 'War and diplomacy', 276–7, and in K. Lo Prete, 'The Anglo-Norman card of Adela of Blois', *Albion* xxii (1990), 569–89. For Theobald's position see M. Bur, *La Formation du comté de Champagne v. 950–v. 1150*, Nancy 1977, 281–3

40 K. Lo Prete, 'Adela of Blois and Ivo of Chartres: piety, politics and the peace in the diocese of Chartres', *ANS* xiv (1991), 131–53; Suger, *Louis the Fat*, 84–5.

41 'Chronica de gestis consulum Andegavorum', in *Chroniques d'Anjou*, i. 145.

uncle's support in his struggles against the king of France and the lords of Le Puiset, while experiencing no difficulties with his neighbour, Count Rotrou. Rotrou himself enjoyed material gains from his wife's dowry and, above all, from the acquisition of Bellême. His association with King Henry gave him a measure of protection and prestige, and, while he respected the outward forms of his relationship with the count of Blois/Chartres, he was politically Count Theobald's equal. Rotrou also enjoyed political influence out of all proportion to the size of his territory or the resources he controlled; this influence is demonstrated by the events of 1118–19 involving Rotrou's nephew, Richer of L'Aigle.

Richer was the son of Rotrou's sister Juliana, the patroness of Tiron, and her husband, Gilbert, lord of L'Aigle in southern Normandy, who had been a loyal servant of King Henry I and had been rewarded by the king with lands in the Sussex rape of Pevensey.[42] When Gilbert died in the mid 1110s his eldest son, Richer, had petitioned King Henry to be allowed to succeed to all his father's lands in both Normandy and England, but the king had planned to give the English lands to Richer's younger brothers, Geoffrey and Engenulf, and he refused Richer's request. Richer was not prepared to let the matter rest and thought he saw an opportunity in the crisis which faced the king in the later 1110s. King Louis VI of France sought to undermine his great rival, King Henry, by pressing the claims of the legitimate heir to Normandy, Robert Curthose's son, William Clitho. He had encouraged the counts of Flanders and Anjou to attack Normandy and there was a groundswell of support for William Clitho's claims among members of the Norman baronage.[43] Richer therefore tried to put pressure on King Henry by threatening to hand over his stronghold at L'Aigle on the southern borders of Normandy to the king of the French, but Henry still remained unmoved. Although beset by what C. W. Hollister calls 'the great military crisis' of his reign, Henry maintained this stance until Rotrou of the Perche pointed out 'in a friendly fashion' (*benigniter*) the consequences of allowing the rebellion to spread.[44] No sooner had Henry received this advice than he agreed to grant Richer all that he and his uncle requested.

The chronology of this episode is far from certain, for Orderic deals with it twice. His first account describes King Henry's decision to grant Richer all his father's lands following an intervention by Rotrou in August 1118. When Rotrou conveyed this news to his nephew, Richer tried to renege on his agreement with the king of France, but was forced to hand L'Aigle over to King Louis after a disastrous siege in early September. In a second reference to these events, however, Orderic places the reconciliation between Richer and the king in mid September 1119, again at the instigation of his uncle,

[42] 'Thompson, 'Lords of Laigle'.
[43] OV vi. 184.
[44] C. W. Hollister, 'The Anglo-Norman succession debate of 1126', *Journal of Medieval History* i (1975), 23, repr. in his *Monarchy, magnates and institutions*, 149; OV vi. 196.

Rotrou.[45] The precise sequence of events is therefore not easily recovered, but the underlying situation is plain. It is clear that, during this time of crisis, Rotrou was frequently at the king's side, and that he used the opportunity to act as a mediator between the king and Richer. In both references Orderic is at pains to point out that Richer's case was forwarded by his uncle and it is not difficult to surmise Rotrou's line of reasoning with the king. He no doubt pointed out to Henry the risks of allowing the vital marcher lordship of L'Aigle to fall into hostile hands and probably hinted that those risks would be increased if he himself were to withdraw his support for Henry. Under pressure from the king of France and his allies, as well as from his own disaffected baronage, and having recently experienced an assassination attempt, Henry was susceptible to Rotrou's persuasion.[46]

Orderic's account of events is detailed and suggests that it was derived from first-hand sources, possibly even Richer himself, for there is criticism of the turn of events which distracted King Henry from the recovery of L'Aigle in September 1118. In October of the same year Rotrou was again at the king's side when he witnessed one of Henry's charters at Arganchy. Despite his alliance with the king, Rotrou seldom witnessed Henry's acts and his presence at Arganchy in the autumn of 1118 is further evidence of the perilous situation in which the king found himself.[47] We do not know the precise circumstances in which L'Aigle was recovered, but Orderic recounts that the French forces retained it for a year, which indicates that King Henry was only able to dislodge them from the borders of the duchy after he had made peace with Count Fulk of Anjou in June 1119. Orderic's account of the count's second intervention shows that, when the time came, Rotrou was still at the king's side and was able to ensure that Henry reinstated Richer in his Norman inheritance and added to it the English lands which he had earlier been so reluctant to grant him.

By the year 1120 Rotrou could look back on considerable achievements. The community at Thiron had established a considerable reputation. His relations with his neighbours, the counts of Blois/Chartres, were cordial and he enjoyed the confidence and favour of King Henry of England, the most powerful ruler of his day. So great was his favour with King Henry that when in 1119 Henry made the peace with his neighbour, Count Fulk of Anjou, Rotrou was allowed to retain the Bellêmois, even though the settlement had involved the restoration of rest of the Bellême lands to Robert of Bellême's son, William Talvas.[48] The only cloud, therefore, on Rotrou's horizon was the

---

45 OV vi. 196, 248–50.
46 For the assassination see C. W. Hollister, 'The origins of the English treasury', *English Historical Review* xciii (1978), 265–6, repr. in his *Monarchy, magnates and institutions*, 214–15.
47 *Regesta regum anglo-normannorum*, ii, ed. C. Johnson and H. A. Cronne, Oxford 1956, no. 1183. For Rotrou's other attestations see nos 1466, 1944, and *CDF*, no. 1054.
48 K. Thompson, 'William Talvas, count of Ponthieu, and the politics of the Anglo-Norman realm', in D. Bates and A. Curry (eds), *England and Normandy in the Middle Ages*, London 1994, 171–2.

absence of a male heir. He had fathered two illegitimate sons, Geoffrey and Bertram, but there is no evidence that he ever intended to make them his heirs and his marriage to King Henry's natural daughter, Matilda, while successful as the means of cementing the alliance, had produced only two daughters, Philippa and Felicia.[49]

Lordship and consolidation

Within three generations then the Rotrou lineage had been securely established in the borderlands between Normandy and the lands of the Thibaudian counts of Blois/Chartres. During Rotrou II's rule it becomes easier to discern the mechanisms by which their ascendancy was maintained. While we can infer that Rotrou's predecessors were wealthy, for example, it is rare for earlier records to demonstrate the deployment of wealth as explicitly as does the reference to the 'eight pounds of his own coin' which Rotrou gave to Lancelin of Fai 'because he had made this gift to his church'.[50] Not all of this 'two-way flow of allegiance and patronage' which the Rotrous, like all other successful kings, princes and lords, controlled involved material wealth, however.[51]

For some of the local lords of the Perche the profits of office under the counts may have been a sufficient inducement to support the Rotrous. Pagan of Saint-Quentin attests several of the acts of Count Rotrou II as his *prepositus*,[52] and the responsibilities of his office secured for him the grant of a burgage tenement in Nogent-le-Rotrou, although his landed resources were probably insignificant since he gave the priory of Chartrage only half an arpent of meadow at Saint-Quentin.[53] Pagan stands for the officials who represented Rotrou power at the most basic level in the localities. There is evidence for the presence of such *prepositi*, who are occasionally called *pretor* or *prefectus*, in a number of locations where the counts had property which needed to be managed.[54] The nature of their tasks might vary from the management of landed property through the control of salt distribution at

---

[49] For Rotrou's daughters and son, Geoffrey, see *Tiron*, no. cxlix. The existence of Rotrou's son, Bertram, can be inferred from the mention in 1131 of his grandson (*nepos*): Geoffrey Bertram: *Documentos para el estudio de la reconquista y repoblación de Valle del Ebro*, ed. J. M. Lacarra, Zaragoza 1982–5, no. 210.

[50] *NLR*, no. xxviii.

[51] D. Crouch, *The Beaumont twins*, Cambridge 1986, 104.

[52] *Tiron*, nos lxii, xxxiii, cclvi; *NLR*, no. xxxii; *Cartulaire de la leproserie du Grand-Beaulieu et du prieuré de Notre-Dame de la Bourdinière*, ed. R. Merlet and M. Jusselin, Chartres 1909, no. 58 as *prefecto*.

[53] *Clairets*, no. i; L. Bart des Boulais, *Recueil des antiquitéz du Perche, comtes et seigneurs de la dicte province ensemble les fondations, bâtiments des monastères et choses notables du dict païs*, ed. H. Tournouer, Mortagne 1890, 136.

[54] BN, MS Duchesne 54, p. 460.

Nogent or Mortagne to the collection of commercial tolls in the major urban centres, although they appear not to have run the count's forest, since officials known specifically as foresters appear before 1094.[55] The terms on which the *prepositi* and foresters operated are not explicit, but it seems likely that they were appointed as farmers and attempted to secure as much revenue as possible from their office, while returning an agreed amount to the count. In the 1120s Rotrou's *prepositus* at Bellême, Pagan of Saint-Quentin, attempted to curtail the trading privileges of the priory of Bellême and Rotrou presided over the court which found against him.[56]

The opportunity to manage comital property was therefore a piece of patronage which many within the Perche would seek to secure, and would enable the Rotrous to form alliances with local families. The Capreolus dynasty were substantial figures with interests throughout the Perche, and they provide the best example of a close association between the Rotrous and particular lineages in the Perche. The precise genealogy of the family remains to be established, but the first recorded Capreolus attested an act of Count Rotrou II, probably in the 1060s, and members of the family continue to appear in the comital entourage from that period onwards. When Count Rotrou II returned from the Holy Land in 1100, two Capreoli, Hubert and Gerald, were on hand to witness his confirmation of grants made to Saint-Denis on behalf of his late father. Gerald Capreolus later accompanied Rotrou on a visit to the court of the count of Blois/Chartres in 1118, while Hubert's son, Warin, also attested acts of the comital family.[57] Around 1112 Hubert Capreolus was the count's steward and took it upon himself to imprison Bishop Hildebert of Le Mans, when the bishop brought messages to Countess Beatrix from her son who had been captured by Count Fulk of Anjou. Even though the countess had received the bishop kindly and given him the kiss of peace, Hubert suspected one member of the bishop's entourage of complicity in the count's capture and confined the entire party.[58] The bishop accused him of lawlessness, but Hubert's action implies a role as guardian of the count's interests and commander of his forces.

Any consideration of the relationship between the Rotrous and the men, such as the Capreoli, who formed the backbone of their fighting forces is speculative, but the incident involving Ivo of Courville in which the relationship was tested and ultimately broke down does throw some light on the personal bonds which linked the counts and the local lords. During the course of the dispute it was asserted on Rotrou's behalf that Ivo had broken an

---

55 *NLR*, no. xviii; *Tiron*, nos xci, cvi.

56 CM*Perche*, no. 22.

57 For the first Capreolus attestation see *NLR*, no. xix; for Rotrou II's return see *NLR*, no. li; BN, MS lat. 17139, p. 56 (1118); for Warin see *NLR*, no. xxvii; *Tiron*, no. xxxiii.

58 'Porro filius ille perditionis Hubertus Capreolus est. Hubertus consilium malignavit adversum me, manus injecit in me, captum tenet me, de dapifero comitis factus dapes diaboli': Hildebert, ep. xviii to Serlo bishop of Sées, PL clxxi. 225–8. See also Geoffrey Grossus, 'Vita Beati Bernardi Tironiensis', col. 1414, and the *Actus pontificum*, 406–7.

association which he had formed with Rotrou and the account of Rotrou's plea neatly lays out the obligations which both sides might expect to incur in such a relationship. When Ivo had acknowledged that Rotrou was his lord he had received material goods, and in return he was expected to promote his lord's interests. Ivo had failed to carry out the latter, for he held Rotrou's men captive and had caused Rotrou harm by violent means.[59]

Courville lies on the River Eure at the very edge of the Chartrain, almost exactly halfway between Nogent-le-Rotrou and Chartres, and its master might reasonably look in either direction for protection. Two generations before, in the mid eleventh century, when Ivo's namesake and predecessor had given property to the abbey of Marmoutier, he acknowledged that he had the whole area of Courville from the viscount of Chartres and his sons ('a quibus habeo totam terram Curvae Villae'). The Rotrou family, however, offered an alternative powerbase, for the donation was also witnessed by Count Rotrou's grandfather, Rotrou I, and the Courvilles must soon have begun an association with the Rotrous.[60] Before 1071 Ivo of Courville attested a donation to the Rotrou family foundation at Nogent-le-Rotrou and in the late 1090s an Ivo of Courville was present at a lawsuit in Chartres, attesting in company with Count Geoffrey II.[61] Count Rotrou II's assertions in the ecclesiastical court suggest that Ivo of Courville had at some point acknowledged Rotrou as his lord. The bond had perhaps been strengthened during the course of Rotrou's conflict with Robert of Bellême, when Rotrou would have been anxious to secure the support of as many fighting men as possible, but Ivo's enthusiasm for his new lord had apparently cooled when Rotrou had begun work on the fortification more or less in his backyard.

For others the lordship of the Rotrou lineage retained its attraction. Perhaps the best illustration of the extension of Rotrou's power is provided by the territory around Ceton (Orne, cant. Le Theil). Here an important family, the Chesnel, was well-established. Their interests stretched from Avezé (Sarthe, cant. La Ferté-Bernard) on the Huisne river along the course of the tributary River Maroisse towards Ceton, where a fine motte survives today. The resources at the disposal of this family were considerable and had been deployed in the foundation of a Cluniac priory at Ceton and in benefactions to the cathedral of Le Mans.[62] At the end of the eleventh century the head of

---

[59] 'Ivo Rotrocum dominum suum diffiduciasset, et praedam ejus prior cepisset, homines suos ea die qua captus est in vinculis haberet, et ad forisfaciendum eidem armata manu militum ea die procederet': Ivo of Chartres, 'Letters', PL clxii, ep. clxxiii. Cf. Fulbert of Chartres's classic fomulation of the obligations of lord and follower: Fulbert, *Letters and poems*, letter 51.

[60] For further links between the Courvilles and the counts of Blois see J.-F. Lemarignier, 'Le Domaine de Villeberfol et le patrimoine de Marmoutier (XIe siècle)', in *Études d'histoire du droit privé offertes à Pierre Petot*, Paris 1959, 347–62.

[61] *SPC*, 314.

[62] *Cartulaire de l'abbaye de Saint-Aubin d'Angers*, ed. A. Bertrand de Broussillon, Paris 1903, no. dcxxx; *NLR*, no. xviii; *VLM*, no. 196.

the family, Walter Chesnel, might look in three directions for lordship. His act of foundation for the priory at Ceton, made before 1094, indicates that he primarily acknowledged the Montgommerys at Bellême and he had been present when King Philip of France (1060–1107) confirmed Robert of Bellême's grant of the church of Saint-Léonard of Bellême to Marmoutier in 1092.[63] There were also long-standing Chesnel links with the Rotrous' rivals, the Gouet family, which controlled the territory to the east of Ceton and had ambitions to the south where they had built a castle at Montmirail (Sarthe, ch.-l. du cant.). Walter's father, Ivo, had been in the Gouet family entourage in the late 1060s and Walter attended the ceremony which marked the formal foundation by William Gouet II of the priory of Châteigniers.[64]

In the closing years of the eleventh century, however, Walter developed an association with the Rotrous. He attested Count Geoffrey II's confirmation to the Cluniac priory at Nogent-le-Rotrou, which was made before 1088, and two other acts in the count's presence and he was involved in a lawsuit in his court.[65] After Rotrou returned from the Holy Land Walter also attended his court.[66] As the twelfth century progressed the Chesnel lineage disappeared and the failure of male Chesnel heirs may have contributed to the ability of the Rotrous to assert their power in this area.[67] None the less, the Chesnels were powerful figures in their own right and the grant of the Bellêmois to Rotrou in 1113/4 will have done much to ensure the extension of Rotrou ascendancy over the Chesnel territory. Walter Chesnel could waver between lords, but his successors had no such option. The grant of Bellême substantially increased Rotrou's power, providing the critical mass which made Rotrou lordship irresistible and Ceton eventually followed the *coutume* of the Perche.

Judicious monastic patronage also contributed to the maintenance of Rotrou's power. Count Rotrou's association with the abbey of Tiron had the effect of drawing the area into Rotrou's sphere of influence and it enabled him to strengthen his links with families which had long-standing connections with the area. The Beaumont lineage, for example, which took its toponymic from Beaumont-les-Autels (Eure-et-Loir, cant. Authon), was very influential to the south and east of Nogent. At the end of the eleventh century the lineage was represented by Geoffrey, whose parents and grandparents had been associated with the Gouet family. Geoffrey had already been drawn into the Rotrou clientele when he attended the court of Count Geoffrey II in the

---

63 *NLR*, no. xviii; *CMPerche*, no. 13.
64 See *Cartulaire Manceau de Marmoutier*, 124, where Ivo witnessed a Gouet benefaction; for Châteigniers see *Tiron*, no. xii; for other acts in Gouet territory see *NLR*, nos lxxxiii, lxxi.
65 *NLR*, nos vii, xxxiv, xxi, xix.
66 *NLR*, nos lxxxi, xi.
67 Walter Chesnel had a son William Barbaleffa (*VLM*, no. 196), but it has not been possible to trace him beyond one attestation (*NLR*, no. lxxiv). A Walter Chesnel who appears in an act dated 1124x37 may be a grandson of the original Walter: *CMPerche*, no. 209. By 1218 Ceton was held by Gerald Capreolus: *Clairets*, no. xiv.

1080s and had conceded the gift which his follower, Giroie of Orme, had granted to the Rotrou family foundation at Nogent-le-Rotrou. This association was developed when he made his own substantial benefaction to Nogent, granting it the church of St Peter of Happonvilliers (Eure-et-Loir, cant. Thiron-Gardais).[68] In the early years of the twelfth century Rotrou's patronage of the new foundation of Tiron presented another opportunity to consolidate the links between the two lineages, with Geoffrey granting Tiron a carucate of land at *Brimont* (?Brémont, Eure-et-Loir, cant. Thiron-Gardais, cme Combres), and by the 1120s Geoffrey's son Robert, who is specifically mentioned among the nobles (*proceres*) of Count Rotrou's court, was also benefactor of Tiron.[69]

Rotrou in Aragon, 1120–35

Late in the autumn of 1120, having survived the great crisis and made his peace with the king of France, King Henry I decided to return to England after four years in Normandy. A great flotilla was assembled at Barfleur to make the crossing and among those who joined the king was Rotrou's countess, Matilda. She may have deliberately chosen to travel with the king's court since she was apparently travelling without her husband. On the evening of 25 November she embarked on the same ship as her brother, King Henry's only legitimate son, William Atheling, and when the White Ship sank she too was drowned. The political consequences of the death of the king's heir were profound and immediate, and the bereavements associated with it extended throughout the highest levels of Anglo-Norman society.[70] In addition to his wife, Count Rotrou lost two nephews, the sons of his sister, Juliana and her husband, Gilbert of L'Aigle, and his subsequent actions suggest that these losses had an important impact on his life. Within three years Rotrou had left the county created by his immediate forbears and settled in Aragon, leaving his sister, Juliana, in control of the Perche.

Although she was the daughter of a king, little is known of Rotrou's wife, Matilda. Her marriage to Rotrou in the earliest years of the twelfth century, shortly after the king's visit to Domfront, suggests that her mother had been a partner of Henry's youth, who had been settled there from the period when Henry took over the town in 1092. It is known that Matilda was half English, for her mother's name was Edith, and that she appears to have shared her father's enthusiasm for Cluny.[71] She appears in five acts with her husband, but

---

[68] *CMD*, no. xlvi; *NLR*, nos lii, lv.

[69] *Tiron*, no. cxxv; *NLR*, no. xl. 'proceres qui ibi aderant, Robertus scilicet dapifer comitis et cognatus ejus et Robertus de Bellomonte': *NLR*, no. liii; *Tiron*, no. lxiii.

[70] William of Malmesbury, *De gestis regum* (RS xc, 1887–9), ii. 497.

[71] Matilda's mother was named Edith: *PR 31 Henry* I, 155. See BL, MS Cotton Vespasian F xv, fo. 171v, for her grant to Cluny.

was perhaps overshadowed by her mother-in-law.[72] It was Beatrix who controlled the Perche before her son returned in 1100 and again around 1112 when he was imprisoned in Le Mans: the assumption of power by a widowed mother was by no means unusual in the Middle Ages.[73]

Matilda is usually described as Rotrou's wife, and in two acts her name is preceded by that of her mother-in-law, while on one occasion Matilda is described as Rotrou's wife and Beatrix is described as the countess.[74] She is also described as 'daughter of the king of the English' which may reflect similar descriptions of Countess Adela of Blois, the daughter of William the Conqueror, and serve a similar purpose of emphasising the prestige which she brought to her husband's family.[75] It is, of course, possible that Rotrou's illegitimate sons predated his marriage to Matilda and that the political alliance between them developed into genuine affection, leading to personal loss for Rotrou when she died. An act in which Rotrou gave 20s. annually from the revenues of Aldbourne to the monks of Lewes mentions his wife Matilda by name alongside references to himself and his mother and father.[76] Alternatively Rotrou may have decided that a conspicuous display of grief was politically wise, since William of Malmesbury tells us that the Atheling might have escaped the wreck in a small boat if he had not insisted on returning to rescue his half-sister, the countess of the Perche.[77]

Rotrou's whereabouts in the closing months of 1120, when the White Ship was lost, are unknown, but before he left for Aragon he founded in 1122 a church, dedicated to the Mother of God, in expiation of a vow he had made when he had himself been delivered from a shipwreck. This information is derived from the traditions of the monastery founded by Rotrou at La Trappe, where the memory was also preserved that Rotrou had endowed the church with relics he had brought back from a second pilgrimage to Jerusalem.[78] Although the tradition is not contemporary it is a useful pointer. Count Fulk of Anjou is known to have made a pilgrimage to Jerusalem at this time, when he made contact with the newly founded order of Templars, and it may be that Rotrou was also in the Holy Land around 1120.[79]

In the years since Rotrou had first ventured to the Iberian peninsula, his cousin, King Alphonso of Aragon, had failed to maintain his hold on the Castillian inheritance of his wife, Queen Urraca, and had separated from her. He had continued his conflict with the Muslims and a council at Toulouse in 1118 led to the formation of a massive army of southern French troops. With

---

[72] NLR, nos xi, lxi, lxxxviii; Tiron, nos lxiv, cvi.
[73] Stafford, Queens, concubines and dowagers, 120ff.
[74] NLR, no. lxxxviii.
[75] NLR, no. lxi. On Adela see Lo Prete, 'Anglo-Norman card of Adela of Blois', 570.
[76] BL, MS Cotton Vespasian F xv, fo. 167v.
[77] Malmesbury, De gestis regum, ii. 497.
[78] La Trappe, 578–9.
[79] OV vi. 310; J. Phillips, Defenders of the Holy Land: relations between the Latin east and the west, 1119–1187, Oxford 1996, 28ff.

its aid Alphonso captured Zaragoza in December 1118 and in February 1119 the city of Tudela fell.[80] Alphonso's success put a premium on reliable men to consolidate the conquests. He had already recruited Gaston of Béarn and Centulle of Bigorre, and some Spanish sources suggest that Rotrou was present during the Ebro campaigns, capturing Tudela. There is, however, no trace of Rotrou in Spanish charters until 1123: by April that year he was Alphonso's governor of Tudela and in 1125 he took part in the campaigns in Benicadell, after which some of his followers returned home, bringing tales of Rotrou's exploits to Orderic's monastery.[81]

Aragonese charters were frequently dated by reference to the king's chief officers and allusions to Rotrou's lieutenants in those charters suggest occasional and well-managed absences from his duties there.[82] Rotrou is known to have visited northern France in 1125, when he witnessed a charter, probably at Chartres, on behalf of his cousin, Geoffrey viscount of Châteaudun, and in 1126 he was in England.[83] He was in King Henry's presence at Woodstock that autumn during the period when the king was seeking advice on the succession to the Anglo-Norman realm, and Rotrou's detailed knowledge of Iberian politics would have been particularly valuable since Castille had been ruled for nearly twenty years by a queen regnant. Although he was again in northern France in 1129, when he witnessed an act in favour of Fontevraud at the ducal court in Rouen,[84] Rotrou's continuing commitment to Aragon is implied in a grant he received from King Alphonso in December 1128 'for the service given and being given every day'.[85] For that service Rotrou received the town and castle of Corella and it is clear that he acted as a focus for northern French fighters in the Iberian campaigns.

Many of the *francos* who can be found in Spanish sources of this period have toponymics that link them to the borders of Normandy. Rotrou's lieutenant, Robert Bordet of Cullei, was subsequently to make a mark on the

---

80 J. M. Lacarra, 'La conquista de Zaragoza por Alfonso I', *Al-Andalus* xii (1947), 79. For the contribution of the French see M. Bull, *Knightly piety and the lay response to the First Crusade: the Limousin and Gascony, c. 970–c. 1130*, Oxford 1993, 96ff.

81 Laliena Corbera, 'Nobles *francos*', 152–6. L. Nelson, 'Rotrou of Perche and the Aragonese reconquest', *Traditio* xxvi (1970), 122–3, 126–7, suggests that the chronicles have been doctored in the light of the later dispute between Navarre and Aragon. For Rotrou in Spain in April 1123 see *Doc. Ebro*, no. 91; OV vi. 400–2.

82 *Doc. Ebro*, nos 136, 140, 142–47, 151 (all 1127), 155, 157, 159 (all 1128). 'Sub eo comite Rotron in Tutela, sub quo Robert Bordet in castello; Duran Pesson iusticia': *Colección diplomática medieval de la Rioja: documentos*, ed. Ildefonso Rodrìgues de Lama, Logroño 1976–9, ii, no. 85, 28 Feb. 1126. 'Comite Pertico dominante et Tutela Gofre Bertran in illo castello de Tutela, Duran Peixon iusticia': *Doc. Ebro*, no. 161, 22 Sept. 1128.

83 CMD, no. clxxvii; *Earldom of Gloucester charters*, ed. R. Patterson, Oxford 1973, no. 109. Orderic (OV vi. 404) says that Rotrou returned from Spain in 1125.

84 *Tiron*, nos cxx, cviii. CDF, no. 1054 is witnessed by Rotrou, and this witness list compares closely with those of acts made at Rouen in 1129: *Regesta*, ii, nos 1580–1.

85 'propter seruitia que mihi fecistis et cotidie facitis': *Doc. Ebro*, no. 164 (Dec. 1128 at Almazán).

politics of the peninsula, but there were also other less well-known men such as Godfrey of Argentan (Orne, ch.-l. du cant), Algrin of Séchrouvre, (now Saint-Ouen de Séchrouvre, Orne, cant. Bazoches-sur-Hoëne), David of Le Mans (Sarthe) and Roger of Falaise (Calvados).[86] With the exception of Algrin of Séchrouvre and Robert Judas, whose plans to follow Rotrou to Spain were recorded by the priory of Saint-Denis at Nogent-le-Rotrou before his departure and by the abbey of Tiron on his return, most of these men did not come from the Perche itself.[87] The grant of property in Tudela to the abbey of Saint-Martin of Sées, a Montgommery family foundation, and the presence of Reginald of Bailleul, a confirmed supporter of the Montgommery family, suggests that Reginald may have led a detachment of men from the Montgommery lands to Spain in the aftermath of his own defiance of King Henry I in 1119.[88] Reginald and Silvester of Saint-Calais returned to their own lands in the 1120s and Rotrou probably assumed command of those men that remained, many of whom he may have fought in earlier border disputes in Normandy.

During Rotrou's absence the Perche was, according to the cartulary of Saint-Denis of Nogent-le-Rotrou, 'in the hand' of his sister Juliana and she can be found presiding over the nobles of the Perche when a dispute was settled.[89] She also witnessed a benefaction to Tiron in the company of her nieces, Rotrou's daughters, Philippa and Felicia.[90] Rotrou returned at intervals, and Juliana appears in a number of acts alongside her brother as if in recognition of her role. It is rare to find a sister engaged in such an active role in the running of any polity in the Middle Ages. Clearly Juliana was a woman of some ability, who was granted the unusual privilege of attesting the foundation charter of a religious community not established by a member of her family.[91] She contributed to the running of her husband's property and it may be that when her own son, Richer, inherited those lands her talents became available for her brother to use, particularly since L'Aigle was at no great distance from the Perche. None the less the ease with which Rotrou was able to spend long periods away from his territory must be an indication of the stable conditions of the 1120s and of the strength of the support enjoyed by the Rotrou lineage.

Rotrou retained his governorship of Tudela until the mid 1130s, when the

86 L. J. McCrank, 'Norman crusaders in the Catalan reconquest: Robert Burdet and the principality of Tarragona', *Journal of Medieval History* vii (1981), 70–1; OV vi. 402; *Doc. Ebro*, nos 161, 177.

87 'volens ire in Hispaniam ad Rotrocum comitem': *NLR*, no. xlv; *Tiron*, no. cxviii.

88 For property at Tudela belonging to Sées see GC xi, instr. col. 171; for Reginald of Bailleul in Spain see OV vi. 402; for his defiance of King Henry in 1119 see OV vi. 214–16.

89 *NLR*, no. xxvii.

90 *Tiron*, no. cxlix.

91 For Juliana see *CMPerche*, no. 22; *Tiron*, nos xxii, xxxiii, cxx. Juliana witnessed the foundation of the priory of Le Désert in 1125: AD Eure, priory of Notre Dame du Désert, MS G165 (cartulaire de Notre Dame Le Désert), fo. 1v.

city passed into the hands of García Ramirez, a descendant of Sancho the Great, king of Navarre.[92] García had married Rotrou's niece, Margaret, the daughter of Juliana and Gilbert of L'Aigle, and their grandson was later to claim rights in Tudela on the grounds that it was Margaret's property, while their daughter is recorded as asserting that Rotrou gave her father 'wide tracts of land in Spain as a dowry, together with his niece, my mother'.[93] García subsequently became king of Navarre on the death of Alphonso of Aragon and the importance accorded to Margaret in García's royal charters also suggests that she had made an important contribution to the family.[94] Since Sancho, the son of García and Margaret, was not particularly young when he succeeded his father in 1150, however, it would appear that the marriage alliance between García and Margaret was made well before Rotrou left Spain in the mid 1130s. It is indeed possible that it was the association between Rotrou and García that provided García with the powerbase to re-establish the independent kingdom of Navarre after the death of Alphonso the Battler.

The reasons for Rotrou's withdrawal from Spain after such a lengthy commitment are nowhere made explicit. The uncertainty after the death without heirs of his cousin, Alphonso, may have been significant, but family circumstance may also have been a contributory factor.[95] Rotrou had made an agreement that he would not remarry and that Helias, the second son of Count Fulk of Anjou, who had married Rotrou's daughter, Philippa, should succeed to the Perche.[96] The marriage was something of a diplomatic coup for it linked the Rotrou lineage with one of the major princely families of northern France and unequivocally underlined the position it had achieved. Although Rotrou had no legitimate son to succeed him the marriage, which was commemorated in a benefaction made by Rotrou to the abbey of Tiron, would ensure that Rotrou's descendants would rule in the Perche.[97] Nothing

[92] For Rotrou at Tudela see *Col. Rioja*, nos 95 (Mar. 1129), 98 (26 Oct. 1130); *Doc. Ebro*, nos 178, 182, 185–88 (all 1129), 192 (1130), 208, 210 (1131); *Col. Rioja*, no. 101 (Mar. 1132); *Doc. Ebro*, no. 217 (1132). For García at Tudela see *Col. Rioja*, no. 103. García was the grandson of Sancho Garces, an illegitimate son of García III of Navarre: E. Lourie, 'The will of Alfonso I, "el batallador", king of Aragon and Navarre: a reassessment', *Speculum* l (1975), 642–43. He was also the grandson of the Cid: de Vajay, 'Ramire II le moine roi d'Aragon', 734 n. 54.

[93] Blanche, daughter of García and Margaret, married the king of Castille. Their son, Alphonso VIII of Castille, in the course of a submission of his grievances against the king of Navarre made in 1177 describes how he sought 'medietatem Tutelae ex causa maternae successionis quam comes Dalperg donauit reginae Margaritae sobrinae suae quae uxor fuit regis Garsiae': *Gesta*, i. 148. For the observations of another daughter, Margaret, see Hugh Falcandus, *La historia o liber de regno Sicilie*, ed. G. B. Siragusa, Rome 1897, 110.

[94] 'Ego quoque Margarita Dei gratia regina simul cum domino meo rege hanc cartam et hoc donatiuum laudo et confirmo': *Col. Rioja*, no. 112 (Oct. 1136). A similar form of words can be found in *Colección diplomática de Irache*, i, ed. J. M. Lacarra, Zaragoza 1965, nos 131, 134.

[95] Laliena Corbera, 'Nobles *francos*', 167, argues that Rotrou probably refused to serve under García, but charter evidence suggests that he had already left Tudela by this date.

[96] William of Tyre, *Chronique*, ed. R. B. C. Huygens, Turnholt 1986, 632–3.

[97] *Tiron*, no. xxxiii.

further is recorded of Philippa, however, beyond the fact that she became the mother of a daughter, Beatrix, and it seems not unreasonable to speculate that Rotrou returned to the Perche in the mid 1130s because Philippa had died, leaving the comital line in danger of extinction.[98]

Rotrou's eldest son, also Rotrou, was probably born around 1135, since he did not come of age until the 1150s, and it therefore seems likely that Rotrou's second marriage, to Hawise daughter of Walter of Salisbury, took place when he returned from Aragon in the middle 1130s. Certainly the scribes of the English exchequer, when compiling the pipe roll in the autumn of 1130, considered that the title of countess of the Perche referred to Rotrou's first wife, for they mention payments to her mother, Edith, from the revenues of Devon, and it is clear that they did not acknowledge Hawise, whose mother was called Sibyl, as the countess. Conventionally, however, Hawise's marriage has been dated before 1126 because her name, the names of witnesses and the year 1126 were all added to an act of confirmation given by Rotrou to the priory of Bellême.[99]

The 1126 date is not unreasonable because Rotrou was in England in that year and he would have had an opportunity to come into contact with Hawise's family. Their interests were centred in Wiltshire, where the dowry lands of Rotrou's first wife lay. He is known to have met Hawise's uncle, Edward of Salisbury, at Woodstock in Oxfordshire in the autumn of that year, and the marriage could have been negotiated at that point.[100] Since it was common practice for charters to be drafted by religious communities and validated by the donor on his next visit, Rotrou may have proposed the Bellême confirmation on his return from England as a means of marking his remarriage, and the charter would then have been drafted with a space for the new countess's name left blank. There may have been some uncertainty about which of Walter's daughters Rotrou might marry or even about Hawise's name. It is quite possible that Hawise, whose paternal ancestry was English, had a name, perhaps that of her paternal grandmother, which was unfamiliar to the scribes at Bellême and which required clarification.

In the event, however, despite the evidence of the Bellême act, it seems that the marriage did not proceed. There may have been a delay because of the youth of the bride, and then the opportunity of the Angevin match arose for Philippa. The details of this latter alliance are preserved in the work of William of Tyre, the historian of the crusader kingdoms of the east, who knew a great deal of the family history of the counts of Anjou because Count Fulk left Anjou, married the heiress of Jerusalem and succeeded her father as king.[101] These events were all related to the diplomacy of the late 1120s when King Henry of England sought a suitable husband for his heiress, the former

---

98   Robert of Torigni, *Chronique*, ii. 28.
99   *CMPerche*, no. 21.
100 *Earldom of Gloucester charters*, no. 109.
101 William of Tyre, *Chronique*, 632–3.

empress, Matilda. In June 1128 she was married to Geoffrey, eldest son of Count Fulk of Anjou and the count left for the Holy Land. The negotiations which preceded the marriage of Matilda and Geoffrey were complex and delicate, taking a year to accomplish, and it is not unreasonable to see the Percheron marriage as part of them. If Count Fulk were to take up a new career in the east so that Geoffrey might become count of Anjou immediately, then he would clearly wish to see the interests of his other children safeguarded. His eldest daughter, Matilda, who had married William the Atheling in 1119 was returned to Anjou and took the veil at Fontevraud.[102] His second son, Helias, may well have been promised the Perche as the husband of Rotrou's heiress, Philippa, although the marriage is unlikely to have been celebrated before 1129 at the earliest since Helias was not born until 1114 or later. Rotrou's visit to northern France in 1129, when he visited the ducal court at Rouen, could therefore have been the result of the wedding.[103]

Rotrou's own projected marriage was then presumably cancelled, since it was a condition of Philippa's marriage agreement that he would not remarry. He returned to Aragon and there he stayed until the mid 1130s, one charter suggesting that he remained as late as January 1135.[104] By December of the same year, however, he had returned to northern France; a stinging letter from his niece, Blanche of Navarre, daughter of Margaret of L'Aigle and García Ramirez confirms that Rotrou had left his post:

> I hear that you do not intend to go back to the place you have just left and I am afraid that you may therefore incur the wrath of the Supreme Judge. For your absence will perhaps encourage the enemy to move against the Christians whom you have so rashly abandoned and it will enable them to attack those helpless people. . . . Be wise therefore and return to the place you have unwisely left. End your life where you spent a good portion of it in the service of God. Out of family affection I would welcome your presence with me, but your spiritual welfare makes me demand from you the fruit of good work.[105]

Blanche's letter was ineffective, however. Rotrou did not return to Aragon, but entered instead on the marriage which he had projected nearly ten years before. It can hardly be described as a political alliance. His first wife had been the (admittedly illegitimate) daughter of a king, but his second bride

---

[102] For the negotiations see M. Chibnall, *The Empress Matilda: queen consort, queen mother and lady of the English*, Oxford 1991, 56. For Matilda of Anjou see OV vi. 330.

[103] The birth of Helias post-dates that of Geoffrey le bel in August 1113: 'Chronicae Sancti Albini Andegavensis', in *Chroniques des églises d'Anjou*, 32. For Rotrou in Rouen see *CDF*, no. 1054.

[104] *Doc. Ebro*, no. 251; OV vi. 448.

[105] *RHF* xv. 512. The letter has been attributed to Margaret, despite the fact that the niece identifies herself with the initial B. It is just possible that the wife of García Ramirez was originally called Beatrix after her maternal grandmother, but more likely that the letter came from her daughter, Blanche.

brought no such great connections. She was descended from the most successful of the English survivors of the Norman conquest, Edward, sheriff of Wiltshire, whose co-operation with the Norman conquerors was to pay important dividends. In 1086 Edward held over 300 hides in nine English counties, and his two sons, Walter and Edward, who both married Norman wives, were to become important figures in the reign of Henry I.[106] Walter succeeded his father as sheriff of Wiltshire for a period and Edward fitz Edward was the standard-bearer at the battle of Brémule. It is hard therefore to escape the conclusion that Rotrou sought a speedy alliance and wished to capitalise on the detailed negotiations already carried out with the Salisburys. The marriage offered the prospect of social advancement for Hawise's family and brought Rotrou the chance of an extension to his English landholdings. In the later twelfth century the Rotrou family were in possession of property which had been held in 1086 by Hawise's great-grandfather, Arnulf of Hesdin, and it was probably secured as a result of the marriage.

Return to the Perche, 1135–44

When Rotrou returned to the Perche the rulers of his own generation were passing – Rotrou was to be present at the deathbed of his ally of more than thirty years, King Henry, in 1135 and King Louis VI was to die in August 1137. Their departures led to opportunities for those who remained, including Rotrou and his slightly younger contemporary, Theobald of Blois. Rotrou was able to exploit the disputed succession to Henry I's realm to his own advantage, while Theobald became chief adviser to the new king, Louis VII. Rotrou was now the senior figure of his generation with a reputation enhanced by his years of successful involvement in Christian warfare. In the summer of 1137 his position was recognised when he was among the entourage of great French lords who accompanied the young King Louis VII to Poitiers for his wedding to the heiress, Eleanor of Aquitaine.[107] Less than ten years later Louis would assume the leadership of the Second Crusade and it is possible that some of his enthusiasm for the project may have been derived from the weeks he spent in the summer of 1137 in the company of the distinguished survivor of the first expedition.[108]

When King Henry died on 1 December 1135, his chosen heir, his daughter Matilda, was at odds with her father over the provisions of her dowry. As a

---

[106] CP xi. 374–6 s.v. Salisbury. See also D. Crouch, *William Marshal: court, career and chivalry in the Angevin empire, 1147–1219*, London 1990, 12–16; A. Williams, *The English and the Norman Conquest*, Woodbridge 1995, 105ff.

[107] 'Chronicle of Morigny', in *RHF* xii. 84.

[108] See M. Bull, 'The Capetian monarch and the early crusade movement: Hugh of Vermandois and Louis VII', *Nottingham Medieval Studies* xl (1996), 25–46, for an alternative explanation.

result she was with her husband in Anjou rather than in either of her father's realms of England or Normandy. Her cousin, Stephen, the son of Henry's sister, Adela, countess of Blois, was better placed in the county of Boulogne and he made a dash to London where he was crowned king before Christmas. Matilda was able to secure only a foothold on her inheritance by taking possession of Argentan and a series of border castles in the south of the duchy of Normandy. The Norman nobles were uncertain whether to accept her as their ruler and her cause was undermined by the behaviour of the troops brought by her husband Geoffrey of Anjou in support of her claim. Matilda therefore found herself isolated in southern Normandy for much of 1136 while she first awaited and then recovered from the birth of a child in June of that year. King Stephen, meanwhile, made no effort to establish himself in Normandy and for more than a year the political situation remained finely balanced.

With neither candidate able to impose themselves on the duchy there was much scope for Rotrou to secure concessions. He might choose either side – he could reactivate the Angevin alliance which had been formalised in the marriage of his daughter, Philippa, and Geoffrey of Anjou's younger brother, or he might prefer Stephen, who controlled England where the lucrative dowry lands of both his wives lay. There is no record of Rotrou's activities in the year 1136 or the opening months of 1137, but it seems safe to speculate that there was considerable negotiation between Rotrou and both parties for he held the key to Normandy. Although the Norman lords had declared their support for Stephen's tenure of the duchy, the king continued to delay in England for more than a year. The absence of active ducal authority resulted in outbreaks of lawlessness in several areas of Normandy and the situation was made worse by a second campaign to assert the claims of the Empress Matilda waged by Geoffrey of Anjou.[109]

In the spring of 1137, when Stephen finally made an appearance in Normandy as its ruler, it was essential that he should secure immediate support. Rotrou and his nephew, Richer of L'Aigle, represented a major threat, for if they were to join the Angevin forces much of the south of the duchy would have been lost instantly. It was precisely the situation which had confronted Henry I in 1118/19 when Rotrou had supported Richer's claims to his father's English lands, and Henry had swiftly complied with Rotrou's request on that occasion. The magnitude of the inducement offered by Stephen to Rotrou and Richer is an indication that Stephen too recognised the strength of Rotrou's hand. Although Henry I and his father the Conqueror before him had insisted on ducal tenure of important castles throughout the duchy, Stephen departed from this policy by assigning the ducal castles of Moulins-la-Marche and Bonsmoulins respectively to Rotrou and Richer.[110] In the eleventh century Norman rulers had struggled to find a reliable

---

[109] Chibnall, *Empress Matilda*, 72–3.
[110] OV vi. 484. For a clear exposition see E. Z. Tabuteau, 'The family of Moulins-la-Marche

castellan for Moulins, which controlled the marches fronting onto the Perche, and even though Henry I had a reliable ally in Rotrou, he still considered the area of such strategic importance that another fortification was constructed at Bonsmoulins around 1130. In April 1137 Richer was with the king at Évreux and the bargain was probably concluded then.[111] The grant of the castles, whose clear purpose was the defence of southern Normandy, was something of a gamble on Stephen's part, but in the event the strategy preserved his rule in Normandy for a further four years.

The precise terms of the grant are not recorded, so it is not known if Rotrou acquired the important ducal demesne nearby. The castle alone, however, would have provided a focal point for Rotrou's power and the grant included control of the settlement at Moulins for Rotrou gave the abbey of Saint-Évroul the right of presentation to the parish church of St Nicholas.[112] Men with toponymics from the area, such as Ivo of Falandres (Orne, cant. Moulins-la-Marche, cme Mahéru) and Walter of Mahéru (Orne, cant. Moulins-la-Marche) also attest the count's later acts.[113] Once again, then, a rapprochement with the ruler of Normandy had secured additional power for Rotrou, and there are signs of Rotrou's goodwill towards his new ally. Rotrou's son was given the name Stephen, for example – a name wholly outside the naming patterns of the families of both Rotrou and Hawise. Rotrou also took over the patronage of a small community of Savignac monks, an order that had its origins in the teachings of the Norman hermit, Vitalis of Mortain, and in which Stephen is known to have been interested.[114] So diligent was Rotrou's support for these monks that later tradition points to him as the founder of the abbey at La Trappe. It was a link which was to associate Rotrou with one of the most famous houses of the western monastic tradition.

In the mid 1130s a local family had decided to give land in the valley of the River Avre for the foundation of a religious community and monks were recruited from a house which was itself only a recent foundation, the abbey of Aulnay in Normandy. Rotrou's nephew, Richer of L'Aigle, had approved the deed of gift in 1136 and the community might have remained a fairly minor foundation but for the intervention of Count Rotrou.[115] He persuaded the community to move to a new site by granting them a church which he had

in the eleventh century', *Medieval Prosopography* xiii (1992), 29–65. For Bonsmoulins see *RHF* xii. 580.

[111] *Regesta regum anglo-normannorum*, iii. ed. H. A. Cronne and R. H. C. Davis, Oxford 1968–9, no. 69.

[112] '. . . Rotrodum comitem Pertici divinae pietatis intuitu dilectis filiis nostris abbati et monachis sancti Ebrulfi presentationem parochilis ecclesiae de Molendinis donavisse: BN, MS lat. 11055, fo. 127.

[113] Ivo of Falandres witnessed *Tiron*, no. cclvi (1141). Walter of Mahéru drafted Hereford, Dean and Chapter archives, MS 798, published as *The original acta of St Peter's abbey, Gloucester, c. 1122 to 1263*, ed. R. B. Patterson (Gloucestershire Record Ser. li, 1998), no. 248.

[114] R. H. C. Davis, *King Stephen*, 3rd edn, London 1990, 100.

[115] AD Orne, MS H725, published as *La Trappe*, 112, 475–6.

founded some time previously. According to the fourteenth-century narrative tradition preserved at La Trappe the house of God ('Domus Dei') was built near a church founded by Rotrou in 1122 to fulfil a vow he had made when in danger of shipwreck.[116] Most significantly, however, the narrative comments that at the time of the foundation 'many lords, barons and not a few noble men, following his pious example, gave generous benefactions from their own property' and, as in the case of Tiron, the generously endowed house at La Trappe became a centre of comital influence at the very borders of the count's territory, as well as underlining the count's commitment to Normandy through his patronage of the Norman Savignac order.

As the 1130s drew to a close Rotrou was at the peak of his power. He had reforged his Anglo-Norman connection, which had been temporarily weakened by the uncertainty about Henry I's successor, and with England and Normandy under the same ruler he could expect to enjoy the revenues of his English property without difficulty. In 1139 he attended the royal court at Oxford and it is tempting to associate this visit with the foundation by his second father-in-law, Walter of Salisbury, of an Augustinian priory at Bradenstoke.[117] It was a significant stage in the rise of the Salisbury lineage and one at which Walter might welcome the presence of his distinguished son-in-law. It is possible too that Rotrou took the opportunity to visit his sister, Margaret, who was living in England in the late 1130s.[118]

Margaret had married into a powerful Norman clan which had worked closely with William the Conqueror and his sons. Her husband, Henry, was a younger son, who made his fortune in the conquest of England and became earl of Warwick, while his elder brother, Robert of Beaumont, held not only the family's lands in Normandy, but also the earldom of Leicester together with the county of Meulan in northern France which he inherited from his mother. As the 1130s drew to a close this kin group secured an ascendancy over the court of King Stephen. Margaret, who had lived in Normandy since the death of her husband in 1119, joined her eldest son in Warwickshire, and in the summer of 1139 a younger son, Rotrou, became bishop of Évreux. Relations between the two branches of the family were cordial and Margaret's links with the Rotrou lineage were not forgotten. Arrangements for the monks of the priory at Meulan to commemorate the deaths of Countess Beatrix, the mother of Margaret and Rotrou, and of Count Rotrou must surely have been put in place by Margaret, and Rotrou's nephew, Earl Roger of Warwick, was later to make a benefaction to Pipewell abbey for the soul of his uncle Rotrou.[119]

---

[116] *La Trappe*, 578–9.

[117] *Regesta*, iii. no. 279; *Cartulary of Bradenstoke priory*, ed. V. C. London (Wiltshire Record Society xxxv, 1979), no. 570.

[118] Crouch, 'Oddities', 136.

[119] BL, MS Cotton Caligula A, xiii, fos 85v–6. I am grateful to David Crouch for drawing this reference to my attention.

By November of the same year Rotrou had returned to the Perche and was engaged on what Orderic describes as the king's business. 'Taken into the king's pay', Rotrou moved against the castle of Pont-Échanfray (Eure) in the valley of the River Charentonne in central Normandy. The castle was occupied by Ribold, son of Baldwin, whose brother, Simon the Red, was based at Échauffour, and from these two centres they pillaged the surrounding area and the lands of Earl Robert of Leicester.[120] Orderic's account suggests that Rotrou's actions were the result of a specific contract with the king and it may well be that Rotrou's visit to England had been used for detailed negotiations between the king and his powerful southern neighbour during which the count had undertaken to enforce order in the border region while the king was preoccupied with the rising of the empress's followers.[121] Equally the earl of Leicester, who was high in the king's favour in the late 1130s and a cousin of Rotrou's nephews, may have influenced the discussions towards the protection of his lands.

It was Rotrou's nephew, Richer of L'Aigle, however, who was most involved with the king's cause. He too was in England in the summer of 1139 and was actively engaged in the raising of troops on the king's behalf. In September 1140 he was *en route* for England with fifty knights when he was intercepted at Lire by the forces of Robert earl of Leicester and imprisoned at the count's castle of Breteuil. Earl Robert's action against Richer is at first sight surprising for both were acknowledged supporters of the king of England, but Robert's hostility was buried in long-standing feuds related to control of territory in central Normandy and, as Stephen's reign progressed, and it became more and more apparent that the king would be unable to maintain the peace in Normandy, so there was ample opportunity for the furtherance of personal quarrels.[122]

This outbreak spurred Rotrou into action. He led his armed men in covert operations against his nephew's captors, and in mid October 1140 he captured Robert of Leicester's chief henchman, Robert Poard and his brother Maurice. Although Orderic Vitalis asserts that in this way Rotrou restored order to the border region, King Stephen was unable to reward Rotrou with the release of Richer, who remained in Earl Robert's prison. Orderic suggests that from this point Rotrou became disenchanted with his alliance with Stephen and it may be that he was in negotiation with the empress's party throughout the autumn and early winter of 1140. His nephew, Robert of Neubourg, the son of his sister, Countess Margaret of Warwick, had already shown some sympathy with the Angevin cause, while Rotrou's own granddaughter, Beatrix, was Geoffrey of Anjou's niece. Rotrou seems to have wasted little time in exploiting these links and as soon as the king was

---

120 OV vi. 512.
121 OV vi. 534.
122 Ov vi. 546–8; Thompson, 'Laigle', 188–9.

captured by the empress's forces at Lincoln in February 1141 Rotrou made his peace with Geoffrey of Anjou.[123]

Rotrou's action was decisive for the future direction of Normandy. Geoffrey had already secured a substantial foothold in the western areas of the duchy and by mid 1141 much of central Normandy had submitted to him too. There are indications that, as a senior and respected associate of King Henry, Rotrou had played a significant part in events. It was in Rotrou's town of Mortagne, in mid Lent, that a meeting of Norman nobles was convened to debate the political options. A substantial proportion of the meeting, led by Archbishop Hugh of Rouen, favoured an approach to Count Theobald of Blois, who was invited to take the inheritance of his uncle, King Henry. Theobald, however, refused, commending in preference an honourable settlement with Count Geoffrey. Rotrou made use of the meeting, however, to enter into negotiations with Earl Robert of Leicester, who held his nephew, Richer of L'Aigle captive. A treaty between Robert and Rotrou followed, which was perhaps not dissimilar to the magnates' peaces of the latter end of King Stephen's reign in England. Earl Robert was persuaded to release Richer, but more important he also secured a truce with Count Geoffrey for himself and his brother, Waleran count of Meulan. These developments clearly unnerved Stephen's Norman supporters. The garrisons of Verneuil and Nonancourt acknowledged Geoffrey and shortly before Easter Bishop John of Lisieux made his peace with the count.[124]

At the end of his long career, then, Rotrou II could look back on a job well done: his county well-established and unchallenged, and three young sons lined up to inherit it. His own personal prestige was high. He had been the faithful friend and counsellor of Henry I, the most successful ruler of his day. He had served with distinction and apparent success in the wars in the Holy Land and the Iberian peninsula. He was associated with one of the most prestigious of the new orders which had taken root in his territory at Thiron and his reputation ensured that he himself moved in the highest circles as his excursion to Poitiers with the young King Louis demonstrates. Finally, in 1141, he had effectively performed the role of king-maker, convening the conference at Mortagne, which arbitrated the Norman succession. Rotrou, his father and grandfather had successively asserted their independence with a greater and greater degree of success, but it was Rotrou's exploitation of his position as a border magnate and whole-hearted espousal of the Norman alliance which set the seal on the family fortunes.

There is every indication, indeed, that the Anglo-Norman alliance suited Rotrou. The stability it brought plainly gave him the confidence to spend a large proportion of his time in Spain and the bargains he made with the rulers of Normandy were always kept. He supported Henry consistently both

[123] OV vi. 548–50. For Robert of Neubourg's earlier flirtation with the Angevin cause see OV vi. 466.
[124] OV vi. 550.

against Robert Curthose and in the serious conflict of 1111/12, when he was captured by Robert of Bellême and may have come close to losing his life. When Henry sought advice on the empress's claim to be his heir Rotrou made his way from Navarre to England and as Henry lay on his deathbed Rotrou was there too, summoned probably to assist the king in what he thought was the forthcoming campaign against his own daughter and her Norman ally, William Talvas.[125] With the old king dead in the late 1130s Rotrou was prepared to enter a similar alliance with his successor Stephen. It was only when it became clear that Stephen had lost all control in Normandy that Rotrou was forced to rethink his policy, withdraw his support from one ruler of Normandy and work effectively to establish another one.

At the beginning of the 1140s Rotrou was an ageing man as a benefaction to Tiron, made in 1141 and involving Baldwin the doctor, suggests, but he was by no means inactive. The La Trappe foundation narrative suggests that in December 1140 he was on the verge of a third trip to Jerusalem. We do not know whether he went, but it is known that, after the business at Mortagne had been conducted and Richer released from prison, Rotrou undertook one final visit to Spain where he attested an act in memory of his niece, Queen Margaret of Navarre, in January 1142.[126] Having made his commitment to Count Geoffrey of Anjou, Rotrou stood by that too. His granddaughter, Beatrix, was married to John of Alençon, son of the most prominent of the empress's Norman supporters, William Talvas, and grandson of Rotrou's old enemy, Robert of Bellême. Finally in 1144, as Count Geoffrey was at the gates of Rouen, Rotrou's support extended even to fighting in the service of the empress's husband. At well over sixty years of age Rotrou must have led a Percheron detachment to Rouen in support of the Angevins, for his death is recorded during the course of the siege of the citadel there. The chronicler Robert of Torigni says only that Rotrou died during the siege, which might imply a natural death, but that is unlikely since Rotrou's obituary was celebrated in early May and the siege was successfully concluded on 23 April. It therefore seems probable that Rotrou had been wounded in the fighting but had not died until some time after it had ended.[127] His place of burial is unrecorded, but it is likely that his body was brought back to the family foundation of Saint-Denis of Nogent-le-Rotrou and laid to rest in its chapter house.

Rotrou had died as he had lived, a great warrior. He was the fourth in a line of formidable fighters and the importance of their military skills in imposing and maintaining the power of the Rotrou dynasty should not be underestimated. Lands and powers had been steadily accumulated over the generations which enabled Rotrou II to seize the opportunities presented in the

---

[125] For the events of late 1135 see Thompson, 'William Talvas', 174–7.

[126] *El gran priorato de Navarra de la orden de San Juan de Jerusalén (siglos XII–XIII)*, II: *Colección diplomática*, ed. S. A. García Larragueta, Pamplona 1957, no. 18, cited in Laliena Corbera, 'Nobles francos', 158 n. 47.

[127] Robert of Torigni, *Chronique*, i. 234; *Obits*, ii. 188, 239.

twelfth century. It was above all his reputation as a Christian warrior which raised the status of the dynasty and allowed him to distance it from the Thibaudian counts who had a less glorious record. Like the Montlhéry, who were ultimately able to secure the kingship of Jerusalem, Rotrou was a member of that network of middling families which made great gains from crusading.[128] Unlike them, however, he did not need to stay in the east to make his gains, but was able to improve the political position of his lands at home.

[128] Riley-Smith, *First crusaders*, 169–88.

4

Rotrou the Less (1144–1191)

In the middle years of the twelfth century the political situation in France changed dramatically when the independent duchy of Normandy collapsed with the fall of Rouen in 1144 to Count Geoffrey of Anjou. In securing the Norman inheritance of his wife, the Empress Matilda, Geoffrey extended his own influence northwards to the Channel coast and laid the foundations for the power of his son who would become King Henry II of England (1154–89). The scene was thus set for confrontation between two great power blocs as the king of France, Louis VII (1137–80), was faced by a prince whose territories significantly exceeded his own. The house of Rotrou had the challenge of adapting to these changed political circumstances while maintaining associations across France which contributed to its own status and power. Initially Rotrou III was to deal with that challenge by seeking security in alliance with his nearest neighbours, the counts of Blois/Chartres, but in the 1170s and 1180s he and his family were able to develop friendly relations with both the Capetian and Plantagenet courts, and to profit from both. Like his father and grandfather before him Rotrou maintained an interest in new monastic movements, in particular the Carthusians and the Grandmontines, and an increasing rate of survival of comital acts from his lifetime suggests a regularisation of the government of the Perche under his rule.

Robert, the king's brother, and the minority of Rotrou III (1144–c. 1150)

Given the difficult political circumstances of the early 1140s it was perhaps unwise of Rotrou II to give such wholehearted support to the Geoffrey Plantagenet's cause as to participate personally in the Rouen campaign during the early months of 1144. He was well-advanced in years in the 1140s, but his sons by Hawise of Salisbury were still little more than children, and his death in the spring of 1144 left his probably young and not well-connected wife to cope with a complex political situation. Rotrou and his immediate forbears had gained much from their alliance with the rulers of Normandy and Rotrou had attempted to prolong that connection by fighting for Geoffrey Plantagenet, but Geoffrey was clearly too pre-occupied to give the newly widowed countess much support. In these circumstances it was natural that she should seek the protection of a second husband and she made an almost immediate remarriage.

It is impossible to know who advised Hawise during the period immediately following her husband's death. Her own family was far away in England and concerned with the maintenance of their traditional influence in Wiltshire as the struggle between King Stephen and the empress dragged on. It is possible that she received some support from her mother's family, who originated from Sourches near Le Mans, but perhaps more likely that she turned for an informed perspective on the politics of the situation in which she found herself to her husband's nephew, Rotrou, bishop of Evreux, and his brother, Robert of Neubourg, who were leading figures in Norman politics of the 1140s. By early in 1145 she had accepted a new husband and married the younger brother of Louis VII, Robert Capet.[1]

Robert was the third surviving son of King Louis VI of France and his queen, Adelaide of Maurienne. Modern authorities nearly always refer to him as Robert of Dreux, although he did not acquire Dreux (Eure-et-Loir), where he established his lineage, until 1152. Little attention has been paid to this early stage of his career in the 1140s when he is more properly described as 'the king's brother', the legend inscribed on his seal.[2] At the time of his marriage to Hawise Robert was some twenty years old and the nearest male heir of his brother, the king, since the intervening brother, Henry, was a churchman. Robert had already had some experience in the service of his elder brother, for he had commanded the soldiers who had seized the property of the bishopric of Châlons-en-Champagne in 1143, but the opportunities available to a Capetian cadet of the twelfth century were strictly limited.[3] There were no great tracts of territory with which he could be endowed as King Henry I (1031–60) had endowed his brother, Robert, with the duchy of Burgundy in the early eleventh century and no heiresses with inheritances as substantial as that of Adeliza of Vermandois, who had married Robert's great-uncle, Hugh, in the 1070s.[4]

Robert's marriage to Hawise, therefore, when it has been noticed at all by historians, has been seen as a similar alliance to that of his father's half-brother, Philip of Mantes, who married the heiress of Montlhéry, and part of an overall pattern of Capetian expedients to provide for younger sons.[5] If that was the rationale, however, then it was essentially a short-term strategy for the alliance gave Robert only temporary custody of the lands of his stepson, Rotrou III. It is more tempting, therefore, to see the marriage as part of a complex set of agreements surrounding the rapprochement between

1   CMPerche, nos 28, 29.
2   A. W. Lewis, '14 charters of Robert I of Dreux (1152–1188)', Traditio xli (1985), 146; 'Sigillum Roberti fratris regis Francie', in L.-C. Douët-d'Arcq, Collection des sceaux, i, Paris 1863, no. 720.
3   Bernard, ep. ccxxi, in Opera, viii, ed. J. Leclerq and H. Rochais, Rome 1977.
4   For Robert duke of Burgundy see Ralph Glaber, The five books of the histories, 158. See also A. W. Lewis, Royal succession in Capetian France: studies in family order and the state, Boston 1981, 46, 52; Bull, 'The Capetian monarchy and the early crusade movement', 31.
5   Lewis, Royal succession in Capetian France, 60.

King Louis, Theobald IV of Blois and Count Geoffrey of Anjou which was finalised in the autumn of 1144.[6] King Louis recognised Geoffrey's conquest of Normandy and at much the same time he also made peace with Theobald of Blois. The installation of his brother Robert in the Perche contributed to both settlements, for it provided a useful check on Geoffrey in Normandy and gave some protection against potential Angevin threat to Theobald's territories, as well as securing useful employment for Louis's energetic younger brother.

Such an arrangement would have been a masterpiece of balance, for as ruler of the Perche Robert controlled the Norman ducal castle at Moulins-la-Marche on behalf of his stepson, while Geoffrey inherited the ducal right to garrison the castle of Bellême which Henry I had retained when he had granted the Bellêmois to Count Rotrou in 1113. An act drafted for the priory at Bellême in the mid 1140s refers to Robert's administration of the area but little can be deduced about the practicalities.[7] It is possible that Robert encouraged the abbey of Saint-Benoît-sur-Loire at Fleury, with which his family had close links, to establish a priory at La Chaise near Eperrais (Orne, cant. Pervenchères). His grandfather, Philip I (1060–1108), had been buried at Fleury and the very earliest endowments of the priory date from 1146 when Robert's influence in the Perche would have been at its height.[8] Robert may also have cultivated the bishop of Sées, the unfortunate Gerard, whose election was disputed by Count Geoffrey of Anjou, the new master of Normandy. Gerard punctiliously dated his acts in favour of the priory at Bellême by reference to Robert's rule there and he gave a church to the new priory at La Chaise.[9]

In June 1147 King Louis's younger brother was among the royal party that set out for the Holy Land on the Second Crusade. After some adventures that demonstrated his impetuous nature, including the abduction of a kinswoman from the Byzantine emperor's court, he returned home ahead of his brother.[10] Letters preserved among the correspondence of the king's regent, Abbot Suger of Saint-Denis, suggest that as soon as he returned Robert began to intrigue for control of his brother's kingdom. One letter in particular, addressed to the count of the Perche, implies that Robert's young stepson was implicated in his activities. It is addressed to Rotrou the Percheron count by Louis VII's chancellor, Cadurc, and an unidentified *E. de Sal* and it gives

---

6   L. Grant, 'Suger and the Anglo-Norman world', *ANS* xix (1996), 61.

7   'regni Francorum gubernacula moderante Ludouico filio Ludouici et fratre ipsius Roberto Belismensi domino et comite Perticensi': *CMPerche*, no. 28.

8   AD Loiret, abbey of Saint-Benoît-sur-Loire, MS H22 (cartulaire de Saint-Benoît-sur-Loire), p. 185, no. 289.

9   For Gerard's election see Arnulf of Lisieux, *Letters*, ed. F. Barlow (Camden 3rd ser. lxi, 1939), xxxiiiff. For Gerard's acts see *CMPerche*, nos 28, 29, and *Recueil des chartes de l'abbaye de Saint-Benoît-sur-Loire*, ed. M. Prou and A. Vidier, Paris 1900–7, i, nos cxxxvi, cxlvi.

10 Odo of Deuil, *De profectione Ludovici VII in orientem*, ed. and trans. V. G. Berry, Morningside Heights, NY 1948, 78.

details of an apparent disagreement over custody of the tower of Bourges between Abbot Suger and the king's seneschal, Ralph of Vermandois.[11] Rotrou is asked to advise Ralph to send a note to Cadurc ordering him to deliver the castle only to Ralph or his forces. The letter then goes on to suggest that Rotrou has some sort of claim, not to say designs, on Bourges: 'civitas vestra Biturica vestra est si hoc faciatis'. There are also hints about the desirability of visiting the countess of Bourbon.

It is hard to relate the contents of the letter to the interests of the young Rotrou, who can have been little more than an adolescent at this period. His family is not known to have had any link with Bourges nor to have had particular claim to access to Ralph of Vermandois. On the other hand Countess Agnes, the wife of Archambaud VI of Bourbon, was the sister of Queen Adelaide and thus Robert's aunt, while Bourges had been the property of the Capetian family since the time of Philip I. His father, Louis VI, had given the citizens a charter which had been confirmed as recently as 1144/5 by Robert's brother, Louis VII.[12] Since Cadurc and his ally were asking the count of the Perche to use his influence with the king's seneschal, the count was clearly a well-connected man whose intervention the seneschal would respect. The political tensions behind the letter, which was probably intended for the king's brother and originally addressed to R the Percheron count, have never been fully disentangled.[13] Suger's view of the king's brother as at best a meddler and at worst a conspirator has generally prevailed, though it is possible that on his return from the Holy Land Robert found himself under pressure to take sides in differences which had arisen in the king's absence between the seneschal and the abbot.

Robert meanwhile pursued his own interests in northern Maine. In the

---

[11] 'Mandaveramus quod abbas S. Dionysii turrim Bituricensem Widoni de Rebrache et militibus suis et servientibus deliberaret, et ut redderem cito mihi mandaverat. Mandamus igitur vobis quod nos fuimus ad Comitem Rodulfum et inde fuimus ad abbatem et locuti fuimus de negotio: et ipse respondit nobis quod abbas non faciebat pro eo hoc, neque praecepto ipsius. Quapropter mandamus vobis ut Comiti Rod. literis vestri significetis, et ut amico vestro mandetis ut ipse Comes mihi Cadurco amico vestro sigillum suum mittat privatim, in quo habeat: Ego Comes Rod. mando tibi Cadurco, ut non reddas turrim Bituricensem alicui homini, sicut jarasti mihi, nisi mihi vel hominibus meis': *RHF* xv. 512–13. Cadurc had been Louis's favoured candidate in the disputed election to the archbishopric of Bourges in 1141: M. Pacaut, *Louis VII et les élections épiscopales dans le royaume de France*, Paris 1957, 94–100.

[12] *Chartes du Bourbonnais, 918–1522*, ed. J. Monicat and B. de Fournaux, Moulins 1952, no. 17. For the development of royal authority in Bourges see Devailly, *Berry*, 382–404.

[13] The letter is known to modern scholarship in the edition prepared by André Duchesne in the 1640s, in which Duchesne states that he had seen the correspondence of Abbot Suger at the Augustinian house of Saint-Denis-les-Puits. It had probably been taken there when the celebrated library at Saint-Victor in Paris was reorganised by the prior of Saint-Denis in the early sixteenth century: L. Delisle, *Le Cabinet des manuscrits de la Bibliothèque impériale*, Paris 1868–81, ii. 228. It may be that Duchesne's copyists incorrectly expanded the 'R' to Rotrou. Lindy Grant thinks the letter is a forgery: *Abbot Suger of Saint-Denis: Church and State in early twelfth-century France*, London 1998, 174–6.

course of 1149, probably before his brother's return in November, Robert had extended his influence westwards, taking the castle of Mont de la Nue (Sarthe, cant. Mamers, cme Contilly) from John, son of William Talvas, count of Ponthieu, a prominent supporter of Geoffrey of Anjou.[14] In his account of the incident the chronicler Robert of Torigni indicates that the castle was taken by treachery and his association of John Talvas with the loss implies that Robert seized the castle while John's father was absent with the Second Crusade. The seizure of the castle was a breach of crusading etiquette and more than a minor irritant for it rekindled powerful local rivalries, since the forbears of William Talvas had been longstanding rivals of the Rotrou lineage and had competed for the Bellême inheritance, particularly during the lifetime of William's father, Robert of Bellême. William Talvas had already lost his share of that inheritance when Bellême had been added to the Rotrous' territory in 1113 and Robert's capture of Mont de la Nue could not be countenanced. William had been unstinting in his support for Geoffrey of Anjou's efforts to secure Normandy in the 1130s and a recompense for that support was now sought.[15]

Geoffrey had spent the turn of the year 1149/50 in Normandy, where he had installed his eldest son, Henry fitzEmpress, as duke before he returned to Anjou to deal with his own troublesome barons. At some point in 1150, probably in the early spring as he made his way southwards towards Anjou and before he began his celebrated siege of the castle of Montreuil-Bellai, Geoffrey retook Mont de la Nue for the Talvas family. Robert's small territorial gain had quickly been lost, but it highlighted all too well the powerful position which Geoffrey of Anjou had established in western France in the second half of the 1140s. Robert's brother, King Louis, newly returned from the crusade, took the opportunity to complain to the pope, protesting that Geoffrey had used military force to enter Robert's land, and he carried out a major reprisal. Gathering a large army he and Robert moved against the southern Norman city of Sées, where the Talvas family had considerable property, and burned it to the ground.[16]

Robert's tenure of the Perche was, however, only temporary, relying on his custody of his wife's eldest son and by the turn of the 1150s Rotrou III must have been nearing adulthood. New arrangements would therefore be necessary and they seem to have taken effect in 1152. In August of that year Robert made a second marriage to Agnes, the heiress of Braine in Champagne, implying that his first wife, Countess Hawise, had died.[17] Hawise's obituary

<hr/>

14 Robert of Torigni, *Chronique* i. 254. This incident has been redated by Dr Grant to 1149, since Pope Eugenius wrote to Abbot Suger for further details before the abbot's death in January 1151: 'Suger and the Anglo-Norman world', 63.

15 For the Talvas family see Thompson, 'William Talvas', and S. Lowenfeld, 'Documents relatifs à la croisade de Guillaume comte de Ponthieu', *Archives de l'orient latin*, Paris 1881–4, ii. 251–5.

16 *RHF* xv, 461; Robert of Torigni, *Chronique* i. 254.

17 *Royal succession in Capetian France*, 62.

was celebrated at Chartres on 13 January, so she could have died in January 1152, leaving Robert free to contract his second marriage.[18] With his second wife Robert gained extensive interests in Champagne, but his presence west of Paris had clearly been useful to his brother and Louis was anxious to retain his services there. Robert was therefore granted the royal city of Dreux as his own possession and it is with Dreux that his name has come to be associated.

Robert of Torigni describes a conference which took place at midsummer 1152 shortly after the marriage of Henry fitzEmpress and Eleanor of Aquitaine in which King Louis, Robert, Henry of Champagne, Eustace of Boulogne, King Stephen's heir and Geoffrey, the younger brother of Henry fitzEmpress sought to co-ordinate their efforts against the man who was now duke of Normandy, count of Anjou and duke of Aquitaine.[19] Although Torigni describes Robert as the Percheron count 'comes perticensis' it is quite possible that Robert's participation was made in his new capacity as the lord of Dreux and that Torigni was using his former title. The campaign against Tillières-sur-Avre and Verneuil (both Eure) on the southern Norman border due west of Dreux, which took place at Robert's instigation later in the same year, certainly suggests the vigour of a new broom, intent on asserting himself in a new situation.[20] The evidence therefore points to Rotrou III assuming responsibility for his inheritance around 1152.

Family ties and frontier conflict, c. 1150–c. 1175

The young count was a newcomer to the political scene of the 1150s, but even the experienced players found themselves dealing with new situations. The alliance between Normandy and Blois, which had been in existence for more than fifty years and had been the mainstay of the policy of Count Theobald IV of Blois, had disintegrated after the death of Henry I in 1135. At first Theobald had tried to work with Geoffrey of Anjou as he had worked with his uncle, Henry I, and in 1141 he had supported, or at least not opposed, Geoffrey's claim to Normandy in return for a promise that the city of Tours would be restored to his family by the Angevins.[21] By the time that Geoffrey secured Normandy with the capture of Rouen in 1144 it was becoming clear that that restitution would not be made and that the count of Blois could look for no special relationship with Normandy under its Angevin master. In 1151 Theobald was still on sufficiently good terms with the Angevins as to knight his cousin, the empress's second son, Geoffrey,[22]

---

18 For the death of Hawise see *Obits*, ii. 33.
19 Robert of Torigni, *Chronique* i. 261.
20 Ibid. i. 269–70.
21 OV vi. 548.
22 Robert of Torigni, *Chronique* i. 253

but there are signs that he had been seeking to strengthen his own position with new allies.

When his (probably) eldest daughter, Isabelle, had made her first marriage around 1140 it had been a very grand alliance with the eldest son of King Roger II of Sicily, but after she was widowed in the late 1140s a husband was found for her nearer home. Theobald's new son-in-law was William Gouet IV, lord of Alluyes, Bazoches and Montmirail, a descendant of the William Gouet I who had been a rival of the Rotrou family in the mid-eleventh century. His territory lay immediately to the south of the Perche on the borders between Theobald's lands and those of the Plantagenet family.[23] It comes as no surprise therefore that another daughter of Theobald, Matilda, became the wife of the young Rotrou III of the Perche. The date of the marriage of Rotrou and Matilda of Blois is not known, but it clearly fits into a pattern of alliances under construction in the late 1140s and early 1150s, as Theobald sought security from the potential Angevin threat to the west by drawing his neighbours into his family.

For Rotrou the marriage alliance reactivated the relationship with the Thibaudian counts of Blois/Chartres which had been weakening since the time of his grandfather, Geoffrey II (1079–99). It formalised links with his most powerful and nearest neighbour at a time of political uncertainty when conflict to the north of the Perche between King Louis VII and his over-mighty subjects, Geoffrey and his son and successor, King Henry II of England, was becoming increasingly common. Within the decade the close alignment with Blois had given Rotrou a major political gain, for in December 1158 King Henry II conceded to Rotrou the castle of Bellême, which his grandfather, King Henry I, had withheld from Rotrou II in 1113.[24] The grant was part of an arrangement negotiated by Rotrou's brother-in-law, Theobald V of Blois (1152–91), through which Henry secured control of several important fortresses on the borders of his lands, including Theobald's castles of Amboise and Fréteval.

In return for Bellême Rotrou was persuaded to give up the castles at Moulins and Bonsmoulins which King Stephen had conceded to his father in the late 1130s. It may well be that the property at Moulins, having been exposed to the repeated conflict along the southern border of Normandy, had fallen in value. The castle of Bonsmoulins had certainly been burned in 1152 by King Henry, while he was still duke of Normandy, as a reprisal against Rotrou's cousin, Richer of L'Aigle.[25] None the less the agreement reveals how closely Rotrou's room for maneouvre had been reduced in comparison with that of his father, for it was part of a package arranged between King Henry

---

[23] Ibid. i. 315. Duke Roger died either on 2 May 1148 (*Necrologio de Liber Confratrum di S. Matteo de Salerno*, ed. C. A. Crombi, Rome 1922, 60) or on 2 May 1149 ('Annals of Montecassino', MGH SS xix. 310). I am grateful to Graham Loud for these references.

[24] Robert of Torigni, *Chronique* i. 315

[25] Ibid. i. 269.

and Theobald V of Blois, and it was probably related to the homage which Theobald performed to King Henry in 1159.[26] Rotrou had made a gain but at a price; he did not lead in negotiations with Henry and his contribution was presumably only to persuade his cousin Richer of L'Aigle to part with Bonsmoulins. The Perche had taken on the role of an associate of Blois, closer to the position of Rotrou's ancestors who had acknowledged the counts of Blois/Chartres as their overlords in the acts establishing the priory at Nogent-le-Rotrou.[27]

This changed position is hinted at in Rotrou's own acts dating from this period, for all those that can be securely dated to the 1150s and 1160s point to a close association between Rotrou and Blois. In 1159, for example, Rotrou gave exemption from comital exactions and rights of *vicaria* at Le Pas Saint L'Homer (Orne, cant. Longny) to the monks of Saint-Laumer of Blois, a Thibaudian family foundation. His grant, which was made with the approval of his wife and sons, was made within the monks' cloister at Blois itself.[28] Other comital acts dating from the 1160s and 1170s indicate a similar deference to the counts of Blois. A confirmation of the privileges enjoyed by the family foundation of Saint-Denis at Nogent-le-Rotrou was made not in Nogent, but in Orléans 'in presentia comitis Theobaldi' and was attested by members of his entourage, including his chancellor, Huldric, and the Chartrain lords, Bernard Decanus, Richard Aculeus and William of Bullou.[29] Rotrou's act of foundation for the new Carthusian house at Val Dieu mentions the 'consilio et auxilio' of his brother-in-law William who was bishop of Chartres at the time,[30] while in 1173 Rotrou exempted the abbey at Bonneval, which was under the protection of the counts of Blois, from all customary payments throughout his jurisdiction. This act was made with the specific participation of his wife, who is described as the daughter of the great prince Theobald [IV] and whose approval was witnessed in the chapter of Bonneval by her elder sister, Isabelle, the former duchess of Apulia and widow of William Gouet.[31]

Although Rotrou's position was in some respects circumscribed by closer links with the Thibaudians, his marriage with Matilda of Blois also had the

---

26 'Continuatio Beccensis', in Robert of Torigni, *Chronique* ii. 174

27 *NLR*, nos v, vi, vii.

28 Gouverneur, *Essais*, 215–16. For the Thibaudian connection with Saint-Laumer see N. Mars, *Histoire du royale monastère de Sainct-Lomer de Blois . . . 1646*, ed. A. Dupré, Blois 1869, 97–132.

29 *NLR*, nos viii, xii. These two acts as preserved in the cartulary of Saint-Denis are substantially the same with only slight variations in the witness list and anathema clause. Count Theobald is known to have been in Orléans in 1164 when he gave property to St Crux: GC viii. 515–16.

30 RCVD, fo. 1.

31 'Rotrodus Perticensis comes et uxor mea Maildis magni principis comitis Teobaldi filia . . . hoc ipsum confirmauit in capitulo Boneuallis uxor mea Maildis. . . . Testes cum ea Ducissa soror ejus': AD Eure-et-Loir, abbaye de Bonneval, MS H619.

effect of enhancing the family's standing, for it brought the house of Rotrou into a new network of family relationships of high status (*see* fig. 2). Matilda's sisters had married the duke of Burgundy, cousin of the Capetian king, and the count of Bar-le-Duc, and in 1160 her youngest sister, Adela, was to become the third wife of King Louis VII. The creation of a new alignment between the Thibaudian family and Louis VII was the major political development of that decade. It presented the Thibaudian counts with an important stake in the future of the Capetian family, for it offered the prospect that a son born of that marriage would be both king of France and their nephew. Other ties were also used to strengthen the links between the two families. Count Theobald V of Blois/Chartres and his brother, Count Henry I of Champagne (1152–81) married respectively Adelaide and Mary, the daughters of Louis VII and Eleanor of Aquitaine, while in 1165 William of the White Hands, a younger brother of Henry and Theobald, became bishop of Chartres, despite his youth, and Count Theobald received the title of royal seneschal.[32]

Throughout the 1160s, then, Rotrou III maintained close ties with Theobald V of Blois and was thus drawn into an alignment with the king of France, but links remained with the Anglo-Norman world. Rotrou's brother, Stephen, for example, was a canon of Rouen cathedral, an office which had probably been secured when their cousin Bishop Rotrou of Évreux had become archbishop in 1165, and an illegitimate brother of Rotrou III became archdeacon of Évreux.[33] Bishop Rotrou's brother, Robert of Neubourg, had been Henry II's justiciar in Normandy and Rotrou's maternal uncle, Earl Patrick of Salisbury, was among King Henry's most prominent servants before his assassination in Poitou in 1168.[34] Just as Henry II had cultivated Count Theobald of Blois with signs of favour including a subsidy on his pilgrimage to Santiago, so he probably made overtures to Rotrou, perhaps through his uncle, Patrick, for the pipe rolls indicate that Rotrou had recovered his father's English lands by the second half of the 1160s. It is even possible that Rotrou's younger brother, Geoffrey, sought employment with the English king, for the chronicler, Geoffrey of Vigeois, describes how King Henry committed the Limousin to the control of the count of Perche's brother, Geoffrey of Neubourg, and William Pantulf in the mid 1150s.[35] The reference is clearly incorrect in using the toponymic 'of Neubourg' for Rotrou's brother and the individual in question was probably Geoffrey of Neubourg, the younger brother of Robert of Neubourg and Bishop Rotrou, who was in fact

---

[32] Robert of Torigni, *Chronique* i. 357; A. Luchaire, *Études sur les actes de Louis VII*, Paris 1885, 47.
[33] For Stephen in the chapter of Rouen see *CDF*, no. 11. For Rotrou see AD Loiret, college of Orléans, MS D668 (cartulaire de Saint-Sulpice-sur-Risle), fo. 9v; RCVD, fos 1, 2v, 10.
[34] W. L. Warren, *Henry II*, London 1973, 95 n. 1; Crouch, *William Marshal*, 34ff.
[35] Geoffrey of Vigeois, 'Chronicon lemovicense', in *RHF* xii. 439.

Figure 2
The in-laws of Rotrou III count of the Perche

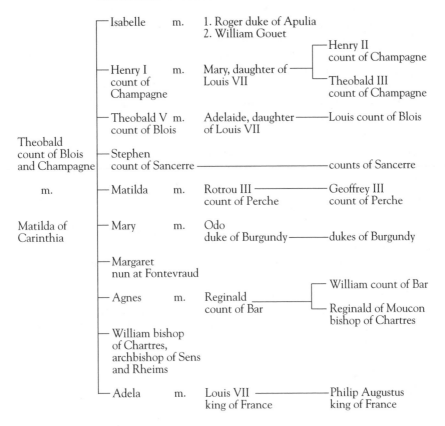

Rotrou's cousin. None the less it does demonstrate that opportunities existed in the service of the English king.

When the Capetian and English kings came to blows, however, Rotrou was always aligned against Henry II. The 1167 campaigning season, for example, saw a Norman raid on Chaumont and a French reprisal towards Andelys in Normandy, followed by a further campaign in the Perche ('in pago Perticensi') where French knights were captured by the Normans.[36] Indeed the direction of King Henry's campaign in the next year, 1168, reveals all too clearly the identity of those he regarded as enemies. After a raid by King Louis on Chennebrun (Eure, cant. Verneuil) Henry's reprisals were aimed firstly at Hugh of Châteauneuf-en-Thymerais, whose castle at Brézolles (Eure-et-Loir, cant. Dreux) was destroyed by the king's forces, and then at the count of the Perche, the greater part of whose lands were ravaged by troops under the

---

36 Roger of Wendover, *Chronica* i. 47.

personal command of the king.[37] The pipe roll for this year records that royal displeasure towards the count of Perche had been felt on his English property, for the stock of the count's Wiltshire manors had been sold and the profits paid into the royal exchequer.[38]

Henry's own perception of the alignment of the Perche is suggested by his construction of a castle at Beauvoir in north-east Maine in 1169 and the erection of earthworks along the border between Le Mêle-sur-Sarthe (Orne, ch.-l. du cant.) and Nonancourt (Eure, ch.-l. du cant.).[39] These works filled the gap left in the defences of Henry's realm after his deal with Theobald and Rotrou in 1158 had secured Moulins and Bonsmoulins on the southern Norman border and Amboise and Fréteval further south. Henry's fortuitous acquisition of the great Gouet castle of Montmirail in 1169, which he bought from William Gouet IV's son-in-law and heir, Hervey of Gien, completed a line of fortresses which protected his lands. Strength in depth behind that line had been provided when the king took the castles of Alençon and La Roche-Mabille from the Talvas family in 1166.[40] It was a military expression of the political blocs that had emerged in the middle decades of the twelfth century and the Perche of Rotrou III lay on the very frontline. When the conflict between Henry and his eldest son, the Young King, came to a head in 1173 it was by way of Rotrou's stronghold at Mortagne that the Young King made his way to the court of Louis VII.[41] Then in the following year Henry received a further illustration of the dangers of a hostile Perche, when a party led by the Young King was able to strike up into Normandy towards Sées in an raid which was an almost exact repetition of that of Rotrou's stepfather, Robert, in the early 1150s, though not as destructive. Rotrou and other members of his family including his brother-in-law, Theobald of Blois, and nephew-in-law, John of Alençon, were among the raiders in the attack which was only beaten off by the energetic efforts of the townspeople.[42]

---

[37] Robert of Torigni, *Chronique* ii. 8.

[38] '. . . instauramento terrae comitis de Perche vendito et de assisa facta super homines ejusdem terre': *PR 14 Henry II, 1167/18.*

[39] Robert of Torigni, *Chronique* ii. 14. For Henry's charter to the men of Beauvoir and two acts given by him there see *Recueil des actes de Henri II roi d'Angleterre et duc de Normandie concernant les provinces françaises et les affaires de France*, ed. L. Delisle and E. Berger, Paris 1906–27, i. 521–3, 573–4, 574–5. For Les Fossés-le-Roi see G. Louise, 'La Seigneurie de Bellême xe–xiie siècles: dévolution des pouvoirs territoriaux et construction d'une seigneurie de frontière aux confins de la Normandie et du Maine à la charnière de l'an mil', *Le Pays bas-normand*, nos cxcix/cc (1990); cci/ccii (1991), ii. 252; A. Lemoine, 'Chennebrun: un bourg castral au coeur des conflits franco-normands du xiie siècle', *Annales de Normandie* xlviii (1998), 525–44.

[40] Robert of Torigni, *Chronique* ii. 15–16. For Alençon and La Roche Mabille see ibid. i. 360.

[41] Ralph of Diceto, *Opera historica*, ed. W. Stubbs (RS lxviii, 1876), i. 355.

[42] Ibid. i. 379.

Running the Perche

For more than twenty years Rotrou III moved within the orbit of his wife's family, the counts of Blois, and in these years the focus of the count's interest lay within his own territory. It was a territory significantly reduced in 1158 by the cession of Moulins-la-Marche and unable to expand at the margins as a result of family alliances with neighbours such as the Gouet family to the south and the lords of L'Aigle to the north. Despite these limited opportunities, however, Rotrou did not follow the example of his father and seek adventure elsewhere. His younger brother, Stephen, enjoyed a brief career in the Sicilian kingdom which was ruled by their cousin, Margaret of Navarre, on behalf of her young son, but there is no record of Count Rotrou moving much beyond his territory. None the less his ambitious plans for a new monastic foundation suggest that he was in touch with new religious developments.[43]

On 29 June 1170 in a grand ceremony Rotrou surrendered his comital rights over a large area of the forest of Réno, east of Mortagne so that a charterhouse could be established at Val Dieu.[44] The Carthusians, inspired by the community founded near Grenoble by Bruno of Rheims in 1084, were dedicated to the contemplative life and avoided contact with the secular world. Each *hirena* or community had clearly defined boundaries beyond which the monks might not pass and the order developed expertise in the production of manuscripts, since, according to the customs of the order, which were codified by Prior Guigno (d. 1136) of the Grand Chartreuse, monks were to preach not by word of mouth but by the production of books. They refused to accept endowments such as churches which would force them to participate in secular life and lived instead off the revenues of their endowment.[45]

Like his father and grandfather before him, then, Rotrou was in the forefront of monastic patronage, supporting the newest initiatives. Where Geoffrey II had promoted the Cluniacs and Rotrou II the new ascetic orders, Rotrou III favoured an order which was in the earlier stages of its expansion. In the mid twelfth century there were only two houses north of the Loire, Mont Dieu in the diocese of Rheims and Val Saint-Pierre in the diocese of Laon.[46] It is difficult to pinpoint an association that roused Rotrou's interest in the order. It is possible that the retirement to the Grande Chartreuse in the late 1140s of the much-respected count of Nevers remained in the mind of

---

43 For Stephen's career see Thompson, 'Family tradition and the crusading impulse', 17–19, and the references cited there.

44 AD Orne, charterhouse of Val Dieu, MS H2621.

45 C. Brooke, *Monasteries of the world: the rise and development of the monastic tradition*, London 1974, 79–80.

46 J.-P. Aniel, *Les Maisons de Chartreux des origines à la Chartreuse de Pavie*, Geneva 1983, 16ff.

contemporaries, but it is also possible that Rotrou was influenced by his brother-in-law, William, bishop of Chartres, who is prominent in the foundation charter.[47] The establishment of a charterhouse involved a considerable commitment of resources; each monk required an individual cell and conventual buildings were necessary for the *conversi* or lay brothers whose task it was to organise material support for the monks. It is not perhaps surprising, therefore, that Rotrou's other acts of religious patronage which can be dated to the first half of his rule were confirmations and exemptions from comital exactions rather than direct grants of property or cash.

In his act of foundation Rotrou promised to acquire additional lands for the house and the process by which that was accomplished can be reconstructed from an episcopal confirmation given by Bishop Lisiard of Sées before 1201.[48] Large sums of money were involved, such as the £45 *angevin* for which Matthew of Fai was persuaded to sell his interests on the River Commeauche, and even where a personal commitment was made money still changed hands. Ivo of La Frette, for example, conceded part of his property for £31 on the understanding that he would eventually join the community when his wife died and that his son would be brought up in the house until ready to make his own decision about entering it. Different considerations influenced other donors. In return for Andrew of Prulai's concession of two holdings within Val Dieu's boundaries the prior placed ('collocavit') his two daughters in religious houses. Similarly before 1183 Mary of Bellavilliers conceded her land in the section of forest known as Bois Roger in return for the Carthusians' intervention to secure a living for her son, Stephen.

Having obtained a piece of property the monks consolidated around it. The interest in Bois Roger which they had acquired from Mary of Bellavilliers was increased when Hugh of Courcerault surrendered his rights there for £20 *angevin*. Then, when Mary's son, Odo, conceded all his interests within the boundaries of the house, the annual payment from Bois Roger to which Odo was entitled also became the property of the monks. Finally, Odo's tenant, Robert Balbet, surrendered his rights as well, giving the monks a valuable package of woodland resources. They also secured several tracts of pasture in the valley of the River Commeauche and River Jambée, mostly from the family and tenants of Ivo of La Frette, who had joined the community.

Val Dieu, like Routrou II's major foundations of Tiron and La Trappe, lay in a heavily forested region at the extremity of the family's territory. Such solitude was desirable for the monks, but the very presence of the community emphasised the lordship of the Rotrou lineage over the area. Their power in the area is apparent, since Rotrou III's predecessors had granted forest rights in Réno to other communities: Geoffrey II had endowed the Cluniacs of Nogent-le-Rotrou and Rotrou II had given some rights to Tiron, but it is clear that they did not hold exclusive rights. Waleran of Le Pin and Hugh of

---

[47] Odo of Deuil, *De profectione*, 14.
[48] RCVD, fo. 16v.

Courcerault, two local men, had interests in the forest which Rotrou had persuaded them to surrender by the time the house was formally founded in 1170 and he continued to use his influence in its favour. He is described as the sponsor of Hugh of Courcerault's subsequent gifts and witnessed Odo of Le Pin's important benefaction. Since Waleran and Hugh are described in the bishop's act as brothers and Waleran and Odo shared a toponymic, it appears that Rotrou had asserted himself to persuade an important kin-group to support the community. Perhaps most significant, however, is the surrender in 1185 by Gervase of Châteauneuf-en-Thymerais of all his rights in the locality which took place at a solemn ceremony in the church at Rivray, attended by the priors of the other Carthusian houses of Mont Dei and Val Saint-Pierre.[49] A hundred years before the Châteauneuf-en-Thymerais lineage had rivalled the Rotrous for influence to the east of the Huisne River; in 1185 Gervase's concession was formally recorded in an act in which he is described as a *fidelis* of Rotrou.

The great diplomas in favour of Val Dieu survive only as cartulary copies, but they are part of a significant corpus of material which survives from the Perche in the second half of the twelfth century, enabling us to reconstruct more of the routine workings of Rotrou III's Perche than is possible for any of his predecessors and reflecting the increasing regularisation of government which took place in the county, as in the rest of western Europe, in the twelfth century.[50] Records of forty-two acts by Rotrou III during his forty-seven years as count have been located, of which six survive in the original. This compares with twenty-five acts from his father's forty-five-year period of rule, of which four survive in the original. Some acts have pious preambles, but most start with a simple, business-like invocation of the Trinity or a statement of notification.[51] Of the forty-two acts located twenty-three are known to have had witness lists, but a small number take the form of an open letter or writ in which the count's wishes are made known and no witnesses are given.[52] There is only one example among the forty-two surviving acts of a charter to which *signa* have been appended in the manner of the great confirmations to the priory at Nogent-le-Rotrou, given by Rotrou's ancestors in the eleventh century.[53]

The increased survival rate for documents of the second half of the twelfth century suggests not only that more documents were produced, but also that preservation was worthwhile, and implies a society in which there was an incentive to record in writing because the record could in some way be guar-

---

[49] 'quicquid iuris ad eum spectabat in nemore de Resno quod continetur infra terminos eorum': ibid. fos 8v, 19v.

[50] Dunbabin, *France in the making*, 277–86.

[51] For pious preambles see *CMPerche*, nos 34, 227.

[52] Château Saint-Jean, Nogent-le-Rotrou, MS A/1; *NDC* i. 218; Château Saint-Jean, MS C/108; AD Sarthe, MS H927.

[53] Gouverneur, *Essais*, 215–16.

anteed. The documents which survive from Rotrou III's lifetime indicate that that guarantee was provided by comital power. Twenty-five of Rotrou's acts make reference to the authority of the count's seal; in contrast only three of his father's acts refer to a seal. The formulaic phrases associated with his seal indicate that it was appended to documents to add strength to the action, and the count's role is made clear in his confirmation for the abbey of La Trappe in which he declares that he has taken all the monks' possessions into his hand, custody and protection.[54] Unfortunately only two examples of the impression left by Rotrou's seal are extant. They show the count on horseback wearing a pointed helm with a shield in his left hand and a sword in his right.[55] There is no counterseal. It is a common image on magnates' seals in the twelfth century and it demonstrates that the basis for the count's control of the Perche lay in his coercive powers, which enabled him to act as protector and guarantor of stability.[56]

The growing use of writing also made it possible to be much more system-atic in the enforcement of comital rights. The act in which Rotrou III confirmed to Robert of Saint-Quentin his own father's grant of a house at Nogent-le-Rotrou to Robert's father, Pagan, itemises the tax exemptions included in the gift: 'ab omnibus bannis, equitationibus, petariis, collectis, talletis nec non etiam ab omni justitia senescalii et praefecti ab omnibus corvetis'.[57] A similar list of named impositions from which the monks of Perseigne are to be exempt while travelling into, out of and across the Perche is given in a writ addressed to all Rotrou's bailiffs, praepositi, farmers and agents.[58] This act is, in fact, our best evidence for the growing regularisation of government in the Perche during the twelfth century for it presupposes a network of officials engaged in the count's business to whom explicit instruc-tions could be sent and it even stipulates a penalty for those who do not comply with Rotrou's instruction. The records of a sale of property at Berd'huis (Orne, cant. Nocé) are also revealing. The act survives in two versions; both detail the property rights on offer by the vendor, Aylmer of Villeray: 'quicquid iuris, consuetudinis et iusticie in terra . . . de Berduis habebat', but the acts vary in the fullness of the exclusion clause covering the count's interests. One version states that the property is to be sold except for the interest which the count will retain: 'saluo ceruagio meo'.[59] The other version is more detailed and specifies 'the manner in which the monks' service shall be performed', including attendance at courts, rendering of produce and the occasions on which tallage may be taken.[60]

---

[54] La Trappe, 587.
[55] AN, MS S2238 (titres de propriété de l'abbaye de Saint-Denis), no. 15, pictured in 'Chateaux forts et guerres au moyen âge', Cahiers percherons lviii (1978), 38.
[56] A. Giry, Manuel de diplomatique, Paris 1894, 647.
[57] Clairets, no. i.
[58] AD Sarthe, MS H927, printed as Perseigne, no. ccclxiv.
[59] AN, MS S2238, no. 15.
[60] Ibid. no. 11.

Rotrou's court remained an important element in the maintenance of the family's power, bolstering the image of the count as the promoter of peace and security. A grant of exemption from the justice of the count's seneschal and *praepositus* implies that these powers were thoroughly enforced and the act recording Aylmer of Villeray's sale at Berd'huis makes it clear that, while cases of minor civil disturbance or even theft might be tried in the abbot's court, cases involving judicial combat (*duellum*) were reserved to the count.[61] The outcome of such a confrontation in Rotrou's court is recorded in an act dating from 1182/3 in which the count states; 'I have ordered the manner in which the dispute was settled before me through an agreement [finem duelli] to be committed to the notice of all by the wording of the present document.'[62]

As the twelfth century progressed there is some evidence of increasing procedural sophistication involving the role of the seneschal.[63] The number of seneschals increased and territorial areas of competence seem to have developed. The earliest dated reference to a seneschal occurs in 1167 and relates to Warin of Lonray, who usually appears in acts concerning the Bellême area. When he attested an act outside this area, Gervase of Châteauneuf's concession to Val Dieu in 1185, he was described as the seneschal of Bellême. Warin usually attested records of gifts or sales transacted in the count's presence, such as Fulk of Colonard's cession of a vineyard to the priory at Bellême in return for £20, or the concession of rights of jurisdiction at Dame-Marie made by Giroie Bastardus to the abbey of Jumièges. This latter act Warin attested together with William, the seneschal of Mortagne, demonstrating that by 1182 when it was given more than one seneschal operated in the Perche.[64] From managing the count's court in his presence, it was but a short step to presiding in his absence. Thus, the efforts of Ivo of Rémalard, who held the office of *dapifer* with authority in the area around Nogent-le-Rotrou, to secure a settlement between Giroie of Orme and the monks of Nogent-le-Rotrou in a dispute about watercourses are recorded in the priory's cartulary.[65]

It is clear that the old practice of beneficiaries drafting records of religious patronage continued in Rotrou's lifetime. Acts relating to the priory of Saint-Léonard of Bellême, for example, continue to have a characteristic preamble: 'Considerantes quam fragilis sit vita mortalium quam labilis memoria modernorum necessarium esse comprobamus scripto commendari quod sempiterna notione volumus retinere', and to make reference to the prior who held office at the time of drafting.[66] However, evidence of experi-

---

61 *Clairets*, no. 1; AN, MS S2238, nos 11, 15.
62 *Chartes de l'abbaye de Jumièges*, ed. J.-J. Vernier, Rouen 1916, no. cxxxiii.
63 For trial by combat see ibid.
64 *CMPerche*, no. 227; RCVD, fo. 8v; *CMPerche*, no. 175; *Jumièges*, no. cxxxiii.
65 *NLR*, no. xcii.
66 AD Orne, MS H2154.

mentation, or perhaps inexperience in the drafting of other acts, suggests that household clerks were also being employed. In 1190 Rotrou notified the transfer of a tithe to the leperhouse at Nogent-le-Rotrou in an act which makes several innovations: it begins as a writ with a salutation, continues with a general notification and concludes with the formula 'me ipso teste et plegio', followed by a witness list.[67] The scribe who drafted Rotrou's act granting to the abbey of La Trappe a vineyard at Vaunoise (probably Origni-le-Butin, Orne, cant. Bellême) must have lacked experience for he placed the clause relating to Rotrou's seal immediately after the opening words 'Ego Rotrochus'.[68]

The latter scribe did not put his name to the act, but one clerk in partic-ular from Rotrou's household, Adam of Loisail, assumed a prominent role in drafting Rotrou's acts and he is, on occasion, described as the count's chan-cellor. Adam spent more than thirty years in comital service under Rotrou and his son, Count Geoffrey III, his last attestation dating from the 1190s, and he may well have travelled to England with the count for an act in favour of Bradenstoke priory is witnessed by Adam the clerk.[69] When he died his property, which included the church of Bubertré (Orne, cant. Tourouvre), half its tithe and 5s. from its altar dues, was given to the Cluniac house at Nogent-le-Rotrou. Since the lords of Loisail had been benefactors of Nogent-le-Rotrou in the early twelfth century it seems likely that Adam belonged to a family with a tradition of support for the comital house and that he was taken into comital service as the need for scribal skills became greater.[70] Another clerk who joined the comital entourage was Gerald Goherius, the priest of Mortagne, who witnessed several acts in favour of Val Dieu as well as Rotrou's grant at Origni-le-Butin; it is possible too that, in the absence of better qualified personnel, he was pressed into service to draft that act, for it appears not to have been made with great ceremony but privately by means of a *cartula*.[71]

From the 1170s, a number of individuals to whom the title *magister* is given attest comital acts, suggesting that the university-trained schoolmen of Paris were beginning to find employment even in the smaller courts of western Europe. This group includes men such as Master Reginald (1170), Master Geoffrey (1185), Master William the Small (1185), Geoffrey Ignard (before 1190), and Master Hugh Vivandarius (1190).[72] There is evidence too for increasing specialisation among the count's officers. Under Rotrou II the

---

[67] Château Saint-Jean, MS C/108.

[68] *La Trappe*, 313.

[69] *Cartulary of Bradenstoke*, no. 655.

[70] 'Actum est hoc publice apud Manves anno ab Incarnatione Domini MCLXXXIX. Datam per manum Adae de Loseel': *La Trappe*, 587–90; AN, MS S2238, no. 15; RCVD, fo. 8v. For autograph: 'Data per manum Adam de Loisello' see AD Eure-et-Loir, MS H619. See *NLR*, no. xi for benefactions made by William of Loisail.

[71] *La Trappe*, 313.

[72] RCVD, fos 2, 8v; Château Saint-Jean, MS C/108; AN, MS S2238, no. 15.

duties of the seneschal/*dapifer* had included command of the count's troops as the career of Hubert Capreolus demonstrates, but under Rotrou III the military and the legal responsibilities of the office seem to have separated and a new officer, the marshal, appears. Clement the Marshal first attests in a comital act dated 1165 and he remained in the count's service until at least 1186 when Rotrou issued an act in favour of Le Mans cathedral in Clement's house at Nogent-le-Rotrou.[73] While Rotrou's acts enable us to deduce the apparatus of comital power through the existence of officers such as the toll-gatherer, bailiffs, farmers and *prepositi*, there is no evidence describing the mechanisms of lordship in the manner in which Bishop Ivo of Chartres' letters illuminate Rotrou II's relationship with Ivo of Courville.

While Rotrou's seneschals tended to be drawn from families with toponymics and traceable links with particular localities, other officials were drawn from humbler stock and would therefore be more dependent on comital favour. For the very able these offices might be the foundation of a family fortune. One such family owed its advancement to the office of *viarius*, or law enforcement officer.[74] Simon *viarius*, who witnessed Rotrou III's foundation of the charterhouse at Val Dieu in 1170, was able to grant to La Trappe a meadow near the mill at Chapelle de Montligeon, together with a quarter of the product (*moltura*) of the mill at Montgiun. He was probably the Simon who attested Rotrou III's act for the priory of Moutiers made in 1159, but the act is of uncertain provenance and the attestation appears as 'Simonis Marii'. Similarly he may be the Simon Mercier/Marnier who attests Rotrou III's act for Chartrage, another act where the text has been transmitted by a seventeenth-century antiquarian.[75] In 1220 a knight called Simon *Viarius* notified that his father Matthew *Viarius* had granted a money fief of 10s. from the *prepositura* of Mortagne to Gervase of Longpont.[76] This would give a family descent over some sixty years of Simon/Matthew/Simon with the 'Matheo Viario' who appears in an act for Val Dieu in 1185 identified with the son.[77] The 10s. money fief from the *prepositura* at Mortagne may have been the count's original retainer. After three generations in comital service, however, the family could afford to dispose of it since Simon had attained knightly status.

[73] *NLR*, no. xiii; *Chartularium insignis ecclesiae cenomannensis quod dicitur liber albus capituli*, ed. A. Cauvin, Le Mans 1869, no. dxxxv.
[74] F. Lot, 'La *Vicaria* et le *vicarius*', *Nouvelle Revue historique de droit français et étranger* xvii (1893), 293.
[75] RCVD, fo. 2; *La Trappe*, 584, 588; Gouverneur, *Essais*, 215–16; Bart, *Antiquitéz*, 131.
[76] *La Trappe*, 11–12.
[77] RCVD, fo. 8v.

New opportunities, c. 1175–87

At the point where the Capetian/Blois coalition appears at its strongest in the 1170s, however, there are indications that the Rotrou family began to look in another direction. A cordiality between the Rotrou and Plantagenet families is first indicated in the pipe roll of 1177/8 which records a visit by Count Rotrou to England made at King Henry's expense. Since the king's writ also covered payments for the expenses of the archbishop of Rheims, who is known to have visited Canterbury on a pilgrimage to Becket's tomb, it seems likely that Rotrou accompanied the archbishop, his brother-in-law, William of Blois, formerly the bishop of Chartres.[78] Henry had financed a similar all-expenses-paid excursion by Theobald V of Blois to Compostella in 1159 when he had been seeking Theobald's support and it may be that he took the opportunity of a similar approach to Rotrou.[79] It is also possible that Rotrou's interest in the Carthusian order was a factor in opening relations. Simon, the prior of Mont Dieu, and Engelbert, prior of Val Saint-Pierre, who had been present at the foundation ceremony for Val Dieu, had already had diplomatic dealings with Henry during the course of the Becket controversy and Rotrou's experience in establishing the house at Val Dieu may well have been useful in taking forward the king's plans for the charterhouse at Witham in Somerset that Henry founded in contrition for the death of Becket.[80]

Count Rotrou had a number of potential links with the court of King Henry II. His maternal cousins, William, earl of Salisbury and William Marshal were well-placed there and Rotrou certainly maintained the connection with the Marshal family, for his cousin, Anselm, a younger brother of William Marshal, attended the foundation ceremony for Val Dieu.[81] Alternatively he might look to his paternal cousin, Archbishop Rotrou of Rouen, but from the mid 1170s relations with King Henry were most readily promoted by Rotrou's brother, Geoffrey, who was frequently in the king's presence, attested his acts and received signs of favour.

Geoffrey of the Perche can first be traced at Henry II's court in the autumn of 1174 when he witnessed the peace treaty between King Henry and his sons, though it is of course possible that he had been in the king's service since the 1150s if Geoffrey of Vigeois's reference to Geoffrey of Neubourg, brother of the count of the Perche, does indeed refer to him.[82] Some weeks after this first attestation he was present on 8 December 1174 when William the Lion of Scotland did homage to King Henry at Valognes.[83] Four of Geoffrey's earliest attestations at the court are made in the company of the

---

78 *PR 24 Henry II 1177/8*, 121; Roger of Howden, *Chronica*, ed. W. Stubbs (RS li, 1868–71), ii. 167.
79 Geoffrey of Vigeois, 'Chronicon', in *RHF* xii. 439.
80 F. Barlow, *Thomas Becket*, London 1986, 179.
81 RCVD, fos 1–2.
82 *Actes Henri II*, ii. 21; Geoffrey of Vigeois, 'Chronicon', in *RHF* xii. 439.
83 *Actes Henri II*, ii. 23.

king's third son, Geoffrey, count of Brittany and three with Richard, so it is possible that Geoffrey had fought with the king's sons in the rebellion of 1173/4 and began to witness royal charters after their reconciliation with their father. From October 1174 onwards Geoffrey attests royal charters regularly, apparently travelling with the king for his attestations are made as far apart as Nottingham, Northampton, Argentan and Angers. In October 1175 he was present when the treaty between Henry and Ruaidrí king of Connacht was ratified at Windsor and throughout the 1170s there are signs of favour in the financial records, including the payment of the substantial sum of £56 on the 1180 Norman exchequer roll.[84] By the mid 1170s Geoffrey was well-established in England, assuming control of his family's English property and securing additional property at Newbury in Berkshire, which he retained until his death some time before September 1180.[85]

There is little direct evidence of Count Rotrou's activities in the later 1170s and early 1180s, though it may have been a period of increasing prosperity for the Perche which permitted the establishment of new religious foundations. In Normandy the urban expansion of Bayeux can be demonstrated by the move of a community of lepers and its institutionalisation on a new site, and it is likely that something similar was occurring in the Perche. By the late 1170s there was a leperhouse outside Nogent-le-Rotrou, to which a tithe in Mâle (Orne, cant. Le Theil) was granted by Odo of Viviers and confirmed by Rotrou in 1179. The master of this house was to attest a number of Rotrou's charters.[86] It was dedicated to St Lazarus and was possibly linked with Louis VII's foundation at Boigny, near Orléans, the French centre of the crusading order of St Lazarus.[87] In the early 1180s a hospital was established within Nogent-le-Rotrou. As with similar institutions which were appearing throughout France in the twelfth century its origins are obscure, but Rotrou was later to claim that it had been founded in memory of his wife.[88]

---

[84] Actes Henri II, ii. 46; Gesta, i. 102–3; Roger of Howden, Chronica ii. 85; PR 21 Henry II, 103. 'Per cartam Regis': Magni rotuli scaccarii Normanniae sub regibus Angliae, ed. T. Stapleton, London 1840–4, i. 39.

[85] PR 21 Henry II, 103; PR 26 Henry II, 46. Well into the reign of John Geoffrey's debts continued to be recorded among the pledges to Aaron of Lincoln.

[86] For the Bayeux community see D. Jeanne, 'Quelles Problematiques pour la mort du lépreux?: Sondages archéologiques du cimitière de Saint-Nicholas de la Chesnaie-Bayeux', Annales de Normandie xlvii (1997), 69–90. For the leperhouse at Nogent see S. Proust, Inventaire sommaire des archives des hospices de Nogent-le-Rotrou depuis leur fondation jusqu'à 1790, Nogent-le-Rotrou 1869, 104. For the master's attestations see AN, MS S2238, no. 15; RCVD, fo. 8v.

[87] M. Barber, 'The order of St Lazarus and the crusades', Catholic Historical Review lxxx (1994), 447ff.

[88] For Rotrou's claim see G. Bry de la Clergerie, Additions aux recherches d'Alençon et du Perche, Paris 1621, 75. In 1182, or possibly 1183 if following old style dating, Rotrou had confirmed the gifts of Philip of Montdoucet 'in fundatione domus elemosinarie de Nog' Rot': Château Saint-Jean, MS A/1. On French hospital foundations see J. Caille, Hospitaux et charité publique à Narbonne au moyen âge, Paris 1978, 31.

These pieties perhaps indicate an awareness on Rotrou's part of his role as count, promoting the welfare of his subjects and protecting the poor, but this is not to suggest that his relations with the Church were always harmonious. In 1183 Pope Lucius addressed a letter to Geoffrey, dean of Chartres, instructing him to defend his Church's property against the inroads of inter-lopers.[89] The pope confers authority on the dean to bring the ecclesiastical sanction of excommunication against any parishioner who injures the Church and its property, and he names the mightiest of the dean's parishio-ners with Rotrou's name at the head of the list. It is hard to escape the conclu-sion that the dean and chapter had specific grievances against Rotrou and the other great lords named, for which they had sought the pope's commission. The nature of the dispute cannot be recovered, but it may have related to the woodlands at Authou. Here Rotrou and the chapter both had interests and it is possible that Rotrou, perhaps in an effort to increase his resources, had sought to exploit the property to the detriment of the chapter.[90]

In 1183, however, the count's fortunes improved markedly when he was granted control of two of his brother Geoffrey's English manors.[91] Since the sheriff accounted £12 18s. at Michaelmas 1183 for property for which he had accounted £19 for the whole year 1181/2, it appears that Rotrou was granted possession some two-thirds of the way through the 1182/3 accounting period. If the writ mentioned in the pipe roll, by which King Henry conveyed the Wanborough property, was indeed despatched in May, then it forms an inter-esting link with the count's activities in Poitou in 1183. In the early summer of that year, Henry II's eldest son and heir, the Young King Henry, irritated that he had a title, but no real authority, in his father's territories, attempted to seize control of his mother's inheritance from his brother Richard. The Young King and his brother, Geoffrey of Brittany, joined forces with malcon-tents who were unhappy with Richard's rule and plundered the monasteries of the area around Limoges, including the abbey of Grandmont for which Henry II had a particular affection. Then in late May the Young King fell ill and, as he lay on his deathbed at the castle of Martel, his father sent him a ring as a token of forgiveness. King Henry's emissaries were Bishop Bernard of Agen and Count Rotrou.[92]

Rotrou was surprisingly well-qualified for the job of peace-making, since he had been a supporter of the young Henry in the great rebellion of Henry II's sons in 1173/4 and he had connections in the area among the fami-lies whom the Young King had sought to persuade to his side. Rotrou's aunt,

---

89 NDC i. 208.

90 NDC i. 221.

91 'de firma Aldiburna et de Wamberga terra Galfridi de Pertico antequam comes frater ejus habuisset': PR 29 Henry II, 1182/3, 128. 'Et comiti de Perch' . . . in catallis de Aldeburna per breve regis': ibid. 129.

92 Geoffrey of Vigeois, 'Chronica', in RHF xviii. 217. The Young King's activities in the south are briefly discussed in R. Benjamin, 'A forty years war: Toulouse and the Plantagenets, 1156–96', Historical Research lxi (1988), 270–85.

Matilda, the sister of Rotrou II, had married successively her brother's crusading comrade, Raymond viscount of Turenne, and Guy of Les Tours, and it was at Martel, the castle of her grandson, Rotrou's cousin, another Raymond of Turenne, that the Young King died.[93] The chronicler, Geoffrey of Vigeois, who is particularly well-informed about these events and saw the passing of the Young King's funeral cortège, implies that Rotrou's role in these conflicts in the Limousin was not confined to this final service to the Young King. For he describes how at that time (*tunc*) Rotrou and the bishop 'were running hither and thither in pursuit of peace' ('discurrebant de pace tractantes') and it seems not unlikely that it was these peace-making activities which prompted the old king to grant the count of the Perche some of his late brother's lands in recognition of his efforts.

There was an additional link between Rotrou and the king of England which may also have contributed to the improvement in relations between the two. Probably as a result of his family connection with Turenne, Rotrou shared the king's affection for the Grandmontine order.[94] It is difficult to trace the beginnings of the Grandmontine house at Chêne Galon just to the north of the forest of Bellême in the Perche, because the Grandmontine rule forbade the monks to hold land other than the immediate surroundings of their house and they therefore kept no records to safeguard their title. The terms of an act of confirmation given by Rotrou III's son in the early thirteenth century, however, indicate that the community had been established by Rotrou.[95]

The rationale behind the friendly relations between the Perche and the Plantagenet realm is apparent. Count Rotrou was as tempted by the English lands offered by Henry II as his father had been by the inducements of Henry I. His opportunities for expansion from the Perche were now limited by the tight network of family relationships in which he found himself. For his part the king of England was returning to the policies of his grandfather by cultivating the friendship of his neighbours. In the years before the 1173 rebellion Henry had ensured the security of his vast realm by military means, both his own energetic activity and the maintenance of a series of castles. The raid on Sées in 1174 undertaken by the Young King, Rotrou and his allies, although not disastrous in its effects, had, however, illustrated how easily such fortifications might be bypassed, as well as showing all too clearly the continuing threat from the Perche.[96] From the 1170s Henry seems to have decided that reliance on border fortresses was not enough, but needed to

---

[93] Geoffrey of Vigeois, 'Chronica', in *RHF* xii. 436; *Gesta*, i. 301.

[94] E. Hallam, 'Henry II, Richard I and the order of Grandmont', *Journal of Medieval History* i (1975), 165–85.

[95] 'Quicquid habent et possident ex dono antecessorum nostrorum scilicet bonae memorae Rotrodi patris mei et Gaufridi fratris mei comitum Pertici': BN, MS Duchesne 54, p. 461.

[96] On castles in the Angevin empire see Powicke, *Loss of Normandy*, 196–204; W. L. Warren, *King John*, London 1961, 73–4.

be combined with the conciliation of his near neighbours and the accommo-dation with the Perche which followed worked well for the rest of the reign.[97] There were no further sorties from the Perche and even in the closing days of the king's life after the meeting at La Ferté-Bernard, when much of northern Maine surrendered to Richard and King Philip, there is no indication that Count Rotrou welcomed Henry's enemies.[98]

Rotrou and the crusade, 1187–91

While the latter years of Count Rotrou's contemporary, King Henry II, were played out against a background of family rivalry and increasing political tension, Rotrou's political and personal fortunes improved towards the end of his life. The hostility of Henry II had disappeared and Rotrou's mission to the Young King in 1183 is an indication of a new role that might emerge for the Perche. At the same time friendly links were maintained with the Thibaudian counts of Blois and Champagne, despite the death of Rotrou's wife, Matilda of Blois, in January 1184, and through them with the royal house. Rotrou's eldest son, Geoffrey, attested a grant made by his uncle, Theobald of Blois, to the Fontevraudine house of Hautes Bruyères in 1183, and in the mid 1180s his second son, Rotrou, was appointed treasurer of the college of Saint-Martin at Tours, a foundation noted for its links with the French crown.[99] The younger Rotrou's translation to the royal bishopric of Châlons-en-Champagne in 1190 is an indication of the continued strength of the Capetian connection, but there was none the less more scope for inde-pendent action by the Rotrous from the 1180s. Rotrou and Geoffrey were to exploit that scope very successfully; in particular Rotrou was to take up with enthusiasm the challenge of the new crusade.

In the autumn of 1187 news reached western Europe of the disastrous defeat of the Christian forces under the command of the king of Jerusalem at the Horns of Hattin. The defeat would lead to the fall of Jerusalem itself and the pope sent out an appeal urging men to take the cross. Throughout Rotrou's life the Christian settlements established in the east after the First Crusading expedition had managed to survive and there had been a steady stream of fighting men who had made their way to the east.[100] His younger brother, Stephen, had died in Jerusalem in 1168/9, and his brother-in-law,

[97] Henry and Richard pursued a similar policy with Robert of Dreux, who received £300 annually from King Henry and £600 from Richard: *Rotuli chartarum in turri Londinensi asservati, 1199–1216*, ed. T. D. Hardy, London 1837, 58.
[98] The material on the closing days of Henry's life is reviewed in Warren, *Henry II*, 623–6.
[99] BN, MS franc 20691 (extraits du cartulaire du comté de Chartres), fo. 560v; Q. Griffiths, 'The Capetian kings and Saint-Martin of Tours', *Studies in Medieval and Renaissance History* ix (1987), 127.
[100] See Phillips, *Defenders of the east*, for the context of relations between the Latin east and the west.

William Gouet IV of Montmirail, was also to die in the Holy Land in the late 1160s. Sons of the Percheron warrior elite also made the commitment. William of Orme, for example, on the point of departure for Jerusalem, was given a leather wallet by the monks of Nogent when he and his brothers settled their dispute with the priory concerning water courses.[101]

In January 1188 the kings of England and France in conference at Gisors agreed to put aside their own quarrels and go to the aid of the Christians in the Holy Land. During their discussions large numbers of the French and English nobles who attended personally took crusaders' vows and among them the chronicler, Rigord, mentions Rotrou count of the Perche.[102] His evidence on this point is of particular value, for it shows not only Rotrou's personal commitment to the crusade, but also reveals his attendance at a particularly important diplomatic negotiation between the two kings, a role which he was to undertake increasingly in the remaining years of his life.

For the next eighteen months the kings of France and England failed to settle their differences and at the time of King Henry's death in July 1189 the whole enterprise appeared to have stalled. With the succession of Richard, however, the political situation was transformed, for Richard was whole-heartedly committed to the crusade and turned his mind to detailed planning. As part of this he sought to conclude alliances which would guarantee his borders. Within three weeks of his accession, on the very afternoon of his installation in Rouen as duke of Normandy, Richard's niece, Richenza-Matilda of Saxony, was married to Count Rotrou's eldest son, Geoffrey.[103] This was a dramatic shift in political alignment, emphasised by the royal rank of the bride. As Richard himself had no children and his sisters were all long since married, the bride was the most senior of the marriageable Plantagenet princesses, and the speed with which the marriage followed Richard's accession, together with the fact that an ecclesiastical dispensation would have been needed for two descendants of William the Conqueror, suggests that the negotiations may have been begun before the death of the old king (see fig. 3).

Matilda was the daughter of Richard's eldest sister, Matilda, and Duke Henry of Saxony. She had been born in 1172 and given the name of her paternal great-grandmother, Richenza, the wife of the Emperor Lothair V. When her parents were exiled to Normandy in 1182 Richenza adopted the name of Matilda, perhaps as a compliment to her maternal grandmother, Empress Matilda, or alternatively because her own name was unfamiliar in western France. When her family returned to Germany in 1185 Matilda had

---

101 'Prior . . . et conventus centum solidos ipsi Gerongio et uni fratri ejus, Roberto scilicet, vinginti; Guillermo vero alteri, Jerosolimam ituro manticam de Cornesio, pro pacis caritatisque benedictione largiti sunt': *NLR*, no. xcii.

102 Rigord, *Gesta Philippi Augusti*, in *Oeuvres de Rigord et de Guillaume le Breton*, ed. H. F. Delaborde, Paris 1882–5, i. 83, para. 56.

103 Roger of Howden, *Chronica* iii. 3.

Figure 3
The family relationship between Geoffrey of the Perche
and Matilda of Saxony

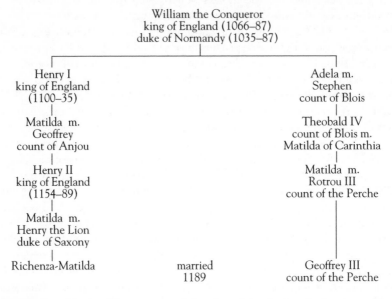

William the Conqueror
king of England (1066–87)
duke of Normandy (1035–87)

Henry I		Adela m.
king of England		Stephen
(1100–35)		count of Blois

Matilda m.
Geoffrey
count of Anjou

Theobald IV
count of Blois m.
Matilda of Carinthia

Henry II
king of England
(1154–89)

Matilda m.
Rotrou III
count of the Perche

Matilda m.
Henry the Lion
duke of Saxony

| Richenza-Matilda | married | Geoffrey III |
| | 1189 | count of the Perche |

remained at Henry II's court and her hand had already been sought in marriage by King William the Lion of Scotland and King Bela of Hungary.[104] She brought with her an enormous dowry, made up of the so-called honour of the constable, centred on the manor of Haughley in Suffolk, and the lands of Henry of Essex.[105] It was the same incentive which Henry I had used to win over Rotrou II nearly ninety years before: a marriage alliance and a parcel of English lands, but in 1189 the contractual consideration was greater. Where Rotrou II's wife had been one among many of Henry I's illegitimate daughters, Richenza-Matilda seems to have been particularly attached to her uncle the king and the honour of the constable was clearly far more substantial than the two Wiltshire manors which had constituted the first Countess Matilda's dowry.[106]

In the light of the Rotrou family's new relationship with the Angevin court it is not surprising that King Philip of France should choose Rotrou as his ambassador to Richard. In the autumn of 1189 Rotrou took the outcomes of a planning conference which Philip had held in Paris to Richard in

---

[104] *Gesta*, ii. 73; K. Jordan, *Henry the Lion*, Oxford 1986, 185.

[105] *Curia regis rolls*, London 1923– , xiii, no. 684.

[106] In September 1189, only two months after her marriage, Richenza-Matilda joined Richard at Geddington: *Gesta*, ii. 87. She joined her grandmother, Queen Eleanor, on 21 Apr. 1199 at Fontevraud, shortly after Richard's burial there: *CDF*, no. 1301; text in *Layettes de trésor de chartes*, i. no. 489.

England; by then his own preparations were well-advanced.[107] Three days after his son's brilliant marriage in Rouen he had confirmed everything that the abbey of Saint-Évroul held in his territory, and he probably issued a charter of confirmation to his father's foundation of La Trappe around the same time, for the Saint-Évroul confirmation is witnessed by Abbot Gervase of La Trappe. He may even have given orders for the redrafting of the act of foundation for his charterhouse at Val Dieu du Réno, for transcripts of the act preserved among the house's archives all include Matilda's name, although she was not born at the time of the original act.[108] There is some disagreement among the chroniclers about the precise date of Rotrou's embassy. Roger of Wendover mentions it in October, while Roger of Howden places it in November, but since Howden was almost certainly not at court at this time Wendover's date is preferable.[109] Rotrou's new daughter-in-law is known to have joined King Richard at Geddington in September 1189, so it is possible that she went directly to court while Rotrou took the opportunity to visit his family's English property. It is also possible that he visited the Augustinian priory of Bradenstoke in Wiltshire, where his maternal grandparents, Walter and Sibyl of Salisbury, were buried, since he granted half a mark of silver to that house in an undated charter.[110]

By May 1190 he had returned to the Perche where he confirmed the conveyance of a tithe which had been bequeathed to the leperhouse of St Lazarus in Nogent-le-Rotrou. Before his departure he was to be joined by his heir, Geoffrey, and his second son, Rotrou, treasurer of St Martin of Tours, in a gift to the hospital of the Maison-Dieu in Nogent-le-Rotrou which included the churches of the two English manors, Aldbourne and Wanborough in Wiltshire, as well as property at Champrond near Nogent. On 20 June he was in Chartres where he made provision of 20s. each annually for the anniversaries of his mother, Countess Hawise, and his wife, Countess Matilda, to be celebrated in the cathedral, and probably granted the annual sum of £10 from revenues of Nogent-le-Rotrou with which a perpetual candle was to be kept burning before the shrine of the Virgin's robe. Rotrou's spiritual preparations were, then, thorough without being extravagant. They favoured the houses in which he took most interest, and they were aimed at the spiritual well-being of his closest family, his wife and his mother.[111]

---

107 Roger of Wendover, Chronica i. 170.
108 GC xi. 823c; La Trappe, 587–90; RCVD, fo. 1–2; AD Orne, MSS H2621, H2622.
109 Roger of Howden, Chronica iii. 19–20; Roger of Wendover, Chronica i. 170; D. Corner, 'The Gesta regis Henrici secundi and the Chronica of Roger, parson of Howden', Bulletin of the Institute of Historical Research lvi (1983), 126–45.
110 Cartulary of Bradenstoke, no. 655.
111 Château Saint-Jean, MS C/108; Bry, Additions, 75. For the anniversaries see NDC i. 221. For an undated text of Rotrou's act concerning the candle see NDC i. 218. It appears to be taken from a vidimus and confirmation of his son, Geoffrey, in which Geoffrey mentions his father's imminent departure. This text has proved impossible to locate. A French trans-

There is no indication of Rotrou's financial preparations for the crusade, but some idea of the scale of expenditure involved is given by the activities of Aylmer of Villeray. A member of a family with ties to the Rotrous going back over a century, Aylmer took extreme measures to raise funds for participation in the crusade. In the count's residence at Nogent, in the presence of Rotrou and his sons, including the treasurer of Tours, he sold his rights over Berd'huis (Orne, cant. Nocé) to the monks of Sainte-Gauburge. For this concession Aylmer received £200 *angevin* and his brother, 100s. Aylmer also raised £35 *angevin* and a further 100s. for his brother from his sale of his rights at Dancé (Orne, cant. Nocé) which Count Rotrou notified in July 1190.[112]

This latter act is valuable evidence for the fact that Rotrou did not join the king of France's party which left from Vézelay on 4 July 1190, but delayed his departure, following the main French forces southwards. It is likely that he took the opportunity to visit Cluny as he travelled, for it was at nearby Mâcon that he issued an act in favour of his family's Cluniac foundation of Saint-Denis of Nogent-le-Rotrou, conceding to the priory the taxes which he had been accustomed to claim over its property in Nogent and granting a tithe of his woodland and pannage revenues.[113] It was a generous gift though not sufficient to justify the remark of his contemporary Ambroise, who composed an eye-witness account of the crusade:

> The count of Perche too who deprived
> himself of everything arrived[114]

None the less the comprehensiveness of Rotrou's preparations does suggest that he did not intend to return.

With the rest of the western European crusaders Rotrou and his eldest son Geoffrey made their way to Sicily, where their particular connections with both the Angevin and Capetian royal houses drew them almost immediately into diplomatic activity. On 4 October 1190 Geoffrey accompanied King Philip on a joint French and Sicilian deputation to King Richard which was to complain about the behaviour of Richard's forces in Messina.[115] In the passage of Roger of Howden's chronicle which describes these events Geoffrey is described as count, and the title is again used of him when he cele-brated Christmas day at the English king's court in Messina. This is a surprising inaccuracy for Howden who was an eye-witness, and can perhaps

---

lation of the act appears in M. O. des Murs, *Histoire des comtes du Perche de la famille des Rotrou de 943 à 1231*, Nogent-le-Rotrou 1856, 523.

[112] AN, MS S2238, no. 15. Aylmer makes no mention of his departure on crusade but his wife, the daughter of Robert de Insula, does so in her later quitclaim: AN, MS LL1158, 411; *CMPerche*, no. 34.

[113] *NLR*, nos ix, xcix.

[114] Ambroise, 'L'Estoire de la guerre sainte', trans. by M. J. Hubert and J. La Monte as *The crusade of Richard Lionheart*, New York 1941, 192, lines 4543–4.

[115] *Gesta*, ii. 128; Roger of Howden, *Chronica* iii. 57.

only be explained by Geoffrey's high status as the king's nephew-in-law, which permitted the use of his father's title as a courtesy.[116] Among the royal clerks who drafted the treaty of Messina that finally released Richard from his engagement to Philip's sister, Alice, however, there seems to be no confusion for the treaty is guaranteed and probably in part negotiated by the count of the Perche.[117]

Rotrou must have travelled with Philip's forces which arrived in Acre in April 1191, for he is mentioned as being among them when the armies of the French and English kings met up on 9 June 1191. Thereafter only two facts are known: that he made a benefaction to the Templars and that he died at Acre. The city finally surrendered to the Christian forces on 12 July 1191, but Rotrou's death probably took place somewhat later, perhaps from wounds sustained in the siege or as a result of an illness contracted in the camp, since his obituary was celebrated at Nogent-le-Rotrou on 27 July. The nature of Rotrou's gift to the Templars is unknown, but it may have been intended as recognition of the fact that the Templars had buried Rotrou's brother, Stephen, in their house in Jerusalem. Alternatively it may have been a deathbed donation since it was immediately confirmed by his son and successor Geoffrey, 'pro remedio anime R patris sui et M matris sui'.[118]

While his father cut a bold figure in the politics of the first half of the twelfth century, Rotrou III gives the impression of a less flamboyant personality who took longer to make his mark. When modern French commentators have described Rotrou II as 'the Great', there is, therefore, a temptation to characterise, Rotrou III as 'the Less'.[119] In many ways Rotrou's career paralleled that of King Louis VII: he was personally devout, the conscientious patron of religious houses and a man much influenced by his wife's relations. Just as the reputation of the French monarchy grew, however, during Louis's lifetime, almost in spite of the king, so the position of the Perche improved in the 1170s and 1180s as Rotrou developed a new relationship with King Henry II and took on a diplomatic role. Towards the end of his life he threw himself wholeheartedly into the crusade, whose attractions he had hitherto managed to avoid, and in his end he was by no means an unworthy son of his father.

During Rotrou's lifetime the structures of more stable government appeared in the Perche, consolidating the new political unit that had emerged. For much of his life it suited Rotrou to remain locked in close alignment with the counts of Blois/Chartres, as had been the situation of his more

---

[116] Other examples of the use of comital titles during a father's lifetime include Waleran, son of Robert II of Meulan and Robert, son of Count Robert I of Dreux.

[117] *Diplomatic documents preserved in the Public Record Office*, I: *1101–1272*, ed. P. Chaplais, London 1964, no. 5.

[118] *Chronicles and memorials of Richard I*, ed. W. Stubbs (RS xxxviii, 1864–5), i. 213; BN, MS Duchesne 20, fo. 230; *Obits*, ii. 396.

[119] De Romanet, *Géographie*, i. 48.

distant ancestors in the early eleventh century. From the 1170s, however, he began to explore the potential of closer links with the king of England and by the end of his life the family stood carefully balanced between the two rival kings, with some members closely aligned to their Capetian relations and the heir, Geoffrey, linked to the Plantagenet family. The Perche was a minor principality but it still stood between power blocs – these blocs differed from those which Rotrou's father had manipulated but none the less Rotrou could play the same game and there are signs towards the end of his life that the pace of that game was quickening.

5

Geoffrey III (1191–1202)

The closing years of the twelfth century saw an intensification of the rivalry between the kings of France and England as King Philip II of France (1180–1223) grew in confidence. Both kings deployed their resources in the struggle and the new ruler of the Perche, Count Geoffrey III, exploited the strategic position of his lands between the two power blocs, securing favour that supplemented the wealth derived from his own territory. The Perche, like all of western Europe, was now more systematically governed, but there are signs that its resources were not sufficient to support Count Geoffrey's aspirations. The princely image of the count and the family's connection with royal and princely houses were major factors in the continuance of the Perche as a separate polity, but expensive to maintain. Around the year 1200, the county attained the height of its power, with Geoffrey III playing an important role in high politics and able to discard any traces of dependence on his Thibaudian neighbours.

The succession of Geoffrey III

Geoffrey's marriage to Richenza-Matilda of Saxony took him to the centre of the Plantagenet family and his actions over the next three years suggest that he was much influenced by the enthusiasm for the crusade which King Richard clearly displayed. In November 1189 Geoffrey was at Westminster with the king and when the crusading armies of King Philip and King Richard met up in Sicily Geoffrey was among those who approached King Richard to complain about the conduct of Richard's troops.[1] Geoffrey spent Christmas with his uncle-in-law at Messina and then he accompanied Richard's party to the Holy Land. He witnessed the marriage settlement between Richard and Berengaria of Navarre, Geoffrey's second cousin, which was made in Limassol in May 1191.[2] The death of Rotrou III in July 1191 and Geoffrey's succession to the county of the Perche did nothing to distract the new count from the crusading project. Unlike King Philip, who abandoned the enterprise soon after the fall of Acre and sailed for home in early August 1191, Geoffrey remained in the east, presumably under the command of his

---

[1] *Acta of Henry II and Richard I, part two*, ed. N. Vincent (List and Index Society s.s. xxvii, 1990), no. 191; *Gesta*, ii. 128, Roger of Howden, *Chronica* iii. 57.
[2] *Les Registres de Philippe Auguste*, ed. J. W. Baldwin, Paris 1992– , i. 469–70.

cousin, the duke of Burgundy. His record was distinguished for its length rather than its glory, however, and crusading sources mention him only once. On the road to Jerusalem in June 1192, when the Christian army was attacked by raiding parties, Geoffrey engaged with the hostile forces in a rather faint-hearted fashion to help repel the attackers.[3]

Nothing more is known of Geoffrey's career until he gave an act of confirmation to the priory at Nogent-le-Rotrou, which is dated 1192 but was possibly given as late as March 1193 if old style dating was in use in the house.[4] During Geoffrey's absence an heir had probably been born between April 1190 and March 1191, for by 1196 a son, Geoffrey, was old enough to witness one of Geoffrey III's acts.[5] The news of Count Rotrou's death must have been brought home by King Philip and his companions, since the count died on or around 27 July and Philip had left Acre on 31 July, sailing from Tyre some days later.[6] In the absence of a count the Perche was the responsibility of the remaining members of the family. Geoffrey's brother, Stephen, and an experienced officer, the seneschal, Warin of Lonray, issued acts jointly in the count's name and their own, and the Countess Matilda had also played a part, acknowledging a benefaction made to the abbey of La Trappe during Geoffrey's absence.[7]

Count Geoffrey's confirmation to the priory at Nogent-le-Rotrou reveals that his home-coming was 'burdened by debt' and Prior Hubert and the community granted him £200 in return for confirmation of his predecessors' grants.[8] A grant to the Grandmontine priory at Chêne Galon on 11 February 1193 also suggests an absence of ready resources. With the approval of his wife and brothers Geoffrey assigned to the priory a regular payment from all his sources of income (*prepositurae*) in the Perche. It was a generous benefaction, intended to clothe the monks, but it was a charge upon future income rather than a payment from current funds. In these circumstances the proceeds of the countess's dowry lands in England would have been an important supplementary source of income, but the political situation that had allowed Geoffrey to acquire those lands had changed since the departure of King Richard in 1190 and was becoming increasingly complex and difficult to read.

---

3   Roger of Howden, *Chronica* iii. 175. 'Jam nimium nostri fatigati pondere belli, fluctuare coperunt, et . . . eo venit, comes de Perche, qui tamen se timide habuit . . .': *Chronicles and memorials of Richard I*, i. 372.
4   *NLR*, no. cx.
5   For the young Geoffrey see *CMD*, no. cciii; *NDC* i. 254.
6   *Obits*, ii. 396.
7   BN, MS Duchesne 20, fo. 230; AD Orne, MSS H5441, H1846 (printed as *La Trappe*, 458).
8   *NLR*, no. cx.

Maintaining the balance I, 1192–7

By February 1193 the links which Count Geoffrey and his father had developed with King Richard were beginning to appear unwise. On his way home from the Holy Land Richard had been captured and held to ransom by the Holy Roman emperor. It was a situation which King Philip would not fail to exploit. Some Norman lords felt the time was right for rapprochement with the Capetians and Gilbert of Vascoeil, keeper of the castle at Gisors, even went so far as to surrender his charge to King Philip. Richard's brother, John, entered negotiations with Philip to be recognised as Richard's successor and Philip moved against Rouen itself.[9]

As the king of France appeared to be gaining the upper hand Geoffrey needed to reaffirm his links with his cousin, Philip. The terms of a treaty concluded at Mantes on 9 July 1193 between King Philip and the Normans suggest that Geoffrey had cultivated his cousin promptly and assiduously. The treaty specifically mentions that the count of the Perche was to have his revenues in England and that the king of England and his men were to keep peace with the count.[10] The reference to the count implies not only that Geoffrey had the ear of King Philip, but also reflects what must have become the count's major preoccupations: the fear of losing his English income and threatened, if not real, conflict with Richard's Norman supporters.

On both sides of the Norman border defences were being strengthened at the end of the twelfth century. At Bellême Geoffrey appropriated three building plots from a local citizen so that he could improve the defences of the castle and he gave the old comital residence to the prior of Bellême in compensation for an area he had embanked.[11] On the Norman side at Moulins-la-Marche the castle had been placed on a war footing, involving the erection of hurdles, laying floors in the towers, constructing terraces and making weaponry.[12] Conflict did indeed break out for the town of Mortagne was burned as Geoffrey indicates in an act of 1195 in which he made a grant to repair the buildings of the hospital there. In Richard's continued absence Philip maintained the pressure on Normandy and, after taking Evreux, Neubourg and Vaudreuil early in 1194, he laid siege to Verneuil, just north of the Perche.[13]

Family connections with King Philip were exploited and in November 1193 Geoffrey's brother, Bishop Rotrou of Châlons-en-Champagne, was among the assembly of bishops which pronounced Philip's marriage to

---

9 Powicke, *Loss of Normandy*, 96.
10 'Comes Particii redditus suos in Anglia integre habebit et rex Angliae et sui pacem ei tenebunt': Roger of Howden, *Chronica* iii. 218. K. Norgate, *England under the Angevin kings*, London 1887, ii. 325; J. Gillingham, *Richard I*, New Haven–London 1999, 241.
11 'veteres aulas comitis': 'Querimoniae normannorum', in *RHF* xxiv/1 (second pagination sequence), nos 135, 164.
12 *Rotuli scaccarii Normanniae*, i. 245–6; Gillingham, *Richard I*, 283 n. 5.
13 Bart, *Antiquitéz*, 156–8; Roger of Howden, *Chronica* iii. 252.

Ingeborg of Denmark invalid.[14] Geoffrey did not abandon all contact with his wife's Plantagenet relations, however, as an agreement made in January 1194 between Philip and Matilda's youngest uncle, Count John of Mortain, shows. It is an agreement that remained, for obvious reasons, unknown to English writers, but was preserved in the French royal archives.[15] In return for King Philip's recognition of John as Richard's successor John made a series of concessions to the French king including the grant of Moulins and Bonsmoulins to Geoffrey. John had no means of enforcing his treacherous grant which would only take effect if he was able to succeed his brother, but the inclusion of Moulins and Bonsmoulins in its terms suggests that Count Geoffrey had links with both King Philip and Count John. It is tempting to assign John's grant to the Templars which Geoffrey witnessed at Rouen between 1192 and 1199 to this period, together with another grant to the Rotrou family foundation at La Trappe; and even if these datings remain speculative the acts are indications of continuing contacts between Geoffrey and John.[16]

King Richard was aware of Geoffrey's activities for he mentions them in the song he composed in prison:

> My comrades whom I loved and still do love
> The lords of Perche and of Caïeux
> Strange tales have reached me that are hard to prove;
> I ne'er was false to them; for evermore
> Vile would men count them, if their arms they bore
> 'Gainst me, a prisoner here![17]

When he finally reappeared from his captivity and made his way to Normandy in May 1194, he was not slow to make felt his displeasure with his niece's husband. The 1194 pipe roll reveals that Geoffrey's worst fears had been realised and he had been deprived of his English lands. For the fourth quarter of the accounting period, that is from late June 1194, his family properties of Aldbourne and Wanborough in Wiltshire are recorded as escheats, while Toddington in Bedfordshire was at farm, so it would appear that Geoffrey had lost these lands in summer 1194.[18] The king's actions could hardly have been more pointed, for it was Geoffrey's family property which had been seized by the king, while Matilda's dowry lands remained untouched.

It was a situation that was not to continue for long. King Richard had a

[14] Roger of Howden, *Chronica* iii. 307.

[15] *Layettes de trésor de chartes*, i, no. 412.

[16] HMC, *Report on manuscripts in various collections*, London 1901–14, vii. 376–7; *La Trappe*, 449.

[17] Gillingham, *Richard I*, 243, based on Norgate's translation of Richard's song, 'Ja nus hons pris'.

[18] *PR 6 Richard I, 1194*, 18, 26, 199.

significant task in recovering the lands that had been lost to King Philip during the years of his crusade and captivity, and he needed to re-establish a network of allies.[19] His displeasure towards Geoffrey was therefore short-lived and by September 1195 the escheats of Geoffrey's English property disappear from the pipe rolls. Richard had made his point and now needed to restore friendly relations. From the next year signs of favour towards the Rotrous begin to reappear: exemptions from taxation for Matilda's dowry lands in Essex, Hertfordshire and Kent were granted by the king's writ and by the mid 1190s the count had recovered his English income.[20] Two surviving confirmations of property show substantial sums being paid to the count in fees. When Geoffrey confirmed property in Wiltshire to Adam de Kenete, for example, he received 30 marks of silver and the countess 3 marks, while a similar confirmation to Geoffrey Perdriz procured 9 marks of silver for the count and one for the countess.[21]

Opportunities were also offered to Geoffrey's brother, Stephen. He had already been granted a portion of the comital revenues, including income from Rivray, Montlandon and Nonvilliers, the proceeds of mills at La Poterie and a share of the salt monopoly at Nogent-le-Rotrou.[22] Following in the footsteps of his uncle, Geoffrey, who had had a role at the Plantagenet court in the 1170s, Stephen supplemented this income by taking service with King Richard and had done so by September 1195. A payment of £266 13s. 4d. is recorded on the Norman pipe roll for that year and further substantial sums followed.[23] The 1198 roll mentions payment of £360 and the payment of arrears on his fee is recorded in 1200.[24] In addition, as the 1190s progressed, Stephen began to accumulate landed property in Normandy. He was granted temporary control of Fulk of Aunou's property in the Hiémois, perhaps during a minority or temporary forfeiture, and in 1198 he owed the Norman exchequer £32 for taxes on it.[25] At some point before 1200 he was also granted property at Chambois (Orne, cant. Trun), which had come into royal hands after being held by several lords, including Ralph of Vermandois and Geoffrey of Mandeville.[26] So great was the favour extended to Stephen that he was allowed to bring a Jew from France to Chambois and enjoy the profits of his

[19] For Richard's recovery see Gillingham, *Richard I*, 283ff.

[20] *PR 8 Richard I, 1196*, 120.

[21] PRO, MS E 326/7482; BL, MS Harleian charter 54.g.26.

[22] BN, MS Duchesne 54, p. 460; AD Eure-et-Loir, abbey of Saint-Vincent-aux-Bois, MS H3907 (Registre de Saint-Vincent-aux-Bois), p. 28; BN, MS Baluze 38, fo. 232v; AD Eure-et-Loir, cathedral chapter of Chartres, MS G1459; *Tiron*, no. ccclxxvii, 160; *Obits*, ii. 389.

[23] *Rotuli scaccarii Normanniae*, i. 137; S. Church, 'The rewards of service in the household of King John: a dissenting opinion', *EHR* cx (1995), 280.

[24] *Rotuli scaccarii Normanniae*, ii. 386; *Memoranda roll 1 John, 1199–1200* (PRS n.s. xxi), 95–6.

[25] *CDF*, no. 310; *Rotuli scaccarii Normanniae*, ii. 396.

[26] *Rot. chart.*, 75b; *Rotuli scaccarii Normanniae*, i, introduction at p. clxii.

moneylending, a privilege normally reserved for the king.[27] In addition he or his brother, the count, also acquired property at *Gaspreia* (probably Gaprée [Orne, cant. Courtomer] some 14 kilometres west of Moulins on the road to Sées), as early thirteenth-century records concerning the knight service owed by the counts of the Perche within Normandy indicate.[28]

Powicke remarks that Richard 'understood the art of giving' and the king certainly deployed that art to draw Geoffrey and his brother into alliance.[29] The most significant of all his gifts, however, has gone unrecorded in any form, either narrative or documentary, and has to be reconstructed from charter evidence. This material shows that Geoffrey's power extended over the castellanries of Moulins-la-Marche and Bonsmoulins on the southern Norman border, indicating that at some point before his death Geoffrey had secured possession of them from the English king.[30] The Rotrou family had had an interest in them for more than fifty years, since Geoffrey's grandfather Rotrou II had been granted Moulins by King Stephen in 1137. In 1158, less than ten years after he became duke of Normandy, King Richard's father, Henry II, had recovered control of the castle of Moulins and its neighbour at Bonsmoulins, which had been held by Richer of L'Aigle, a cousin of the Rotrou lineage. Henry's constables continued to hold both castles for the rest of his reign, yet Richard was prepared to alienate not only the castles but also surrounding ducal demesne, for Geoffrey gave the chapel within the castle at Moulins to Saint-Évroul, while granting rights to its tenants throughout the *baillia*. It is clear therefore that Geoffrey not only had custody of the militarily important fortresses, but had also secured the ducal rights and revenues associated with the area. The date that Geoffrey received this major concession from Richard cannot be established beyond the very broad limits of 1195 and 1198.[31] While Richard expended subsidies on the rulers of the Low Countries and cash to secure the election of his nephew Otto as king of Germany, the concession of a couple of castles and some ducal rights on the southern border to his nephew-in-law might well have seemed a good bargain.[32]

---

[27] *Rot. chart.*, 75b.

[28] 'Scripta de feodis', in *RHF* xxiv. 706

[29] Powicke, *Loss of Normandy*, 118. See Gillingham's comments on Richard's largesse: *Richard I*, 261–2.

[30] AD Orne, MS H721.

[31] *Rotuli scaccarii Normanniae*, i. 244, records Warin of Glapion's tenure of Moulins. By 1198 Moulins has disappeared from the roll.

[32] Roger of Howden, *Chronica* iv. 19–20. *Rotuli scaccarii Normanniae*, ii. 301 (count of Boulogne), 302 (count of St Pol).

Energetic lordship: the initiatives of Geoffrey III

The complexity of the external political situation was not the only problem to confront Count Geoffrey III in the 1190s. The burden of his crusading debt was increased by the conflict with his Norman neighbours. The costly rebuilding of the hospital at Mortagne in the mid 1190s and the additional work on the castle at Bellême are the most visible demands on his resources, but his concern about the continued receipt of his English revenues reveals the underlying anxieties of his position. The county he had inherited was small with no major centres of population. His major objectives must therefore have been to maximise the available resources and to press comital power to its furthest extent. There were few opportunities for expansion on the scale offered by the acquisition of Moulins and Bonsmoulins, though Geoffrey was probably able to make small increases to his lands such as his acquisition of the settlement of Bresollettes (Orne, cant. Tourouvre) from the abbey of Saint-Laumer of Blois in return for an annual payment of £25.[33]

A particularly well-documented initiative by Geoffrey is his assertion of his power in the forest to the north-east of the Perche. At some point after 1194 Geoffrey obtained from the abbey of Saint-Évroul the settlement of Marchainville (Orne, cant. Longny) and associated property, some twenty kilometres from the Norman outpost at Verneuil-sur-Avre, which had been the key to Normandy when Richard had returned in 1194.[34] The abbey retained the church at Marchainville and received in return Geoffrey's service and an annual render of four pounds of wax. The arrangement is never specifically described as an exchange, but by the same charter Geoffrey gave the monks the church of St Nicholas of Maison Maugis, with existing tithes, tithes over any inroads into the forest of Réno and sundry other associated property. It was a substantial package and, while some of it may have been intended as a benefaction, it is also an indication of the value he attached to Marchainville.[35]

At first sight Geoffrey's primary motivation appears to have been economic. In the subsequent process of development Geoffrey managed his new resource carefully, issuing a charter to its inhabitants to encourage settlement. The charter was destroyed in a fire, but Geoffrey's brother, the count-bishop William issued a replacement which enables us to reconstruct it.[36] The men of Marchainville were to be free of all comital dues and to have rights to fuel, timber and pasture within the comital woodlands in return for an annual payment of 12d. Geoffrey's act significantly refers to the residents of Marchainville as *burgenses*, suggesting that he sought more than the agricul-

[33] *La Trappe*, 451–2.
[34] Powicke, *Loss of Normandy*, 100–2.
[35] AD Orne, abbey of Saint-Évroul, MS H702 (printed as De Romanet, *Géographie*, ii. 205–7). OV iii. 150–4.
[36] BN, MS Dupuy 222, 127–8.

tural development of the forest, and his attempt to encourage settlement, which was similar to those undertaken by his cousins, the counts of Champagne, must have been in some measure successful for he was later able to endow his own *anniversarium* using the resources of Marchainville.[37]

Rather more political motives are indicated, however, by the fortification at Marchainville which is first recorded in 1211/12.[38] Since such a fortification is unlikely to have been built by Geoffrey's son, who was still a minor in 1211/12, its construction implies a military or political purpose behind Geoffrey's activities. Marchainville lay far to the north-east of any territory mentioned in the acts of Geoffrey's comital predecessors and Count Rotrou III's grant of land and jurisdiction to the priory of Moutiers in 1159 is, in fact, the only surviving family act which indicates comital power in the lands east of the River Huisne before the end of the twelfth century. It is significant, therefore, that Geoffrey's acts are witnessed by a number of lords whose toponymics link them with this area between the Huisne and the forest of Senonches, implying a new recognition of his power in the locality. Geoffrey's castle at Marchainville had a military purpose in that it controlled the road from La Ferté-Vidame, Verneuil and southern Normandy along which hostile forces may have travelled during King Richard's absence in the early 1190s, but it also demonstrated acknowledgement of the count's power over the area.

Much of the credit for attracting the magnates of this uncertain area between the territories of the counts of the Perche and the lords of Châteauneuf-en-Thymerais must go to Rotrou III's foundation of the charterhouse at Val Dieu, which drew benefactions from the forested uplands. Among the unfamiliar toponymics appearing in Geoffrey's acts of confirmation for Val Dieu are those of Miles of La Charmue (Eure-et-Loir, cant. La Loupe, cme Manou) and Vivian of Feillet (Orne, cant. Longny, cme Le Mage).[39] By far the most significant act however is the guarantee from Count Geoffrey sought by Gerald of *Boceio* for the grant of 60s. from his *prepositura* at Longny which he proposed to give to the convent of Belhomert.[40] Gerald's origins are uncertain; some historians have suggested that he may have come from Boissy-Maugis, but he is as likely to have taken his toponymic from Boissy-lès-Perche, due north of the Perche and only 14 kilometres from Verneuil in Normandy. All his acts and the toponymics of the men who attest them, including those of his two seneschals, Robert of Monceaux (Orne, cant. Longny) and William of La Lande (La Lande-sur-Eure, Orne, cant.

---

[37] For the counts of Champagne see T. Evergates, *Feudal society in the baillage of Troyes under the counts of Champagne, 1152–1284*, Baltimore 1975, 41–59; AD Eure-et-Loir, MS H3907, 42.

[38] AN, MS J399, no. 16 (printed as De Romanet, *Géographie*, ii. no. 2).

[39] RCVD, fos 10v, 13.

[40] AD Eure-et-Loir, MS H5211.

Longny) link Gerald with the area to the north-east of the Perche.[41] His request for Geoffrey's confirmation for this and another act in 1201 reveal therefore that the boundaries of Geoffrey's jurisdiction lay beyond Longny in the north-east and subsequently both the seneschals, Robert of Monceaux and William of La Lande, were themselves to appear in comital acts.[42]

Extension of comital influence in this region inevitably meant that neighbours were obliged to redefine their relationships with the counts. The lords of La Ferté-Ernaud (now La Ferté-Vidame, Eure-et-Loir, ch.-l. du cant.), for example, must have viewed the increasing influence of the Rotrous with some concern. In terms of territory, their own influence was not widespread, but they were benefactors of Tiron, patrons of the order of the Temple and counted Archbishop Hugh of Tours (1136–49) among their younger sons.[43] They had received an annual payment of 100s. from the comital *prepositura* at Mortagne during the twelfth century and William of La Ferté had witnessed a grant by Count Geoffrey in the 1190s, but the developments at Marchainville brought the counts much closer.[44]

Similarly the lords of Châteauneuf-en-Thymerais seemed to be entering a new relationship with the counts of the Perche. Although they had no comital title themselves, the family had been the equals of the Rotrous in the eleventh century and had interests which stretched into the territory of the counts of the Perche, including, in the eleventh century, a castle at Rémalard. At the turn of the century the lordship of Rémalard had come into the hands of Gerald of *Boceio*, though there is no further mention of the castle, and, as we have seen, Gerald had clearly acknowledged the power of Count Geoffrey. In a benefaction to the Carthusians at Val Dieu in 1185 Gervase of Châteauneuf had been described as Count Rotrou's *fidelis* and Count Geoffrey also found means to express increasing influence through religious patronage.[45] A chapel was established at La Loupe on the road to Châteauneuf and he extended his patronage to religious houses traditionally associated with the Châteauneuf family, such as the Fontevraudine convent of Belhomert and the Augustinian canons of Saint-Vincent-aux-Bois.[46]

It is on the south-eastern reaches of the Perche, however, that Geoffrey made the most telling assertions of comital power. In this region, where the Perche shades into the Chartrain, Count Rotrou II (1099–1144) had experienced a setback in the opening years of the twelfth century when Ivo of

[41] For Robert of Monceaux see ibid. For William of La Lande see *Cartulaire de Saint-Jean en Vallée de Chartres*, ed. R. Merlet, Chartres 1906, no. 183.
[42] For Robert see AD Orne, abbey of Saint-Évroul, MS H721; for William see *Clairets*, no. xiv.
[43] *Tiron*, no. ccvi; *SPC*, 610–11
[44] *La Trappe*, 9–10; BN, MS lat. 10089 (cartulaire de Saint-Euverte d'Orléans), p. 391.
[45] RCVD, fo. 8v.
[46] BN, MS franc. 24133, Guillaume Laisne, prieur de Mondonville, mémoires généalogiques, p. 264; AD Eure-et-Loir, MS H5211; BN, MS lat. 5480, p. 352; AD Eure-et-Loir, MS H3907, 42.

Courville had thrown off his lordship in the acrimonious dispute in which the pope himself was involved. As the twelfth century passed another lineage, that based at Illiers, which had been prominent in the acts of Count Geoffrey II (1079–99), ceased to attest the Rotrous' acts. It is significant, therefore, that Robert of Vieuxpont, whose family had acquired the lordship of Courville, can be found among the witnesses of an act issued by Geoffrey in 1196. By his attestation Robert of Vieuxpont, lord of Courville, accepted that Geoffrey would in the words of the act 'hold in his hand all the inhabitants of Chuisnes and all its property, whether belonging to the monks or the men of the settlement, and would defend them as his own property'.[47]

Geoffrey had been cultivating his links with the families of the locality for some time and they were to be strengthened by crusading. It is possible that Geoffrey formed these ties at the court of his uncle, Count Theobald of Blois, for he witnessed an act there in 1183 in company with Ivo of Vieuxpont, whose family held the lordship of Courville.[48] Subsequently Geoffrey and the Vieuxponts were to fight at the siege of Acre and to make gifts to the Templars.[49] Geoffrey also had ties with the lineage based at Friaize (Eure-et-Loir, cant. La Loupe), which lies just off the road from Courville to Nogent-le-Rotrou, and in 1189 he, Ivo of Vieuxpont and his brother, Robert, witnessed a grant to the convent of Belhomert, made by Erembourg of Friaize.[50] In 1202, when Erembourg's brother, John of Friaize, was preparing to embark on the Fourth Crusade, the lineage's loyalties were revealed, for John sought the approval of Stephen of the Perche, the brother of the recently deceased Geoffrey, when he made benefactions to the cathedral of Chartres and to the abbey of Saint-Père.[51]

The success of Geoffrey's attempts to assert comital power was in good measure a product of his personal qualities of leadership. His decision to remain with the Third Crusade after the departure of the French king reflected well on him, and similar qualities of energy and tenacity are hinted at in his pursuit of comital business. Over ninety acts can be traced from Count Geoffrey's time (1191–1202) as against less than fifty from nearly fifty years of his father's rule (1144–91). He confirms religious benefactions, arbitrates in disputes and authorises transfers of property, and such was his power that it was considered worthwhile to preserve his acts. Geoffrey's success may also owe something to his ability to secure the patronage of the English king for his followers. Another member of the Friaize lineage, Warin, the brother of John and Erembourg, was, for example, to be associated with Stephen of the Perche in the fighting between Richard I and Philip Augustus. The

47 *CMD*, no. cciii.
48 BN, MS franc. 20691, fo. 560v.
49 For Geoffrey at Acre see BN, MS Duchesne 54, p. 454. See also *Les Templiers en Eure-et-Loir: histoire et cartulaire*, ed. C. Métais, Chartres 1902, no. xviii.
50 BN, MS franc. 24133, p. 307.
51 AD Eure-et-Loir, MS G1459, printed as *NDC* ii. 22; *SPC*, 670.

Norman pipe rolls show that, while Stephen received a money fee of £360 from the Norman exchequer in 1198, Warin of Friaize was given the by no means insignificant sum of £220.[52]

Access to the wealth of the Anglo-Norman realm, either directly through ownership of property in England and Normandy or indirectly through royal patronage, was to be vital to Geoffrey, for the resources of the Perche itself may not have been adequate to support comital ambitions. It was not a new situation: Geoffrey's grandfather, Count Rotrou II had resorted to an expedition to Aragon in the first decade of the twelfth century on the promise of 'generous wages', and the family apparently made little use of the direct grant of land to their followers.[53] Only one comital act relates to the specific grant of a fee, that which Rotrou III gave to Guy of Vaugrineuse, and there is no evidence of the assignment of major blocs of territory, nor indeed of castles, whose custody was to form such an important part of the patronage of other territorial princes.[54]

The chief sources of patronage available to the counts were grants against comital revenues. Often these might be payments in kind from comital mills or the profits from markets. Rights of access to the comital forest were clearly prized and might form a useful means of rewarding service to the counts. More than twenty years after the extinction of the comital line a right to gather fuel granted by Geoffrey was being pursued by the beneficiary's heirs.[55] Sometimes significant sums might be involved, such as the £10 paid to Osanna from the revenues of La Perrière, or a share in the produce of a comital *medietaria* might be given.[56] The *medietaria* of Ponte (probably Pont Malbroue, Orne, cant. Le Theil, cme Mâle), given by Countess Matilda to the nunnery of Les Clairets, was burdened with such charges and its subsequent history is that of the release of those burdens through benefactions to the nunnery.[57] Occasionally too the counts might alienate an entire source of comital revenue, such as the grant of salt sales at Nogent.[58]

The profits of office also remained an attraction and the Capreolus dynasty, for example, still had a firm grasp on the office of seneschal (*dapifer*) which had been held by members of the family from the early years of the twelfth century.[59] Similarly the Lonray family derived power from the office

---

[52] *Rotuli scaccarii Normanniae*, ii. 386.

[53] OV vi. 296.

[54] *Clairets*, no. xxxiv. For castle custody as an item of comital patronage see B. Bachrach, 'Enforcement of the *forma fidelitatis*: the techniques used by Fulk Nerra, count of the Angevins (987–1040)', *Speculum* lix (1984), 796–819.

[55] 'Querimoniae normannorum', no. 139.

[56] *Clairets*, no. ii.

[57] For the countess's grant see ibid. no. iv. For charges on it subsequently given to the nunnery see 'Gofer de Bruieira unam minam bladi ad mensuram Belismensi in medietaria de Ponte' (no. xiv).

[58] *Obits*, ii. 389.

[59] *NLR*, no. xciii.

of seneschal of Bellême, which was held first by Warin of Lonray from the 1160s and then by his son, William.[60] Perhaps the best example of the importance of a grant of office, however, is that given by the career of Gervase of Prulay in the 1190s. Gervase, who took his toponymic from Prulay, which lies between Bellême and Mortagne,[61] first comes to prominence when he accompanies Count Geoffrey to the Holy Land in 1190/2 and seldom appears to have left his side thereafter. In 1193 he witnessed the count's grant to the Grandmontine priory at Chêne Galon and in 1196 a confirmation to the Maison Dieu at Nogent-le-Rotrou. In the 1190s he was seneschal of Mortagne and a benefactor of the Maison Dieu there.[62] During this time the fortunes of his family had been assiduously advanced. Philip of Prulay, his uncle, acquired the revenues of the cell which the abbey of La Couture in Le Mans possessed at Parfondeval (Orne, cant. Pervenchères) and laid the foundations of a successful ecclesiastical career which would make him a canon of the countess's new foundation of Toussaints at Mortagne and an important ecclesiastic in the 1220s.[63] Gervase himself purchased a vineyard at Nogent-le-Rotrou, strengthening his family's interests in the south of the county, and seems to have acquired the extensive fee of Champs by marriage to its heiress, Mabel.[64]

Service to the counts of the Perche could, then, be a route to advancement and even a minor office had its value. A later legal pleading indicates, for example, that Count Thomas (1202–17) had deprived one Odo Hervey of the custody of the count's meadows in the parish of Saint-Jean at Mauves, which was worth the annual sum of 20s., and Odo considered the loss suffi-

---

[60] CMPerche, nos 63 (William), 227 (1167), 64 (1194) (his two sons, Warin the seneschal, and Gervase), 64, 42 (1212) (William nephew of Gervase). Philip Augustus gave property to William of Longuo Radio in April 1214: Recueil des actes de Philippe Auguste, ed. H. F. Delaborde and others, Paris 1916–79, no. 1329.

[61] AD Loiret, MS H22, no. 288; RCVD, fo. 1v.

[62] RCVD, fo. 9v; Bart, Antiquitéz, 158.

[63] For Philip's career in the 1220s see Cartulaire des abbayes de S. Pierre de la Couture et de S. Pierre de Solesmes, Le Mans 1881, nos clxxx, clxxxi; La Trappe, 139; CMPerche, nos 140, 212.

[64] Clairets, no. xxviii (1229), gives details of the purchase of the vineyard by Gervase and his wife Lucy. La Trappe, 401, reveals another wife: 'concedente Gervasio de Prulai et Mabilia heredi et domina feodi de Campis'. Mabel later married Matthew of Montgoubert: ibid. 459 (<1208), and subsequent lords of Champs were their descendants: see ibid. 117, 455. The implication is that Mabel was Gervase's second wife, and Gervase's name and property descended to the children of his first wife. Mabel had no children by Gervase and was subsequently remarried to Matthew of Montgoubert, to whose descendants the fee of Champs then passed. In the 1230s, after the death of Hugh of La Ferté-Bernard, the legitimacy of his children was challenged by their consanguinei, Gervase, Andrew and Joanna of Pruillé in the diocese of Sées: L. Charles, Histoire de la Ferté-Bernard, Mamers 1877, 51–2. Since the names Gervase and Andrew had already occurred in the Prulay family and Prulay does indeed lie in that diocese, the Prulay family must be indicated which raises the question of their relationship with the lords of La Ferté-Bernard. The most plausible explanation seems to be that Lucy was a member of that family, since the name Lucy recurs in the dynasty, and would imply that Gervase's first marriage was as advantageous as his second.

ciently serious to warrant redress more than thirty years later.[65] None the less Geoffrey III's grant of an entire agricultural operation (*medietaria*) to Lawrence of Champfaye and his alienation of the salt monopoly at Nogent hint that the price of service was rising, and the need to make the Perche run efficiently was consequently becoming more pressing.[66]

Exploiting the Perche

An analysis of the politics of the 1190s demonstrates that Geoffrey's comital power had extended on several fronts and that he used the Anglo-Norman connection to secure additional property in England and on the Norman border, but it tells us little about his attitude to the Perche. Are there any signs that Geoffrey attempted to exploit more efficiently the comital resources he had inherited? The answer to this question is not easily found. No account rolls survive for the landed estates of the Rotrou family and there is no way of measuring the revenues derived from customs, the administration of justice or taxation. None the less there is a hint of more rigorous comital procedures in Geoffrey's act of confirmation to the priory of Nogent-le-Rotrou, in which he asserts that he has had an inquiry made into the monks' rights before confirming them, and it is possible to reconstruct something of the apparatus of comital power from surviving acts.[67] In the absence of precise statistical data, therefore, it is from an impression of comital business and the changes taking place within it that conclusions have to be derived.

Across Europe, as the twelfth century drew to a close, there is evidence of a growing cash economy and the Perche is no exception. Where Count Rotrou II gave a tithe of his storehouses to the abbey of Tiron in the early twelfth century, Geoffrey III gave the leperhouse at Nogent 20s. from the revenues of the town.[68] The counts of the Perche had always had access to cash at the places where tolls were collected, but it is likely that traditional renders and customs were increasingly being exchanged or 'commuted' for payments. Geoffrey III's exchange of his right to hospitality at Chuisnes for an annual cash payment has already been discussed in the context of his links with Chartrain families and it may well be that traditional payments to the Rotrous as landlords were also increasingly made in cash.[69] The rents from the Perche properties in England too are unlikely to have been rendered in kind and must have enhanced the count's cash resources, but this is not to suggest that the counts relied completely on cash payments. It was plainly

---

[65] 'Querimoniae normannorum', no. 217.
[66] BN, MS Duchesne 54, p. 454; *Obits*, ii. 389.
[67] 'Diligenter inquisita libertate ecclesie sue a sapientibus viris et prudentibus': *NLR*, no. xc.
[68] *Tiron*, no. xxii; Château Saint-Jean, MS C/112.
[69] *CMD*, no. cciii.

desirable to retain direct control of some provisioning as Geoffrey's grants of measures of wine from his vineyards to Saint-Vincent-aux-Bois and Val Dieu demonstrate.[70]

It is even possible that Count Geoffrey tried to harness the power of coinage itself by launching a Percheron coinage. In the eleventh and twelfth centuries a number of currencies are specified within charters given in the Perche, including Angevin, Manceau, Tournois, Chartrain and Dunois reckonings.[71] A specifically Percheron coinage, however, is attested by surviving pieces, which have been assigned to a type descending from the coinage of the Thibaudians at Chartres.[72] Their first appearance has been tentatively dated to the 1150s, but the first documentary reference to Percheron money (*monete perticensis*) does not appear in comital acts until the late 1190s and it is tempting to see the coinage as an expression of the position of influence and independence achieved by Geoffrey III at a point when silver had become more widely available after its discovery at Freibourg.[73] An act dated July 1198 in which the priory of Saint-Denis at Nogent-le-Rotrou conceded to the archdeacon of Chartres their rights over the church of Notre Dame in Nogent specifically gives the sum involved as 'seven pounds of Percheron pennies' ('pro septem libris perticensium denariorum').[74] Although the great diversity of weights and alloys of the so-called feudal coinage could hamper exchange, there were considerable advantages in control of a mint. Profits might be made from changes of the coinage at regular intervals and revenue could even be derived by imposing taxes instead of a mutation, which was usually deeply unpopular. There is no evidence to suggest that the Percheron coinage was manipulated in such a sophisticated way. It was a late-comer among the feudal coinages and it never achieved the success of the Champagne or Flemish currencies. The few surviving examples imply that it was a short-lived issue, but Count Geoffrey III may have been encouraged to introduce it by the minting practice of his Thibaudian cousins and the even more lucrative expedients of the Anglo-Norman rulers.[75]

---

[70] BN, MS franc. 24133, 264–5; BN, MS Duchesne 54, p. 450.

[71] A. Chédeville, 'La Role de la monnaie et l'apparition du crédit dans le pays de l'ouest de la France xie–xiiie siècles', CCM xvii (1974), 307; P. Spufford, *Money and its use in medieval Europe*, Cambridge 1988, 200; F. Dumas, 'Les Monnaies normandes (xe–xiie siècles)', *Revue numismatique* 6 sér. xxi (1979), 98.

[72] F. Poey d'Avant, *Monnaies féodales de France*, Paris 1858–61, 262–3; A. Blanchet and A. Dieudonné, *Manuel de numismatique française*, IV: *Monnaies féodales françaises*, Paris 1936, 322; F. Dumas, 'La Monnaie dans le royaume au temps de Philippe-Auguste', in Bautier, *La France de Philippe-Auguste*, 564.

[73] For Percheron money in comital acts see MS lat. 10089, p. 381; AD Sarthe, abbey of Perseigne, MS H930. See also Spufford, *Money*, 105.

[74] *NLR*, no. cvii.

[75] There appear to have been no Percheron coins in hoards recently recovered and published in *Revue numismatique*, nor did a hoard dating from around 1150, which was discovered at Nogent-le-Rotrou in the nineteenth century, contain Percheron coins: *Bulletin de la Société dunoise* iv (1881–5), 367–8, cited in Chédeville, *Chartres*, 434 n. 17. For

There are hints too of a drive for greater efficiency in the management of the woodlands which covered much of the Perche. In an aristocratic society they were important as hunting grounds, providing both food and training in skills vital for a horse-borne military elite, and it was presumably in the interests of conserving the stock that Count Geoffrey specifically forbade hunting in the parishes of Eperrais, Mauves, Courthioust and Saint-Ouen de la Cour.[76] In exploitation for fuel, building materials and livestock production, however, the woodlands also generated substantial income for counts, and formed one of the major components of their grants to favoured religious houses. During the course of the twelfth century there was a substantial movement towards land clearance or assarts into the woodland.[77] Count Rotrou III gave some of the profits of such a clearance to the priory at Nogent-le-Rotrou in 1190 and Count Geoffrey clearly had them in mind in his act describing his acquisition at Marchainville. The act makes provision for the grant to the abbey of Saint-Évroul of tithes over existing cultivated lands and over those which might be cultivated in future in all the extensions (*amplificationibus*) to the forest of Réno.[78] This replacement of the traditionally managed woodland with arable land increased the value of remaining woodland, particularly of its timber products. Demand rose for building timber and for wood products such as stakes for fencing arable land or for use in vineyards and cooperage. Around the year 1130 Count Rotrou II had casually granted whatever wood was considered necessary to establish a vineyard, but Geoffrey III was more cautious about access to his woodland. When he gave the monks of Saint-Évroul resident at Maison Maugis and in the priory of St Lawrence at Moulins-la-Marche various rights he specified that they could take them without the foresters' oversight ('sine liberatione forestriorum'), implying that strict controls on foraging were in place.[79]

There is also an indication that Geoffrey's comital powers were being strictly enforced. Several of his benefactions to favoured religious communities in the Perche took the form of a grant of the services of an individual. Sometimes these grants have been recorded in the most terse form. The grant of a 'certain man exempt and free of taxes, customs and other exactions' to the prior of the leperhouse at Mauves, for example, is recorded only in the records of a later lawsuit when it was alleged that the man had been unjustly taxed.[80] More explicit grants are recorded to the monks of Saint-Évroul at

manipulation of coinage see T. N. Bisson, *Conservation of coinage: monetary exploitation and its restraint in France, Catalonia and Aragon (c. AD 1000–c. 1225)*, Oxford 1979.

[76] 'Querimoniae normannorum', no. 163.

[77] G. Duby, *L'Économie rurale et la vie des campagnes dans l'occident médiévale*, trans. as *Rural economy and country life in the medieval west*, London 1968, 144.

[78] 'Explanationum nemoris factarum et faciendarum quod dicitur les Clairetz': *NLR*, no. xcix; AD Orne, MS H702 (printed as De Romanet, *Géographie*, ii. 205).

[79] 'Ad construendum quicquid vineis comprehenditur esse necessarium': *Tiron*, no. xxxiii. For Geoffrey III see AD Orne, MSS H702, H721.

[80] 'Querimoniae normannorum', no. 225.

Maison Maugis, who received the service of William Serera; to the abbey of La Trappe, which received that of Robert Ingun of Mortagne; and to the abbey of Perseigne, to which Baldwin Bovet of Nogent's service was granted. By far the most detailed record of such a transaction is that conveying the service of Simon le Bret of Moulins-la-Marche to Saint-Évroul, which describes the location of Simon's house and Simon's own gifts.[81] These grants of exemptions suggest that the 'taxes, customs and other exactions' were heavy burdens from which immunity would be welcome. In the words of a modern commentator: 'What rulers at any level had to do was to make their subjects pay dues and accept controls on the land they already held – acknowledge in effect that their property was held under government.'[82] Some of Geoffrey's other grants provide an index of the kinds of impositions which the count might make. Such impositions are mentioned in earlier comital acts, but seldom with the specificity with which they appear in Geoffrey's. In the 1190s, for example, at various locations Geoffrey's agents sought to impose customs and tolls, charges for foot traffic, guard duties, aids, taxes to fund the count's military forces ('exercitu et equitatu'), carting services (carragiis), wall-repair (muragiis), ditch maintenance (fossatis) and duties to provide oats for the count's horses (avenagiis).

There is evidence too of attempts to make comital officers work more efficiently. When a count wished to make a payment he assigned revenues from a particular source of income, usually described as a prepositura. At some point after 1160, but before 1191, for example, revenues which the count received from the mills and bakehouses of Mortagne were directed to a third party, Simon of Vove.[83] Count Geoffrey's acts frequently laid a penalty clause on his bailiffs for failure to make disbursements at the appointed time and in one benefaction to the abbey of La Trappe he instructs the bailiff of Mortagne to use compulsion manfully and energetically ('cogat viriliter et strenue') against the toll-gatherer of his castlery in case of non-payment.[84] By the end of the twelfth century greater recourse to the prepositi for the disbursement of cash may also have led to administrative changes. For in the 1190s the word castella begins to appear in the comital acts in a quasi-administrative sense and under Count Thomas (1202–17) and Count William (1217–26), in the form castellania, it does indeed convey a clearly defined area.[85] A list of such castellania appears in an act of Count Geoffrey III, where they are gathered in three groups: four castles in the Corbonnais, four in the Bellêmois and six

81 AD Orne, MS H702; La Trappe, 16–17; AD Sarthe, MS H930 (printed as Perseigne, no. ccclxv); AD Orne, MS H721.
82 S. Reynolds, Fiefs and vassals: the medieval evidence reinterpreted, Oxford 1994, 131.
83 Bart, Antiquitéz, 132.
84 La Trappe, 16–17.
85 Ibid.; AD Orne, priory of Bellême, MS 2164; Clairets, no. xiv; La Trappe, 136.

others.[86] Later Count Thomas was to supplement the list with Moulins-la-Marche and Bonsmoulins which had been granted to his father.[87]

The act which groups Count Geoffrey's castles so tidily describes his benefaction to the Grandmontine house at Chêne Galon and there is a possibility that it is not a contemporary document. The act survives only among the transcripts of the seventeenth-century antiquarian, André Duchesne, and the Grandmontine order was notable for later reformulations, since the early canons forbade written deeds of gift.[88] The language used in the act could therefore reflect organisational arrangements contemporary with its drafting rather than from Geoffrey's time. None the less, other more reliably transmitted acts of Count Geoffrey do refer to castles as administrative units and castles were indeed associated with several of the sites in his Chêne Galon act. In 1172 Geoffrey's uncle, Count Henry I of Champagne, had undertaken a great inquest into the fiefs of his territory which had been arranged under *castellaniae* and it may be that Geoffrey was emulating the methods and terminology of his uncle, who possessed one of the wealthiest of the territorial principalities of France.[89] It would make sound economic sense if revenues derived from the hinterland of each castle were gathered and guarded within his castles.[90]

The increasing use of writing enabled Geoffrey to pursue comital business more effectively and there is some evidence that he made arrangements for appropriately qualified staff when he founded a new College of Saint-Jean at the castle of Nogent-le-Rotrou. The foundation again mirrors the actions of his uncle, Henry I of Champagne, who established the College of Saint-Étienne within the new palace complex which he built at Troyes in 1157.[91] The clergy resident in such foundations would always be available to provide clerical services when the count was in residence and at other times could process comital business for his attention when he returned. Individuals to whom the title *magister* is given also brought specialist skills to comital service. Master Reginald, for example, was the head of the Maison Dieu at Nogent-le-Rotrou, and it therefore seems likely he was the Reginald *medicus* who attests an act of Count Rotrou III and had been retained for his medical

86 BN, MS Duchesne 54, p. 460.

87 Ibid. p. 459.

88 Ibid. p. 460; Hallam, 'Henry II, Richard I and the order of Grandmont', 172–3.

89 *Documents relatifs au comté de Champagne et de Brie, 1172–1363*, ed. A. Longnon, i, Paris 1901, 1–172.

90 On the administrative functions of castles see Powicke, *Loss of Normandy*, 198–204. For castles at Longpont see Louise, 'Bellême', ii. 261; at Bellême, ibid. 62–7. For remains of *un tertre circulair* see Montisembert, 'Querimoniae normannorum', no. 122, and Louise, 'Bellême', ii. 235. For Rivray see Decaëns, 'La Motte de Rivray'.

91 For Geoffrey's foundation see AD Eure-et-Loir, MS G3485 (nécrologe de Saint-Jean de Nogent-le-Rotrou), fo. 13v. For Henry's foundation see P. Heliot, 'Sur les résidences princières bâties en France du Xe–XIIe siècle', *Le Moyen Âge* lxi (1955), 39–41.

skills.[92] He may also have been the Reginald who later became the countess's chaplain.[93] Most significant of their number is one Robert of Loisail. He began his service to the counts of the Perche under Geoffrey III and ended it as Count William's (1217–26) representative in the county. Master Robert appears prominently in comital witness lists as Count Geoffrey III's chaplain and around the turn of the century he seems to have become the countess's chaplain.[94] By 1203 he apparently held a prebend at the new foundation of Toussaints, Mortagne, and by 1220 had advanced to the highest office, describing himself in a letter written in that year, as 'generalis procurator totius terre comitis Pertici'.[95]

Although the source material needs careful handling, it is possible then to make some observations on Geoffrey's exercise of comital power. The impression is of a vigorous ruler who asserted his power energetically and was prepared to learn from his contemporaries. None the less it must be remembered that his territory was not large and the organisation of his household reflects that fact. There are no references, for example, to officers who controlled the provisioning of the comital household, such as a *dispensator* (household steward) or a *pincerna* (butler). It is just possible that a family founded by William Malenutritus and represented at the turn of the twelfth century by Reginald Malnori were comital *dispensatores*, since such ironic nicknames were used for other household officers, but equally it may be significant that the only strictly domestic officers to be discerned are cooks.[96] The implication is that the comital household moved from demesne property to demesne property, where it was serviced by the *prepositus*, and it therefore had no need for specialists to organise food supplies, only those who could prepare it to the counts' individual tastes. Similarly chamberlains seldom appear in the Rotrou family *acta*.[97] The absence of these officials, whose

---

[92] *The cartularies of Southwick priory*, ed. K. A. Hanna, Winchester 1988, 87–8; *NLR*, no. xcii.

[93] *Clairets*, no. iv.

[94] BN, MS lat. 10089, p. 381; *Monasticon*, vi. 565; *La Couture*, no. clxv. As the countess's chaplain see AN, MS S2238, no. 34 (1201); *Clairets*, no. ii (March 1202). As Master Robert of *Losello* see *Cartularies of Southwick*, 87–8.

[95] *NLR*, no. cix; *CMPerche*, no. 211. For Robert as 'generalis procurator domini Cath' in comitatu Pertici', see Château Saint-Jean, MS C/116.

[96] On butlers see B. English, *The lords of Holderness, 1086–1260: a study in feudal society*, Oxford 1979, 92–3. On the *dispensator* see *Charters of the honour of Mowbray, 1107–1191*, ed. D. E. Greenway, London 1972, lxiii. For the cooks see *NLR*, nos xiii, lxxxviii; *CMPerche*, no. 21; *Tiron*, no. XCV; 'Querimoniae normannorum', no. 215. For the Malnori family see *Tiron*, no. cxviii (William); *Chart. cenom.*, no. xxv; AD Orne, abbey of La Trappe, MS H1846 (1191/2). For a similar wordplay for chamberlain see D. Crouch, 'The administration of the Norman earldom', in A. T. Thacker (ed.), *The earldom of Chester and its charters: a tribute to Geoffrey Barraclough, Journal of the Chester Archaeological Society* lxxi (1991), 81.

[97] *VLM*, no. 609 for Alberic; *NLR*, no. lxxiii for 'Oddo camerarius'; *Tiron*, no. xxii for Arbert, son of Odo the chamberlain; *Jumièges*, no. xxxiii, for 'Guillelmo de Clif, camerario'; *Tiron*, no. cclxxvii, pp. 156–7, for 'Roberto camerario comitis R. Perticensis'.

primary role was to handle cash for immediate use, again suggests that the counts travelled frequently around their *prepositure*, where cash would be readily available.

Some of the problems Geoffrey faced were common to all the rulers of his day, in particular the inflation of the late twelfth century, but Geoffrey's inheritance was not large territorially and it was far removed from the Seine/Rhône axis which was becoming increasingly important economically in the twelfth century. While Geoffrey and his family might grant fairs to their favoured religious foundations and take the profits of their own, those fairs were never to develop into the major mercantile gatherings of Champagne, and the urban centres of the Perche would not develop the industrial traditions of the Low Countries.[98] The Perche was not well-placed economically, but it was strategically positioned to benefit from the rivalry of the Capetian and Plantagenet kings, and it was that opportunity which Geoffrey took. Internally he could do little more than ensure that the Perche ran efficiently and that the resources available to him were fully exploited.

Maintaining the balance II, 1198–1202

By the second half of the 1190s Geoffrey appears to have struck a fine balance between the French and English kings. He remained on good terms with his cousin, King Philip, while holding lucrative English property from his wife's uncle, King Richard. Geoffrey's confidence in his connections is clearly visible in his act in which he outlines the arrangements for his acquisition of Marchainville from the abbey of Saint-Évroul. In his charter to the monks he anticipated no difficulties in obtaining confirmatory documentation from the two kings, declaring that he has sworn an oath to seek charters from the king of the French and the king of England: 'super sacrosancta juravi quod perquirerem cartas regum Francorum et Anglie'. He also appears to have enjoyed similar good relations with the ecclesiastical powers for he promises confirmations from the archbishops of Rouen and Sens, the bishops of Chartres and Sées, the abbot of Blois and the prior of Nogent-le-Rotrou, and there are indeed no indications of friction between the count and church authorities. In 1194 a dispute over tithes at Saint-Julien-sur-Sarthe had been resolved in his court in favour of the cathedral chapter of Sées, and Bishop Lisiard of Sées (1188–1201) had given an episcopal confirmation to the family foundation at Val Dieu.[99] The bishop of Chartres was Geoffrey's cousin and they had both taken part in the Third Crusade. In 1193, shortly after their return, the bishop had conceded to the priory of Nogent-le-Rotrou the right of presentation to its churches at the request of his 'most beloved nephew', Geoffrey, and a comfortable working relationship between the

[98] For fairs see Château Saint-Jean, MS A/6; AD Orne, MS H721.
[99] LBSMS, fo. 75; RCVD, fo. 16v.

secular and ecclesiastical authorities in the Perche is also suggested by Geoffrey's act of 1197 notifying the cession of the abbey of Pontlevoy's cell at Brénard (Orne, cant. et cme. Bazoches-sur-Hoëne) to the chaplain of Geoffrey's brother, Rotrou, bishop of Châlons-en-Champagne.[100]

None the less it has to be said that Geoffrey's relations with his cousin seem to have been stronger than those with his uncle by marriage. In April 1198 he was at the Capetian court at Melun where he and King Philip's other cousins, Robert count of Dreux and William count of Bar, stood surety for the king when he accepted the homage of yet another cousin, Theobald III, the new count of Champagne.[101] Where Richard's favour was expressed in grants of land, Philip's took the form of family advancement. The promotion of Geoffrey's brother, Rotrou, to the royal see of Châlons-en-Champagne in 1190 had been followed by the appointment of another brother, Theobald, as dean of Saint-Martin of Tours, a foundation noted for its closeness to the Capetians.[102] Yet another and probably the youngest Rotrou brother, William, was established at an early age at another royal bishopric, Chartres, where their cousin, Reginald of Mouçon, held the see by the French king's gift.[103] The implication therefore seems to be that the family practised a division of labour in preserving the balance between its powerful neighbours, with Countess Matilda and Stephen of the Perche looking to King Richard while Count Geoffrey, Bishop Rotrou and Dean Theobald maintained the Capetian links.

In the autumn of 1198, however, the rivalry between the French and English kings entered a new and more intense phase. The death of King Philip's ally and Richard's former gaoler, the Holy Roman emperor, Henry VI, in September 1197 had opened up new opportunities for the English king. While Philip pressed for the election of Henry's younger brother, Philip of Swabia, as his successor, Richard sought to isolate the French king by procuring the election of his own candidate. By July 1198, through a combination of diplomatic pressure and bribery, Richard's nephew, Otto of Brunswick, brother of Countess Matilda of the Perche, was elected king of Germany.[104] To support this new diplomatic situation Richard put together a new alignment of princes from the Holy Roman empire and persuaded a number of French lords to his side. The English chronicler, Roger of Howden, names the counts of Boulogne, the Perche, Saint-Gilles (Toulouse), Blois and Brittany as deserting Philip ('relicto rege Franciae') and joining Richard.

---

100 *NLR*, no. c. Reginald was the son of Reginald count of Bar and Agnes of Blois, sister of Geoffrey's mother, Matilda. AD Loir-et-Cher, abbey of Pontlevoy, MS 17 H 55.

101 *Recueil des actes de Philippe Auguste*, no. 581.

102 Griffiths, 'The Capetian kings and St Martin of Tours'.

103 Theobald is listed among Geoffrey III's brothers (*NDC* i. 254–5) and appears as dean of Tours (GC xi. col. 692). For William of Perche see *Obits*, ii. 40.

104 Powicke, *Loss of Normandy*, 118–20.

Howden stresses that these lords swore a pact with Richard not to make peace with the King of France except by common consent.[105]

We do not know whether the count of the Perche was actively engaged in the flurry of conflict between Philip and Richard which broke out in September 1198. Geoffrey owed Richard knight service for Bellême, so it is possible that Percheron troops served in these campaigns, and it is almost certain that Stephen of the Perche, who was with the English king at La Roche D'Orival on 13 August, was directly involved as Richard sought to press his military advantage against the French king.[106] By the spring of 1199 a settlement was being sought by Cardinal Pietro Capuano, who had been sent by the new pope, Innocent III, to settle the quarrels of the two kings and promote the new crusade proclaimed by the pope.[107] The death of King Richard in a minor engagement at Châlus in Poitou in April 1199 threw all into confusion, however. There was uncertainty as to whether Richard's nephew, the twelve-year-old Arthur, duke of Brittany, or his brother John would be accepted as his heir.

In the weeks immediately after Richard's death John had to work quickly to ensure his own succession. Mindful perhaps of King Stephen's rush to Winchester in 1135, John made straight for Chinon where the family treasure was kept, and secured a number of castles in the Loire valley, but he was not welcomed everywhere. While the queen dowager, Eleanor of Aquitaine, favoured him and could influence her lands in his favour, the lords of Anjou, Maine and Touraine declared for Arthur.[108] The inclination of the count of the Perche during this period is unknown, but the 1199 pipe roll refers to a writ issued after John's first coronation granting a tax exemption for the count of the Perche's lands in Essex, which suggests that contact had been made with the man who would be the new king of England.[109] The most likely link was Countess Matilda, who journeyed to Fontevraud to meet her grandmother, the Queen Dowager Eleanor, perhaps in time for Richard's burial on 11 April. After spending Easter nearby at Beaufort, John is known to have joined Eleanor, Matilda and Richard's widow, Queen Berengaria, at Fontevraud.[110] On 21 April he witnessed his mother's charter making provision for the celebration of Richard's obituary annually at the abbey of Turpenay, and the Essex tax exemption may well have been a favour granted

[105] Roger of Howden, *Chronica* iv. 54.

[106] For knight service see *Rotuli de liberate ac de misis de praestitis regnanate Johanne*, ed. T. D. Hardy (Record Commission xxx, 1844), 74. For Stephen see *CDF*, no. 310.

[107] Roger of Howden, *Chronica* iv. 80.

[108] Ibid. iv. 86–7.

[109] *PR 1 John, 1199*, 180.

[110] For John's movements see Roger of Howden, *Chronica* iv. 87, supplemented by Adam of Eynsham, *Life of St Hugh of Lincoln*, ed. D. L. Douie and H. Farmer, London 1961–2, ii. 137–46.

to Matilda at that time, particularly since the Essex lands were the countess's dowry, rather than the family property of her husband.[111]

John then turned northwards to secure Normandy and England, but the Angevin heartland of the Loire valley and Maine remained doubtful. John's sister-in-law, Duchess Constance of Brittany, had entered into alliance with King Philip to further her son's claims.[112] Journeying to Tours, probably in the days immediately after Richard's death, she had placed her son in the custody of King Philip, who despatched the young man to Paris and seized all the cities and fortifications which had declared for Arthur, placing his own men in them.[113] Even as John journeyed north from Fontevraud towards Rouen for his investiture as duke on 25 April, Constance attempted to capture him at Le Mans and he only escaped by the skin of his teeth, according to Adam of Eynsham, the biographer of Bishop Hugh of Lincoln, who was staying in the city at the time. For its adherence to his nephew's cause John made an example of Le Mans, where he did extensive damage to the fortifications and imprisoned citizens, before making his way to England for his coronation on 27 May.[114] In these circumstances, although the Countess Matilda had renewed her connections with the Plantagenets, it was by no means certain that her husband would support her uncle. King Philip himself was in the Perche at Montlandon in May 1199 where he confirmed two of Arthur of Brittany's acts as ruler of Anjou and Maine, and Arthur was probably returned to his mother at that time, for a charter in favour of the Cistercian abbey of Perseigne was issued in Arthur's name in June 1199, and the castle of Langres was granted to Robert of Vitré.[115]

Count Geoffrey's own act extending his protection over the property which the cathedral chapter of Le Mans held at Courgenard (Sarthe, cant. Montmirail) sheds light on his dilemma during these difficult months.[116] In a ceremony in the cathedral of Le Mans Count Geoffrey acknowledged responsibility for the territory held by the canons of the cathedral at Courgenard. His father, Count Rotrou III, had guaranteed a mortgage of rights of jurisdiction there, but Geoffrey's act defines precisely the nature of comital authority

---

111 *CDF*, no. 1301.

112 *Life of St Hugh*, 147–8. Adam implies that Hugh left John's presence on the Monday after Easter, 19 April, and was in Le Mans by the evening of that day. On the next day Matins was interrupted by the duchess's attempted attack on John, who had left at dawn. This sequence of events cannot be correct, since charter evidence indicates that John was still at Fontevraud on 21 April. Since Adam was writing fourteen years later, his recollection of the precise timing may have been inaccurate.

113 Roger of Howden, *Chronica* iv. 87.

114 Ibid. iv. 86–7. Howden's placing of this incident suggests that John's actions against Le Mans took place before Easter, but this seems unlikely since John was at Chinon by 14 April, which would hardly give the citizens time to declare for Arthur: *Life of St Hugh*, ii. 137. It seems more reasonable to suggest that John took reprisals against the city in the month between his investiture as duke of Normandy and his coronation as king of England.

115 *Recueil des actes de Philippe Auguste*, nos 607, 608; *CDF*, nos 1030, 1305.

116 *Chart. cenom.*, no. xxv.

136

and the obligations it imposes.[117] He undertakes to provide security for the canons' men, at all times in peace and in war 'as if they were my own men of Nogent', and not to exact unjust payments for his protection. His contract (*pactio*) with the canons was guaranteed by local notables with toponymics linking them to the south-east of the Perche and by his brother, Stephen's, letters patent and was approved by his wife, Matilda's seal.

The act might simply be a guarantee procured by the canons from a potentially overbearing neighbour but for Geoffrey's final undertaking that he would, when the opportunity presented itself, secure letters patent from the king of France, concerning the protection of the property. Since Courgenard lies in north-eastern Maine, well within the traditional lands of the Plantagenets, where the confirmation of the king of France had not been customary for more than two hundred years, Geoffrey's act is unlikely to have been given at any other time than the summer months of 1199 when King Philip controlled those parts of Anjou, Maine and Touraine which had supported Arthur. His explicit reference to protecting the property in time of war probably indicates the anxieties of the canons, who would already have experienced King John's reprisal against the city of Le Mans and probably feared a long-drawn-out conflict between the two kings. Their strategy of seeking Geoffrey's protection suggests that he was, at the point when the act was given, closely identified with the king of France, and it is plain that Geoffrey did maintain contact with his royal relatives. On 1 July 1199 he attended the wedding at Chartres of his cousin, Count Theobald of Champagne, and Blanche of Navarre, which took place in the presence of the French queen dowager, Adela, Geoffrey's aunt, and he may have used the occasion as an opportunity to re-establish links with the Capetian court after his earlier support for Richard. His grant of 60s. from the revenues of Nogent-le-Rotrou to the church of Franchard certainly suggests a conciliatory gesture, for Franchard, a hermitage at Bière (Seine-et-Marne) in the forest of Fontainebleau, was much favoured by the queen dowager and King Philip himself had patronised it in 1197.[118]

Count Geoffrey cannot be traced with certainty from this date until late in 1199. King John returned from England in late June 1199 and spent the next two and a half months in Normandy.[119] Geoffrey may have been among the nameless counts and barons of the French kingdom who had been adherents of Richard ('adhaeserunt Ricardo regi Angliae') and who subsequently came to John offering allegiance in the summer of 1199.[120] In August 1199 John

---

117 For Rotrou's act see ibid. no. dxxxv (abbreviated version, with corrections and longer witness list, of no. xxviii).

118 *Layettes de trésor de chartes*, i, no. 497. See BN, MS lat. 11089, p. 391 for Geoffrey's grant. For Queen Adela's interest in the house see G. Estournet, 'Les Chartres de Franchard, prieuré de l'ordre de Saint-Augustin près Fontainebleau', *Annales de la Société historique et archéologique du Gâtinais* (1913), 275–369.

119 *Rot. chart.*, 1–23.

120 Roger of Howden, *Chronica* iv. 95. On 28 August 1199 John and Reginald of Boulogne

made agreements with Count Reginald of Boulogne and Count Baldwin of Flanders, and authorised the transfer of Bolsover in Derbyshire with its *castellaria*, which was worth £250 sterling a year, to Theobald count of Bar.[121] There is no record, however, of an agreement with Geoffrey of the Perche for as long as John remained confined in Normandy.

In September, however, there was a breakthrough for John, when he concluded an agreement with William des Roches, the leader of Arthur's forces. Towards the middle of the month John moved south and on 16 September he was at Bourg-le-Roi (Sarthe, ch.-l. du cant.), just south of Alençon.[122] On 18 September the agreement with William des Roches was concluded at Angers, and according to the chronicler Howden William then handed Le Mans over to King John.[123] Accompanied by Arthur and his mother, John must have made his way to Le Mans at the end of September, for he gave charters there and it was to Le Mans that Aimery, viscount of Thouars came, at John's instruction, to surrender custody of the castle of Chinon and the office of seneschal of Anjou, which John had given him in the spring.[124] Howden then recounts that Aimery fled from the royal presence the very next evening, taking with him Arthur and the Duchess Constance, but before he departed he had given the king an undertaking to remain John's liege man and the notification of that undertaking was witnessed by a Count Geoffrey.[125] Since this Count Geoffrey attests immediately after the archbishop of Bordeaux and the bishop of St Andrews, but before the major Anglo-Norman magnates, Earl Robert of Leicester, Count Baldwin of Aumale and Count Ralph of Eu, a figure of some status is indicated and Geoffrey of the Perche is the most likely candidate.

The sudden appearance of Count Geoffrey at King John's court suggests a reappraisal of the political situation by him. The accommodation between the king and William des Roches had strengthened the king's position and made it likely that John would eventually secure all of King Richard's lands. It would therefore be in Geoffrey's interests to give a pointed acknowledgement of John's power in Maine by making a formal appearance at Le Mans, and almost within days Geoffrey's calculation paid dividends, for an army brought to Maine by King Philip was driven out by John's forces in October 1199.[126] The process by which Geoffrey was persuaded to declare his support for John cannot be detected, but it is possible that some preliminary negotiations were carried out by the king's close associate, Hugh of Gournay, who was often in

agreed not to make peace or a truce with the king of France without consulting each other: *Rot. chart.*, 30.

121 Ibid. 30, 11. The castle was Bolsover: *Memoranda roll 1 John*, 26.

122 *Rot. chart.*, 18b, 23b.

123 Ibid. 30b; Roger of Howden, *Chronica* iv. 96.

124 *Rot. chart.*, 23–4; Roger of Howden, *Chronica* iv. 97.

125 *Rot. chart.*, 31.

126 Roger of Howden, *Chronica* iv. 97.

King John's presence during this period. Both Geoffrey and Hugh showed interest in the great Cistercian abbey of Perseigne in northern Maine, which was at the height of its fame under its abbot Adam. Geoffrey witnessed Hugh's grant to Perseigne in company with Gerald of Fournival, one of John's tenants in England and it is possible that some negotiation was carried out then.[127]

In the next month, November 1199, Count Geoffrey was again at John's court for he witnessed the king's confirmation of a benefaction made to the monastic community at Grandmont by King Richard. Geoffrey's attestation was made at Niort (Deux Sèvres) in Poitou in an area where he is not known to have had lands or connections of any kind.[128] The implication is that the count had specific business with the king of England and they seem to have remained in regular contact for the next six months. A commercial agreement between them was notified by the king at Barfleur on 5 February 1200, shortly before he set off for more than two months in England.[129] King John conceded immunity from all customs and commercial taxes to Geoffrey's agent (*hospes*) William of Brion, a citizen of Rouen, while Odo Sirebon of Mortagne entered the king's allegiance and was granted immunity from Geoffrey's customs and taxes. When King John returned to Normandy at the beginning of May 1200 Count Geoffrey must have hurried to his court, for he was with him at Le Goulet less than two weeks later on 16 May as the king made arrangements to continue the subsidy which had been paid to Geoffrey's near neighbour, Robert of Dreux.[130]

The Treaty of Le Goulet, which was approved by John and Philip some days later on 22 May 1200, settled the Plantagenet succession.[131] The nagging question of Arthur's rights was finally settled and John was recognised as Richard's heir, but at the price of acknowledging the implicit superiority of Philip of France as overlord and the payment of a relief.[132] The agreement was to be sealed by the marriage of John's niece, Blanche of Castille, to Philip's son, Louis, and elaborate provisions were made for her dowry. The treaty was guaranteed on both sides by the oaths of nobles and among Philip's guarantors was the count of the Perche. At Château Gaillard two days later King John made a major grant of English property to Geoffrey, increasing his income by £1,000, while the remaining rights possessed by the heirs of the counts of Vermandois in the property at Chambois which had

---

[127] For Hugh at the royal court see *Rot. chart.*, 1–30 passim; *CDF*, no. 1027; AD Sarthe, MS H930 (printed as *Perseigne*, no. lxvii).
[128] *Rot. chart.*, 62.
[129] Ibid. 35.
[130] Ibid. 58.
[131] *Diplomatic documents*, no. 9.
[132] For an analysis of the assertion of feudal rights by Philip and the shift in political balance see Holt, 'The end of the Anglo-Norman realm'.

been given to Stephen of the Perche were surrendered to the king, and presumably passed on to Stephen.[133]

In his conveyance John gave Geoffrey an annual sum of £1,000 made up from a number of sources, the most substantial element of which was represented by the lands of all those who had been granted property on the honour of Henry of Essex since the new enfeoffment. Geoffrey held the honour as the *maritagium* of his wife and the annual value of these alienations, made in the thirty years previous to Geoffrey's tenure, were now to form part of the sum assigned by the king to the count of the Perche, while their tenants were to be compensated.[134] In addition the king conceded the revenues of the royal manor of Shrivenham in Wiltshire until land of an equal value could be found and the balance of the £1,000 was to be found from the exchequer.[135]

The evidence is clearly circumstantial but it does appear that Geoffrey and possibly his brother, Stephen, too, had acted as an intermediary between his two lords, both of whom desired a settlement, but were beset by personal difficulties.[136] John needed legitimation for his claim to the Plantagenet inheritance in preference to Arthur and Philip was in serious trouble with the Church as a result of his repudiation of Queen Ingeborg. Geoffrey's immediate fortunes were enhanced by the Château Gaillard grant and any standing which he had lost with the French king as a result of his joining Richard's alliance in 1198 was more than restored. At Sens in May 1201 the confidence of the French king was again acknowledged when Geoffrey witnessed Philip's acceptance of the countess of Champagne's homage during the minority of her son Theobald.[137]

Stephen of the Perche meanwhile continued in the service of the English king. After Le Goulet, John made his way south for progress around the duchy of Aquitaine. He was in Angers in June 1200 and in July 1200 appointed Stephen of the Perche castellan of Châteauneuf-sur-Sarthe (Maine-et-Loire), north of Angers.[138] The appointment indicates the confidence of the king and it was probably as a result of this new responsibility that Stephen gave up his land in Normandy at Chambois, for by September 1200 it was in the hands of his cousin, William Marshal.[139] Stephen was particularly closely associated with the king in the autumn of 1201 as arrangements were made to

---

133 *Rot. chart.*, 58, 96. The main business of the treaty is enrolled on membrane 35 and Geoffrey and Eleanor of Saint-Quentin's acts are enrolled on the dorso.

134 Ibid. 64b.

135 Geoffrey's own notification of the grant is also enrolled ibid. 96.

136 A similar role is proposed for Constance of Beaumont, wife of Roger of Tosny, in the settlement between John and Arthur made at Le Mans in 1199 (A. Richard, *Histoire des comtes de Poitou [778–1204]*, Paris 1903, ii. 359), but Constance only petitioned for and received her own *maritagium: Rot. chart.*, 20b.

137 *Recueil des actes de Philippe Auguste*, ii. no. 678.

138 *Rotuli Normanniae in turri Londinensi asservati, 1200–1205*, ed. T. Hardy, London 1835, 28.

139 *Rot. chart*, 75b.

settle Anjou and he witnessed both a royal charter and acted as a guarantor of the king's agreement with one of the great lords of Maine, Juhel of Mayenne, who had supported Arthur of Brittany in 1199.[140] When the Jews bought a confirmation of their bonds from the king for 4,000 marks in 1201, it was Stephen of the Perche who was responsible for their transport to Geoffrey fitzPeter and the pipe roll for 1201 records the cost, 22s., of transporting his men and gear.[141]

The crusading impulse

By the summer of 1200 Geoffrey's diplomatic manoeuvrings were over and he was free to take an interest in a new crusading initiative. In 1198 a new pope, Innocent III, had been elected and he had made a new commitment to the Holy Land. He sought to harness the enthusiasm generated by popular preachers such as Fulk of Neuilly and he sent a papal legate, Cardinal Pietro Capuano, to promote peace between the English and French kings. The nobility of northern France enthusiastically embraced the new call to arms, after a lead had been given by Geoffrey's cousin, Count Theobald of Champagne.[142] William the Breton, the French chronicler, asserts that Geoffrey and other nobles who had deserted King Philip for King Richard feared for their position and took the cross after Richard's death, but the evidence of Geoffrey's movements and his participation in the treaty of Le Goulet suggests otherwise.[143] Moreover, Geoffrey of Villehardouin, the chief source for the Fourth Crusade, indicates that Count Geoffrey was not among the first to take the cross, placing the event some time after the beginning of Lent 1200. It seems likely therefore that Geoffrey did not commit himself to the new expedition to the east until after the settlement between King Philip and King John.[144]

Geoffrey's motives for participation in the new expedition to the east then were almost certainly not a desire to escape from a political miscalculation, but rather a personal or social commitment. He may even have felt that his own contribution to the Third Crusade had been inadequate. Geoffrey is rarely mentioned in the accounts of the crusade and the comment on his

[140] *Cartae antique rolls 1–10*, ed. L. Landon (PRS n.s. xvii, 1939), 88–9; *Foedera*, ed. T. Rymer, 2nd edn, London 1816, i. 40.
[141] *Rotuli de oblatis et finibus in turri Londinensi asservati tempore regis Johannis*, ed. T. D. Hardy, London 1837, 133; *PR 3 John, 1201*, 283.
[142] D. Queller, *The Fourth Crusade: the conquest of Constantinople, 1201–4*, Leicester 1978, 2–3.
[143] William the Breton, 'Gesta', in *Oeuvres de Rigord et de Guillaume le breton*, ed. H.-F. Delaborde, Paris 1882–5, i, 211.
[144] Geoffroi de Villehardouin, *La Conquête de Constantinople*, ed. and trans. E. Faral, 2nd edn, Paris 1961, i. 12.

performance in the *Itinerarium* suggests he could have done better.[145] Geoffrey, like his great-grandfather, Stephen-Henry count of Blois, may therefore have wanted another try and, also like Stephen-Henry, he clearly had few qualms about leaving his county in the hands of his wife as regent for a young son. Surviving documents make it clear that in the closing months of 1201 and the beginning of 1202 Geoffrey was fully engaged in preparations. King John gave him permission to take mortgages on his lands in England and Normandy and he borrowed heavily to pay for his expenses. An obligation of 300 silver marks is recorded to his cousin, William Marshal and he also borrowed £300 from a wealthy townsman of Mortagne, Lawrence Flaaut.[146]

The preaching of the Fourth Crusade was a response to the sense of shame caused by the loss of Jerusalem in 1187 and the failure of the Third Crusaders to recover it. It reflected developments in contemporary Christianity which emphasised the individual's spiritual development.[147] After the success of the First Crusade nearly a century of access to the holy places of Christianity, where Christ had lived and died, had made western Europeans more aware of the humanity of Christ and the need to follow his example. Geoffrey's religious benefactions give some hints that his own piety was affected in this way. He supported, for example, the hospitals and leperhouses of the Perche, making grants to the Maison Dieu at Mortagne and the leperhouses at Mauves and Nogent-le-Rotrou.[148] He gave money to fund the mass at Southwick and outside Newbury he founded a house of Augustinian canons, a secular order which worked in the community, but he directed no personal patronage towards the great Cluniac and Benedictine foundations of the Perche: the priory of Saint-Denis at Nogent and the priory of Saint-Léonard at Bellême.[149]

Geoffrey's surviving acts seldom contain lengthy preambles, but statements in two of them underline this attitude to almsgiving. In an act in favour of the abbey of La Trappe Geoffrey declares: 'Since I have heard that God prizes a cheerful giver and since I am unwilling to lose the fruit of my alms through too great a delay in rendering them', while in making a grant to the abbey of Saint-Évroul he asserts 'Since almsgiving opens paradise'.[150] This greater awareness of the individual is also reflected in Geoffrey's

---

145 *Chronicles and memorials of Richard I*, i. 372.

146 'G. comes Pertic' possit cui uoluerit inuadiare terras suas quas de nobis tenet in Anglia et in Normannia quia ipse crucesignatus est . . .': *Rotuli litterarum patentium in turri Londinensi asservati, 1201–1216*, ed. T. D. Hardy, London 1834, 7. For Geoffrey's debts see *Rot. litt. pat.*, 9b; AD Loiret, MS H22, pp. 185–6, no. 290.

147 C. T. Maier, 'Crisis, liturgy and the crusade in the twelfth and thirteenth centuries', *Journal of Ecclesiastical History* xlviii (1997), 631ff.

148 Bart, *Antiquitéz*, 156–8; 'Querimoniae normannorum', no. 225; Château Saint-Jean, MS C/112.

149 *Cartularies of Southwick*, 87–8; *Monasticon*, vi. 565.

150 *La Trappe*, 16–17; AD Orne, MS H721.

preoccupation with the celebration of his *anniversarium*, for which he made provision at Belhomert, the Grand Beaulieu of Chartres, Chêne Galon, Saint-Pierre de la Couture in Le Mans, Tiron and Saint-Vincent aux Bois, and his wife added the cathedral at Chartres.[151]

In the event, however, Geoffrey was to be given no opportunity to take up the cross for a second time. In Lent 1202 he was taken seriously ill and by Easter he was dead.[152] The speed of his final decline and death is manifest in the acts of his widow, Countess Matilda. In a donation to the Cistercian abbey of Perseigne she declares that he had intended to make a benefaction to the abbey, but had failed to confirm it with his seal.[153] He had also laid plans to make a substantial religious foundation in the Perche, and on his deathbed he instructed Matilda that she was to undertake this task for him.[154] As soon as the seriousness of his illness became apparent Geoffrey summoned his brother, Stephen, and handed responsibility for the Percheron crusading effort on to him. King John had clearly thought highly of Stephen's abilities and had entrusted him with responsibilities in Anjou. Like his brother, however, Stephen was prepared to shelve his own interests temporarily in order to participate in the new crusading initiative and was in the process of raising the necessary resources which involved the mortgage of his Angevin property at Langeais (Indre-et-Loir, ch.-l. du cant.) in January 1202.[155]

Two surviving acts are known to date from the last days of Count Geoffrey's life: a benefaction to the chaplain at Perchet and a grant to the waiting woman (*domicella*) Osanna which was made at Le Theil in March 1202, suggesting that Geoffrey died at the comital residence there.[156] The latter act is attested by two men who are described as his knights and appear with some frequency in the witness lists of his charters: Reginald Pessat and Odo. These men were among Geoffrey's closest companions. The service of Reginald, who appears in eight of Count Geoffrey's acts, was recognised by the award of a fee and marriage to a wealthy wife, and in 1195 he was suffi-ciently important to have witnessed an act on behalf of the seneschal of the Perche, Hubert Capreolus.[157] Odo was probably Odo of Lormarin, who

151 BN, MS franc. 24133, p. 303; *Cartulaire de la leproserie du Grand-Beaulieu*, no. 153; BN, MS Duchesne 54, 460; *La Couture*, no. clxv; *Tiron*, no. cclxxvii, 164; AD Eure-et-Loir, MS H3907, 42; AD Eure-et-Loir, MS G1459 (printed as *NDC* ii, 21).

152 Villehardouin, *La Conquête de Constantinople*, i. 46–8.

153 'Comes G morte preuentus hanc donationem sive elemosinam monachis supradictis propter negligentiam eorum non confirmauit sigilli sui appositione': AD Sarthe, MS H930.

154 'vocante domino viam carnis ingressus est universae dum in lecto aegritudinis accubaret multis viris honestis praesentibus abbatibus videlicet et aliis religiosis viris personisque illustribus et famosis moriens non vocavit et ad perficiendum quod proposuerat sub fide nostri matrimonii nos adurans . . . obligavit ad hoc effectui mancipandum': *Clairets*, no. iv.

155 *Rot. litt. pat.*, 4b.

156 *Pièces detachées pour servir à l'histoire du diocèse de Chartres*, ed. C. Métais, Chartres 1899–1904, ii. 419; *Clairets*, no. ii.

157 It is just possible that Reginald was related to the Durand Peisson who appears in *Doc.*

witnessed seven and possibly eight of the count's acts. His toponymic is hard to identify with certainty. It could refer to the manor of L'Ormarin on the River Erre, near Nocé, or it might refer to Lormarin in the Eure.[158] The presence of these two witnesses suggests that a further act dates from this same period. It records Geoffrey's gift, with the approval of his wife and his brother, Stephen of the Perche, of £15 to the priory of Belhomert. It was made for his sister Oravia and cousin Matilda who were both nuns there and, like the grant to the family retainer, perhaps reflects the preoccupations of the count as he lay dying at Le Theil, surrounded by his family and his knights.[159]

Geoffrey's obituary was celebrated on 5 April in the cathedral at Chartres and in his own collegiate foundation of Saint-Jean at Nogent-le-Rotrou, but the abbey of Saint-Évroul, to which he had been particularly generous, celebrated it on 6 April with that of King Richard.[160] His place of burial is unknown although it is likely to have been the family foundation of Saint-Denis of Nogent-le-Rotrou. The loss of such an energetic and able ruler, followed by the departure of his brother Stephen and his death in the east some three years later were to be serious blows for the Perche. Count Geoffrey of the Perche had been remarkably useful to the king of England, whether that king were Richard I or John, but the king of France could hardly do without him either, with the result that around the year 1200 the Perche reached its apogee. The importance of the county was based for the most part on the exploitation of its strategic position between the lands of the kings of France and England, but in the last decade of the twelfth century that exploitation had been effected with considerable energy and intelligence. Where in the eleventh century the counts of the Perche had asserted themselves by taking advantage of their position between emerging territorial principalities, in the twelfth century they performed the same feat but the power blocs were larger and more significant, and all the indications are that the inducements which had to be offered were of an altogether higher order. Some counts of the Perche were better at exploiting this position than others, and there can be little doubt that Geoffrey III played that role to near perfection. But the role was not without its dangers and with the accession of Geoffrey's young son, Thomas, in 1202, the Perche was to be tested to the full.

Ebro, nos 161, 177. M. Defourneaux, *Les Français en Espagne aux xie et xiie siècles*, Paris 1949, 216, suggests that Durand went to Spain with Rotrou II. See *Cartulary of Bradenstoke*, no. 235; *Monasticon* iii (1673), 66; vi (1846), 565. See also 'f. Reginald Pesar quod tenet a comite et maritagium quod cepit cum prima uxore sua': De Romanet, *Géographie*, ii. 21 (1230). For similar rewards see Church, 'The rewards of service', 287–92; *NLR*, no. xciii.
[158] *Cartulary of Bradenstoke*, no. 235; PRO, MS E 210/1532; *Cartularies of Southwick*, 87–8; *Monasticon* iii (1673), 66; vi (1846), 565; AD Eure-et-Loir, MS H5211; BL, MS Harleian charter 54.g.26. Odo's toponymic is illegible in *Clairets*, no. ii.
[159] BN, MS franc. 24133, p. 303.
[160] *Obits*, ii. 55, 391; *RHF* xxiii. 486.

6

The Perche in the Kingdom of France,
1202–1226

At the turn of the thirteenth century the Perche appeared completely secure in its new role as a distinct unit of power whose strategic position, although occasionally precarious, could be exploited by its rulers, and it seemed to be acknowledged by more powerful neighbours. Count Geoffrey III had ruled his inheritance with energy and intelligence, exercising his lordship successfully, and he had manipulated his family relationships with the kings of both France and England, while remaining apparently well-regarded by both. The death of the count at Easter 1202, however, left the Perche without an adult ruler during the period of major upheaval when King John allowed Normandy, Anjou and Touraine to slip from his control into that of Philip Augustus. The Perche under the rule of Geoffrey's widow, Matilda, and his son, Thomas, would be surrounded by territory directly under the control of the French king and a newly strengthened monarchy was emerging. The Rotrous were a family of some standing whose members had occasionally attained European stature: in the thirteenth century they were to find it necessary to capitalise on that standing in order to develop a new relationship with the French crown.

Countess Matilda and the Perche, 1202–10

The situation in which the countess of the Perche, Matilda of Saxony, found herself after Geoffrey's death in 1202 was remarkably similar to that of Hawise of Salisbury some sixty years before. She was to be responsible for the Perche during the minority of a young son in a period of upheaval in nearby Normandy, but unlike her predecessor Matilda was much better equipped to cope. The dowager countess, who was exactly thirty when widowed, was a woman of education and religious conviction, as is demonstrated by her connection with the noted Cistercian, Adam abbot of Perseigne.[1] Her late husband's confidence in her ability to rule during the minority of their son, however, did not rest solely on her personal qualities. The countess possessed not only the important advantage of royal blood, but her standing with the Plantagenets was further enhanced by personal ties. She appears to have

---

[1] Adam of Perseigne, *Lettres*, Paris 1960, 236–49.

spent much of her childhood with her Plantagenet relatives owing to her father's exile from Germany and to have been particularly close to Richard, though she was equally able to procure favour from her other uncle John.[2] With the well-connected countess acting as her son's regent the preservation of the Rotrou lineage was among the least of Geoffrey's concerns in the final weeks of his life and his belief that the Perche could continue as a viable political unit apparently never wavered.

In the immediate aftermath of Geoffrey's death the confidence of the family did not falter. The major pre-occupation of its members was to continue the count's crusading plans. Geoffrey's brother, Stephen, took command of the Percheron contingent and in May 1202 King John issued notifications to the Templars and the Hospitallers that he would stand surety for a further advance of £500 to Stephen.[3] In June 1202 the countess joined Stephen in Chartres. At midsummer that year the city was crowded with intending crusaders in the final stages of their preparations. Count Louis of Blois, a cousin of Geoffrey and Stephen of the Perche, was one of the acknowledged commanders of the expedition and the papal legate, Cardinal Pietro Capuano, was in the city. Despite the recent loss of the count the Rotrou family played its part to the full. Numerous grants were made to local religious foundations by those who were about to depart, including Stephen of the Perche. Matilda's spiritual concern was with her husband's eternal well-being, however, and she arranged for masses for Geoffrey's soul and her own to be offered at the cathedral. An act in favour of the community at Tiron made by one of Stephen's crusading companions, Geoffrey of Beaumont, and jointly confirmed by Matilda and Stephen must also date from this time.[4]

From the summer of 1202, however, Matilda was on her own. Her brother-in-law, Rotrou, bishop of Châlons-en-Champagne, had died in 1201 and, after Stephen's departure for the east, her husband's nearest surviving male relatives were his brothers, Theobald and William.[5] Both men were churchmen: Theobald was the dean of St Martin's of Tours, a centre of Capetian influence in the lands of the Plantagenets, while William was provost of the cathedral of Chartres. Both therefore could offer practical administrative advice but no adult male in the family possessed military experience. By Easter 1202 relations between Matilda's uncle, King John, and King Philip of France had deteriorated substantially and John had been summoned to Paris to answer charges in Philip's court. In retaliation John

---

[2] For her relations with John, who called her 'karissime neptis', see *Rot. norm.*, 87. On attitudes to Jewish financiers see G. Langmuir, '*Judei nostri* and the beginning of Capetian legislation', *Traditio* xvi (1960), 203–39.

[3] *Rot. litt. pat.*, 11.

[4] *NDC* ii. 21; *Tiron*, no. ccclxxvii, 160.

[5] Alberic of Trois-Fontaines, 'Chronicon', MGH SS xxiii. 879.

made ready to defend his duchy and the summer of 1202 was an uneasy one when fighting might erupt at any time.[6]

King Philip's attitude to events in the Perche is not recorded but it is unlikely that he would have allowed the death of such a prominent figure as Count Geoffrey to pass without some intervention since he had used every similar opportunity to his advantage. His settlement with King John at Le Goulet after the death of King Richard, for example, had reaffirmed the principle that a relief should be paid on succession and as recently as 1201 he had secured concessions from the countess of Champagne on the death of her husband, Theobald III.[7] There is no record of a payment from the Perche to the French crown in or around 1202, but the almost immediate remarriage of the widowed countess must be significant. As early as 1203 Pope Innocent III had written to Philip Augustus mentioning Philip's kinsman, I of the Perche, ('consobrinum, J de Pertico') and the title count of the Perche was used by Enguerrand of Coucy in an act which can be dated between 6 April 1203 and 25 April 1204.[8]

It is, of course, possible that the countess had chosen to marry Enguerrand. Tension was mounting between the Capetian and Plantagenet power blocs and a second husband could provide the military leadership unobtainable from her clerical brothers-in-law. Enguerrand was, moreover, closely connected with the French royal house through his mother, Alice of Dreux, the daughter of King Louis VI's son, Robert, who had been the second husband of Countess Hawise. Countess Matilda's second marriage would therefore have provided not only a protector for herself and her young son, but also a link to the Capetian family. There is, however, some reason to think that Matilda was unhappy with the match and that it was not of her making. She never refers to her second husband in her surviving acts and he appears to have played no part in the running of the Perche. Although Enguerrand refers to his wife, the countess of the Perche, in two of his acts and used variants on the title 'lord of Coucy and Count of the Perche' there is no documentary evidence of his involvement in the affairs of the county.[9] A Percheron coin survives bearing the legend 'I Comes Pertici', which the French numismatist, Poey D'Avant, assigned to James of Château Gontier, but James, who inherited some of the comital demesne property, never received the title of count. It is more likely, therefore, that the coin was struck during the minority of Count Thomas, when Enguerrand was technically his

6 Powicke, Loss of Normandy, 148–9.
7 J. Bradbury, Philip Augustus, king of France 1180–1223, London 1998, 232–3.
8 RHF xix. 436–8; Cartulaire de l'abbaye de Notre-Dame de Ourscamp, ed. M. Peigné-Delacourt, Amiens 1865, no. 735.
9 For Enguerrand's references to his wife see A. Duchesne, Histoire généalogique des maisons de Guines, d'Ardres, de Gand et de Coucy, Paris 1621, 356, 359. For his title see BN, MS lat. nouvelle acquisition 2309, no. 38.

Figure 4
The house of Dreux and its relation to the house of Rotrou

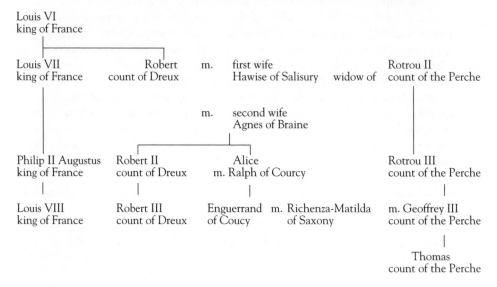

guardian, and suggests perhaps that Enguerrand received the profits of the mint.[10]

Matilda's second husband was a member of a dynasty which had been a constant thorn in the side of the Capetians. Enguerrand's grandfather had been the infamous Thomas of Marle, the archetype of the evil baron, and Enguerrand has been described as a good fighter, but a troublesome magnate.[11] At the turn of the thirteenth century he was a young man anxious to make his way in the world. He had already inherited his own family property and had paid an aid recorded in the first surviving Capetian budget, but he was clearly anxious to supplement his resources with a good marriage.[12] There is some evidence that he had already been betrothed to one wealthy woman, Eustachia of Roucy, and he was to go on to bid for much richer pickings in 1211 when he sought to marry Joanna, the young countess of Flanders. In 1219 he would be specifically excluded from the selection of husbands for another important heiress, Agnes, the daughter of Hervé of Donzé.[13] It there-

[10] *Monnaies féodales*, 262–3.
[11] Baldwin, *Government*, 333, 203. For Thomas of Marle see Guibert of Nogent, *Self and society in medieval France*, ed. J. F. Benton, New York 1972, 184–5; E. Hallam, *Capetian France*, London 1980, 115–16. On the marital adventures of the dynasty see G. Duby, *Le Chevalier, la femme et le prêtre*, trans. by B. Bray as *The knight, the lady and the priest*, London 1984, 153–4. Enguerrand lived on until 1242.
[12] *Le Premier Budget de la monarchie française: le compte générale de 1202–1203*, ed. F. Lot and R. Fawtier, Paris 1932, clxxix, c.1.
[13] *Layettes de trésor de chartes*, i. no. 706n.; *Recueil des actes de Philippe Auguste*, iii, no. 1227; *Catalogue des actes de Philippe Auguste*, ed. L. Delisle, Paris 1856, no. 1941.

fore seems likely that the marriage between Countess Matilda and the young Enguerrand was the price extracted for King Philip's recognition of the succession and that King Philip had used it as a piece of patronage to placate his energetic cousin.

In the months following Geoffrey's death Matilda turned to the business of running the Perche, and a series of transactions which can be dated to the period support this view of Matilda's second marriage. Her initial task was the clarification the count's financial affairs. Geoffrey had borrowed heavily to finance the crusade and these debts would have made it particularly difficult to find a substantial sum for a cash relief. King John had allowed Geoffrey to mortgage his English and Norman property for up to two years and the count had also borrowed 300 marks from his cousin, William Marshal.[14] Matilda set to work immediately after the count's death, for King John's notification that she had taken over Geoffrey's debt to William Marshal is dated 22 April 1202 and another act in which she settled Geoffrey's debts to Lawrence Flaaut of Mortagne was made before Stephen's departure in the summer of 1202.[15]

Meanwhile in the great confrontation between the kings of France and England, King John had scored a notable success in capturing at Mirebeau his nephew, Arthur of Brittany, whom King Philip had set up as an alternative to John. Matilda would therefore need to reinforce her relationship with her uncle and it is clear that she did so, for on 8 September 1202 John extended a truce to his 'most beloved niece'.[16] With John temporarily in the ascendant relations with the English crown continued in a cordial manner. A case involving Rotrou tenants in England was heard in the English courts and the efficiency of the organisation maintained by the countess on her son's behalf is demonstrated as the defendant, Stephen of Erdecot, pleaded that he held the disputed land by Count Geoffrey's gift and had a charter from Thomas, his son and heir, to prove it.[17] Within the Perche itself the normal apparatus of comital government continued. In July 1203 the countess confirmed a sale of property and sealed an act notifying it, and she also confirmed her husband's grant to the monks of Perseigne, which had been left improperly documented through the monks' negligence after her husband's death.[18]

During the course of 1203 Matilda continued her programme to commemorate her first husband. In March she issued a formal act establishing and endowing a collegiate foundation at Mortagne where two priests were to pray for Geoffrey's soul. It was dedicated to Toussaints (All Saints), an unusual dedication in France, and may recall another Augustinian foundation with

[14] *Rot. litt. pat.*, 7.
[15] 'Et Matill' comitissa de Pertico uxor praedicti comitis predictam pecuniam susceperit in se eidem comite Willelmo reddendam': ibid. 9b; AD Loiret, MS H22, pp. 185–6, no. 290.
[16] 'Sciatis quod dedimus karissime nepti nostre M comitiss' de Pert' et feodo suo treugas de nobis et hominibus nostris': *Rot. litt. pat.*, 18.
[17] *Curia regis rolls*, iii. 241.
[18] BN, MS Duchesne 54, p. 454; AD Sarthe, MS H930.

that dedication, patronised by the countess's Angevin forbears in Angers itself.[19] She also implemented his intention to make a religious foundation. Geoffrey left no specific instructions concerning a religious order, so his wife, having taken the best advice available, decided upon a nunnery with the Savignac affiliation to the Cistercians.[20] Although Count Geoffrey had patronised the Fontevraudine house at Belhomert and Count Rotrou II had supported the Cluniac nunnery at Marcigny, the Rotrou dynasty had not hitherto established a house for women and it may be that the countess intended to retire there herself in due course. While at La Loupe in June 1204 she formally established the house at Les Clairets in the forest south of Nogent-le-Rotrou. To her husband's deathbed bequest of *Boveria* she added other endowments, including revenue from her manor of Haughley in England, so it is clear that, even as late as 1204, she saw no reason why the cross-Channel connection established by her husband and herself in the 1190s should not continue indefinitely.

In the years which followed Matilda ruled the Perche on her son's behalf, but no later acts have survived and there are no measures by which the king of France's influence over the Perche in the years after 1204 can be tested. It may be significant, however, that there are no surviving comital acts for the period 1205–11 and that a benefaction to the charterhouse of Val Dieu in 1209, which is acknowledged to be in the jurisdiction of the count of the Perche ('in foeudo comitis Pertici'), was confirmed by Bishop Sylvester of Sées, but not by the count or his mother.[21] It may be that the countess was less adept than her husband at maintaining the balance between the Capetian and Plantagenet kings. Certainly she lacked the extensive family network which her husband had been able to deploy in fostering the family's position. Of his four brothers, only William, the provost of Chartres cathedral, remained close at hand and the absence of references to Enguerrand of Coucy suggests that Matilda did not exploit successfully the potential link with the French court provided by her second husband.

The countess's preferred strategy was to place her reliance on her own family and she exploited her access to King John to the full in her attempts to keep together the family's cross-Channel interests. In 1204, for example, she negotiated to preserve the Rotrous' English interests, using her connections with the English royal house to buy the right to hold her English property while the war between the kings of England and France continued.[22] Her relationship with the Plantagenet dynasty was inadequate protection against

---

[19] AD Orne, College of Toussaints, Mortagne, MS IG 1071/30 (inventaire des pièces justicatives . . . de l'église collegiale et royalle de Toussaints de la ville de Mortagne au Perche), p. 1, supplemented by Bart, *Antiquitéz*, 160–1; *L'Abbaye Toussaint d'Angers des origines à 1330: étude historique et cartulaire*, ed. F. Comte, Angers 1985, 17, n. 11.

[20] 'communicato cum episcopis abbatibus et aliisque viris prudentis et honestis tam clericis quam laicis consilio': *Clairets*, no. iv.

[21] RCVD, fo. 11.

[22] 'quamdiu warra durabit inter regem et regem Francie': *PR 6 John, 1204*, 33.

the events of summer 1204, however. The so-called 'dispossession of Normans', which John carried out as soon as his loss of the duchy became apparent, extended even to his own niece, and the lands which the Rotrou family held by royal favour, including Toddington, Newbury and Shrivenham were repossessed by King John.[23] For nearly three years the Rotrou lands in England remained in the king's hand, until finally in 1207 the countess contracted to pay 2,000 marks to hold her husband's property and to have custody of her son.[24]

Over the next three years Matilda prudently managed the difficult relationship with her uncle. She made careful payments to the English crown, including 800 of the 2,000 marks she had fined for her husband's lands and she paid off some long-standing debts, but on her death in January 1210 her uncle severed the Plantagenet connection with the house of Rotrou and repossessed her lands.[25] The accounts rendered by Fulk of Kantelou for the family's English lands between 1210 and 1212, which are punctiliously recorded in the pipe rolls as the lands of the countess of the Perche, indicate that large sums of money might be obtained from the property and such sums would have been welcome to King John as the second decade of his reign progressed.[26] The English dimension of the Rotrous' fortunes had thus been eradicated and the young count was now forced back upon the traditional foundations of his family's power.

Count Thomas (1210–17)

In 1210 Count Thomas was probably in his mid teens. He cannot have been born much before the end of 1193 since his father did not return from the Holy Land until late in 1192 and he had an older brother, Geoffrey. In the thirteenth century the customary age of majority was twenty-one years and the survival of a series of acts dating from 1215 suggests that Thomas had recently come of age at that point. The death of his mother had left him with few friends. The contribution of his step-father, Enguerrand of Coucy, to the running of the Perche remains completely untraceable and by 1211 Enguerrand seems to have severed his connection with the county. In the

---

23 *Rotuli litterarum clausarum in turri Londinensi asservati*, ed. T. D. Hardy, London 1833–44, i. 3b; *Rot. norm.*, 131, 142; *PR 7 John, 1205*, 175.

24 *PR 9 John 1207*, 100. On John's exploitation of his rights over minors see T. K. Keefe, 'Proffers for heirs and heiresses in the pipe rolls: some observations on indebtedness in the years before the Magna Carta', *Haskins Society Journal* v (1993), 108. It seems to have been easier for women to retain their lands in both England and Normandy after 1204. See the discussion of family and tenurial relations in W. Stevenson, 'England and Normandy, 1204–1259', unpubl. PhD diss. Leeds 1974, 207.

25 For payments see *PR 10 John, 1208*, 5, 29; for John's actions on her death see *PR 12 John 1210*, 204. The date of her death is given in *Obits*, ii. 281.

26 On John's financial problems see R. V. Turner, *King John*, London 1994, 87–114.

spring of that year he was involved in the action against the Albigensians and some months later was seeking a new bride.[27] Thomas's chief support is therefore likely to have been his uncle, William, provost of the cathedral at Chartres, and Thomas's acknowledgement in a document of 1216 that he acted with the advice of 'our venerable father, the lord William of the Perche' suggests that William had indeed taken on this role.[28]

Twenty-five acts or records of acts issued in Thomas's name form the greater part of the evidence for Thomas's rule in the Perche, since there are few chronicle references. All but two were issued between 1215 and 1217. Only one act preserves a witness list and most take a writ form with a general greeting. Using them a similar apparatus of comital rule can be traced to that which had supported the power of Thomas's predecessors. The comital court can be seen at work in an act notifying the settlement of a dispute between the abbey of La Trappe and the brothers, Nicholas, Robert, William and Hugh of Buat, and the count's agent at Mortagne was able to supply ready sums of money to support Thomas's arrangements with the abbey of Saint-Laumer of Blois.[29] Comital exactions continued to be made across the Perche for Thomas granted the Grandmontine house at Chêne Galon the services of three men who were exempt from all such dues.[30] The extensive woodlands of the Perche were at the count's disposal as his confirmation of Aucher's Assart to the abbey of La Trappe indicates.[31] In addition Thomas still held Moulins and Bonsmoulins in Normandy, which his father had obtained before King Philip had taken Normandy in 1204 and Thomas was also careful to establish his own relationship with the community at Marchainville by confirming his father's grant of privileges.[32] Seven of the twenty-five surviving acts are confirmations of those of Thomas's predecessors: in April 1216, for example, the monks of Saint-Evroul sought and acquired Thomas's confirmation of his father's grants, suggesting an acknowledgement of the effectiveness of Thomas's power by those with interests in the Perche.[33]

Thomas's religious patronage suggests an energetic assumption of power by the new count. There are no radically new acts of piety, but he set to work establishing relationships with those houses in which his family had an historic interest. An act in favour of the priory of Bellême clarifies earlier benefactions and there are confirmations of his father's grants to Chêne Galon and Saint-Évroul, but above all Thomas concerned himself with the

---

[27] Peter of Vaux de Cernay, *The history of the Albigensian crusade*, trans. W. A. Sibly and M. D. Sibly, Woodbridge 1998, 110; *Recueil des actes de Philippe Auguste*, iii. no. 1227.

[28] *Clairets*, no. ix.

[29] *La Trappe*, 408–9; AD Loir-et-Cher, abbey of Saint-Laumer de Blois, MS 11 H128 (cartulaire de l'abbaye royale de Saint-Laumer de Blois), 628–30.

[30] *CMPerche*, no. 44; BN, MS Duchesne 54, p. 461.

[31] *La Trappe*, 235.

[32] BN, MS Duchesne 54, p. 459; BN, MS Dupuy 222, pp. 127–8.

[33] AD Orne, MSS H702, H722.

completion of his mother's religious patronage, in particular of the nunnery at Les Clairets. No less than three acts of confirmation were issued for Les Clairets, each of which increased the endowment.[34] He also visited the great Benedictine house of Saint-Laumer at Blois to which he made various concessions in August 1216, and which may hint at the maintenance of ties with his cousin, Count Theobald of Blois/Chartres.[35]

Among Thomas's acts are two which suggest that, in taking a grip on the Perche, he was anxious to maximise the resources available to him. An agreement with Odo Grandin, who had redeveloped the comital mills outside Nogent-le-Rotrou, has the flavour of settling outstanding issues which had accumulated over a number of years. Acting on the advice of his uncle and other prudent men, Thomas conceded a quarter of the mills to Grandin and precise arrangements were made concerning Grandin's rights to take timber from the comital woodland as well as Thomas's responsibilities in the maintenance of the mills.[36] A further act dating from 1217 indicates that he could be scrupulous about the enforcement of his rights, for in confirming the benefaction of his predecessors to the priory of Bellême he defined the exact usage of his forest which the monks might claim, specifying the types of trees which might be taken and the means of its taking, four ass-loads three times a day.[37]

Nevertheless Count Thomas's resources were much reduced from those enjoyed by his father and he lacked the great revenues generated by the fairs in the county of his infant second cousin, Theobald IV of Champagne, or the widespread interests of his other cousins, the counts of Blois/Chartres.[38] The prosperity of the Seine basin and the Champagne region, which had become more marked at the turn of the thirteenth century, was not to spread towards the Perche. Markets, such as that which Thomas granted at Bonsmoulins, and fairs within the Perche were unlikely to raise even a small proportion of the income which the king might derive from similar activities in the Île de France.[39] Yet Thomas was subject to the process of bureaucratic definition which faced all the nobility of France as communities sought to reduce the arbitrary demands of their lords to a clearly specified requirement. In the lordship of Bellême, for example, he was persuaded to recognise that a tallage

---

34 *Clairets*, nos v, vii, x.

35 AD Loir-et-Cher, MS 11 H128, 628–30.

36 *Clairets*, no. ix.

37 *CMPerche*, no. 44.

38 On the Champagne fairs see R. H. Bautier, 'Les Foires de Champagne: recherches sur une évolution historique', *Recueils de la Société Jean Bodin* v (1953), 97–147; Bur, *Champagne*, 299–307. Some of their conclusions about the role of Theobald IV (of Blois) (II of Champagne) have been challenged by H. Dubois, 'Le Commerce et les foires au temps de Philippe-Auguste', in Bautier, *La France de Philippe Auguste*, 689–711.

39 For Thomas's activities see *Clairets*, no. ix; AD Loir-et-Cher, MS 11 H128, pp. 628–30; 'Querimoniae normannorum', no. 236. On the commercial situation in Philip's reign see Dubois, 'Le Commerce et les foires', and M. Bur, 'Rôle et place de la Champagne dans le royaume de France au temps de Philippe-Auguste', in Bautier, *La France de Philippe Auguste*, 243.

could only be collected on the fees of his knights on four occasions: his own knighting; his first capture in warfare; the knighting of his son; and the marriage of his daughter.[40]

There is a hint too, in Thomas's marriage, of decline in the family's standing. While his grandfather, Rotrou III had married a daughter of a powerful neighbouring dynasty and his father had secured the granddaughter of a king and the sister of the Holy Roman emperor, Thomas was unable to profit from these connections by an equally glamorous match. Instead his wife was the daughter of a lesser noble who was an associate of the counts of Champagne and his match was much closer to that of his ancestor, Geoffrey II, who had married Beatrix of Roucy from the same area to the north of the Île de France.

Thomas's bride was Helisende of Rethel, the daughter of Hugh count of Rethel and his wife, Felicia. Although her father is chiefly known for his harassment of the archbishop of Rheims in the opening years of the thirteenth century, Helisende's lineage was distinguished. A distant uncle, Baldwin of Le Bourcq, had taken part in the First Crusade and had become count of Edessa in 1100. In 1118 this Baldwin had secured the crown of Jerusalem as King Baldwin II. In addition to this relationship with the royal house of Jerusalem, Helisende's father was a cousin of Frederick II who was re-establishing Hohenstaufen power in the 1210s.[41] It is possible that the marriage between Thomas and Helisende was arranged by Thomas's stepfather, Enguerrand, whose own brother, Thomas of Vervins, was married to Helisende's sister, and that it was intended to strengthen the Coucy/Dreux/Perche ties after the death of Countess Matilda. Alternatively the king may have made the match with the well-connected Thomas as a means of favouring Helisende's family. The effect of the marriage, however, was to link Thomas to the lesser nobility of the lands under Capetian influence rather than to create a new alliance beyond those circles.

Thomas also faced a political situation unknown to his predecessors. King Philip's success in repossessing Normandy, Maine, Anjou and much of Poitou meant that the Perche no longer lay in a frontier zone, but was surrounded by the lands of a newly powerful and confident king of France. A new working relationship between the ruler of the Perche and the king therefore had to be developed. As early as the year 1211/12 the king secured Thomas's promise that he would render to King Philip, whenever the king required it, his fortress of Marchainville (Orne, cant. Longny).[42] The castle lay on the extreme north-easterly edge of the county in an area where Thomas's father had made considerable efforts to increase his influence in the 1190s, and

---

[40] CMPerche, no. 43.

[41] For the genealogy of the Rethel family see Alberic of Trois-Fontaines, MGH SS xxiii. 817, 822–3, 353.

[42] AN, MS J399, no. 16. A printed version appears in Layettes de trésor de chartes, i. 379 with a note that this document is no longer in the archives, although Delisle appears to have seen it: CPA, no. 1293.

would be particularly useful to the king if John were ever to regain Normandy.[43] In the light of John's diplomatic activity in the early 1210s the king's interest in Marchainville is hardly surprising, but his power was now such that the count of the Perche could not deny him. So keen was the king on ensuring access to the castle that Thomas's uncle and nearest heir, William, bishop of Châlons-en-Champagne, would be obliged to make the same promise in 1217 during Thomas's lifetime.[44]

The extension of the king's power is also apparent in the delivery of justice. The record of a dispute concerning a wood and the ovens at Bellême reveals that the dispute was settled, not as might be expected in the count's court, but in that of the king which sat at Bellême in 1212.[45] Since Bellême was technically held of the king of France by the duke of Normandy, Philip could claim that he was asserting the rights of the Norman dukes to which he had succeeded by dispossessing John in 1204. The extension of royal justice into a part of the Perche also presented the opportunity to develop relationships with the local families of the Perche, as Philip was doing elsewhere in France.[46] The Bellême plea, for example, shows the *bailli* of Verneuil, Bartholomew Drogo, an experienced royal officer, working with Fulk Quarrel, a member of a local Percheron family, which had in the past acknowledged both the Rotrou family and the Montgommery-Bellême before them.[47] Where previous generations of local families had assisted the counts in the running of the Perche, they were now being enlisted by the king. By 1214, when Fulk described himself as 'baillivus domini regis in Belineso et in Corboneto', he had apparently learned enough from his joint sessions with the king's *bailli* and was apparently able to act alone 'in curia domini regis'.[48]

While Fulk's career shows how a Percheron lord was encouraged into the king's service through office, others received material inducements such as the £46–worth of lands formerly belonging to Robert of *Coudre*, which were granted by the king in 1214 to William of Lonray, a member of the family which had frequently held the seneschalcy of Bellême under the Rotrous in the twelfth century.[49] King Philip also fostered his relations with the Percheron families by grants of money fiefs. Payments from the royal

[43] Dr Coulson estimates that there are at least forty such written promises of rendability in the royal archives dating from the period 1202–12: 'Rendability and castellation in medieval France', in *Château-Gaillard*, VI: *Actes du colloque internationale tenu à Venlo . . .*, Caen 1973, 59–67. See also *Layettes de trésor de chartes*, i. no. 1207.

[44] Ibid. i. no. 1008.

[45] CMPerche, no. 42. For the English crown's extension of jurisdictional superiority into Wales and Scotland see R. R. Davies, *Domination and conquest: the experience of Ireland, Scotland and Wales, 1100–1300*, Cambridge 1990, 103–5.

[46] Bradbury, *Philip Augustus*, 233.

[47] For Bartholomew Drogo see *RHF* xxiv/1, 124–6. Fulk Quarrel is listed among the knights of the Perche in Philip Augustus' Register A: *RHF* xxiii. 684.

[48] AD Loiret, MS H22, no. 297.

[49] *Recueil des actes de Philippe Auguste*, iii. no. 1329.

revenues at Mantes-la-Jolie (Yvelines) were made regularly to Guy of Montdoucet, Gervase of Prulay, William of Lonray, Robert Karrell, Fulk Quarrel and Matthew of Coismes, all of whom had interests in the Perche and three of whom, William of Lonray, Guy of Montdoucet and Fulk Quarrel, appear among the knights of the Perche in the knight service returns compiled for the French king after the recovery of Normandy.[50]

It was timely therefore for the Rotrou lineage itself to reassess its position with a view to developing a new partnership with the king of France and there is every indication that that partnership was being worked out. In 1215, at the point when Thomas came of age and could take over the running of the Perche, his last surviving uncle, William, had been elevated from his position as provost of the cathedral at Chartres to the regalian see of Châlons-en-Champagne, an office formerly held by his brother, Rotrou. The position was an important one and indicates royal confidence, for the see was both wealthy and powerful. It had accrued some comital powers within the locality and in 1201 after the death of Rotrou of the Perche the bishop's revenues amounted to £2,047 provins, although only £1,527 were rendered.[51] King Philip had been particularly successful in his efforts to assert his authority over the counts of Champagne and the presence of a bishop committed to the Capetian cause at Châlons would have been an additional source of royal influence within Champagne.

While his uncle served the king as the bishop of a regalian see, the young Count Thomas committed himself to military action with Philip's forces. His father Count Geoffrey had left a considerable legacy of prestige, as Villehardouin's assessment of him shows, and Thomas himself was well-regarded as a knight.[52] Although Roger of Wendover's suggestion that Thomas was with the king's troops at the battle of Bouvines in 1214 must be discounted for want of support from the major sources for the battle, the count did play a prominent part in his cousin Prince Louis's expedition to England in pursuit of the English crown.[53] Louis had arrived in England in the spring of 1216 to lead the rebel barons against King John and quickly secured much of the eastern part of the country. Thomas was not apparently among the original expedition which set out on Louis's great adventure, for

---

[50] Les Registres de Philippe Auguste, i. 202, 311. On Philip's use of the money fief see Baldwin, Government, 273. For Guy of Montdoucet see VLM, no. xxv, and Clairets, nos xiv, xi; for Gervase of Prulay see BN, MS Duchesne 54, p. 454, and VLM, no. xxv; RCVD, fo. 9v; La Trappe, 401; for William of Lonray see BN, MS Duchesne 54, p. 454; La Trappe, 470; NLR, no. xciii; for Fulk Quarrel see AD Sarthe, abbey of Saint-Vincent du Mans, MS H93; Tiron, no. II; La Trappe, 24; Perseigne, no. ccxxi; for Robert Karrell see AD Eure-et-Loir, MS H5211; BN, MS Duchesne 54, p. 454; Canterbury, Dean and Chapter archives, MS carta antiqua R62; for Matthew of Coimes see Clairets, no. xiv.

[51] Bur, Champagne, 181–5. Le Premier budget de la monarchie francaise, CLII, c.1. Actes Philippe-Auguste, no. 727.

[52] RHF xviii. 361.

[53] Roger of Wendover, Chronica ii. 109.

his name does not appear on either list of the prince's followers at embarkation given in the *Histoire des ducs de Normandie* nor in the chronicle of the anonymous of Béthune.[54] As Louis made headway against the English, however, Thomas suddenly appeared with reinforcements, at a particularly opportune moment, during the siege of Dover when other commanders had withdrawn.[55] Among those reinforcements were probably the Percherons, Gervase of Condeau and William of Bruyère, who are known to have accompanied Thomas to England.[56]

Service with the Capetian forces did not of course preclude the satisfaction of Thomas's own ambitions, among which he presumably included the recovery of his family's English property. Thus when south-eastern England was abandoned to the French during the course of 1216, Thomas saw his opportunity. He was quick to assert his right to the Kentish portion of the honour of the constable, which was his mother's *maritagium*, and he announced the fact by confirming an act his parents had made in favour of the Premonstratensian house of St Radegund at Bradsole.[57]

If Count Thomas had been late in joining the invasion, however, he was soon to make up for that tardiness by his enthusiasm. He must have returned to France after the truce of late 1216, for he was at Marchainville in 1217 where he settled a dispute with the priory of Bellême and he also made a benefaction to the nunnery at Les Clairets, but after his winter at home Thomas returned to an active part in the campaign.[58] It is possible that he arrived in England in the entourage of Prince Louis, who returned on 23 April 1217, for he suddenly comes to prominence when he led the French forces sent by Prince Louis to relieve the earl of Winchester's castle of Mountsorrel. The brutality of the Thomas's soldiers was noted in the annals of Dunstable and his opponents withdrew ahead of him.[59] From Mountsorrel Thomas's forces made their way to Lincoln where the castle was still holding

---

54 *Histoire des ducs de Normandie et des rois d'Angleterre*, ed. F. Michel, Paris 1840, 165; BN, MS nouvelle acquisition franc. 6295, 'Chronique d'un anonyme de Béthune' (excerpt) in *RHF* xxiv/2, 771.

55 'Mais la encontre arriva li cuens de Perche od x chevaliers qui pas ne crut tant l'ost que cil la descrurent Anonymous of Béthune': ibid. xxiv/2, 773.

56 For Thomas in England see *Annales monastici*, ed. H. R. Luard (RS xxxvi, 1864–9), iii. 49. For Gervase of Condeau see 'Gervasius de Condeto miles conqueritur quod cum esset in Anglia in servicio comitis Pertici . . .': 'Querimoniae normannorum', no. 119. For William of Bruyere see 'Guillelmus de Bevraria miles de Verreria conqueritur quod cum esset in Anglia in servicio comitis Pertici': ibid. no. 123.

57 *Monasticon*, vi. 941. King John had given a general confirmation to the house in 1199: *Rot. chart.*, 12.

58 For the truce see D. Carpenter, *The minority of Henry III*, Berkeley, CA 1990, 25–31; AD Orne, priory of Bellême, MS H2153 (= *CMPerche*, no. 44), *Clairets*, no. x.

59 *Annales monastici*, iii. 49. The background to the siege of Mountsorrel is covered in E. J. King, 'Mountsorrel and its region in King Stephen's reign', *Huntington Library Quarterly* xliv (1980), 1–10.

out against Gilbert of Gant and other supporters of Prince Louis under the command of its hereditary castellan, Nicola de la Haye. Thomas was clearly very pleased with himself and the success of the expedition. Matthew Paris stresses the pride of the French commanders, but William Marshal, as rector of the English kingdom, was about to move against them.[60] He approached the city of Lincoln from the north and drew up his forces on the plain there on the morning of 20 May 1217.[61] The count of the Perche, accompanied by the earl of Winchester and Simon of Poissy, undertook a reconnaissance and, as Roger of Wendover recounts, they seriously misjudged the size of the forces ranged against them.[62] Over-estimating their enemy's numbers, they declined battle and opted to remain inside the city walls. As a result, when the Marshal's army found a way to break into the city, the advantage of numbers was lost in the confusion and the combined forces of the rebels and the French were overcome in vigorous fighting in the streets. In the heat of the battle on the sunny May Saturday Thomas was killed by blow to the eye.

On so much the sources are agreed, but the precise details vary according to the account.[63] A poem, produced in the Marshal's household, 'L'Histoire de Guillaume le maréchal', gives the Marshal's version of events.[64] It indicates that Thomas took a stand in the area between the castle and the cathedral, where he came to blows personally with his cousin, the Marshal. The hard-pressed Thomas, surrounded by his men, was holding his own against the English when the Marshal rushed forward and seized his horse by the bridle. At that moment the count took a spear-blow, struck by Reginald Croc. The spear penetrated his helmet vizor and he was mortally wounded, but he was still able to strike three blows at the Marshal's helm, before falling dead from his horse. His assailant, Reginald Croc, did not survive to corroborate the Marshal's tale, however, for he too was killed in the battle.[65] The account is contradicted by that of the annals of Dunstable which asserts that Thomas's horse was killed under him as he valiantly defended himself in a graveyard.[66] Roger of Wendover, the prior of Belvoir on the Lincolnshire border, gives a further version, asserting that, as the battle swung in favour of

---

[60] 'comes Perticensis et Franciae marescallus superbientes et eorum consiliis obsecundare dedignantes': Matthew Paris, *Historia minor*, ed. F. Madden (RS xliv, 1866–9), ii. 210. For the Marshal's strategy see Crouch, *William Marshal*, 122.

[61] *Histoire de Guillaume le maréchal*, ed. P. Meyer (Société de l'histoire de France, 1891–1901), lines 16340–59.

[62] Roger of Wendover, *Chronica* ii. 214.

[63] For the sunshine ('Fulsit in armatas solaris gratia turmes') see Carpenter, *Minority*, 37 n. 8, citing *The political songs of England*, ed. T. Wright (Camden Society, 1839), 25. The precise details of the battle have never been disentangled: T F. Tout, 'The fair of Lincoln and the "Histoire de Guillaume le maréchal" ', *EHR* xviii (1903), 240–67.

[64] *Histoire de Guillaume le maréchal*, lines 16704–68.

[65] For the death of Croc see Roger of Wendover, *Chronica* ii. 217.

[66] *Annales monastici*, iii. 50.

the English, Count Thomas was surrounded. He refused to surrender to the English who, he declared, were traitors to their own king and he was killed by a blow through his eye which penetrated his brain.[67] The king of England's forces under William Marshal carried the day and Thomas was hurriedly buried with two of his companions in the orchard of a hospital outside the walls of Lincoln.[68]

The precise whereabouts of Thomas's burial are unknown. The most likely location is the grounds of the Malandry, which had been founded by Bishop Remigius of Lincoln, though it is possible the burial took place in the grounds of the hospital of the Holy Sepulchre.[69] Such obscurity is surprising since his death was noted by many contemporary English commentators, including the annalists of Tewkesbury, Burton, Winchester, Waverley, Dunstable and Worcester, and a donation to Saint Bartholomew's Hospital in London was even dated by reference to it.[70] The Rouen chronicler suggests the formidable reputation that the young knight had achieved by describing how many grieved for him, and his death was reported in the continuation of William of Tyre by Eracles, as well as in German sources which were familiar with the Saxon ancestry of Thomas's mother and his connection with the Emperor Otto IV.[71] Thomas was mourned by his leader, Prince Louis, who remarked 'If everyone had stood as he did, then I would have triumphed gloriously', and shortly after his death his second cousin, Count Theobald of Blois, set up a window in the newly rebuilt choir of Chartres cathedral in his memory.[72]

If Prince Louis had succeeded in taking the kingdom of England, then Thomas's reward would no doubt have been the restoration of all the family's English property and probably a considerable increase to it. It was a not unreasonable gamble for the count, but in the event not only was Louis driven out of England, but Thomas was killed, leaving as his successor his uncle, Bishop William of Châlons-en-Champagne, who could father no legitimate heir. Thomas's attempt to reconstitute the cross-Channel connection of his ancestors was therefore not only a failure, but a disaster for the dynasty. By the 1210s Thomas had little alternative to his decision to take service with the Capetians and his rashness in the English campaign may have owed something to a desire to make up for the lateness of his lineage's commitment to the French kings. His passing was a glorious episode held up by the Capetian heir, Prince Louis, as the pattern for all the nobility, but the lineage

67 Roger of Wendover, *Chronica* ii. 216.

68 Matthew Paris, *Historia minor*, ii. 213

69 J. W. F. Hill, *Medieval Lincoln*, Cambridge 1948, 343, 345.

70 *Annales monastici*, i. 63, 224; ii. 78, 287; iii. 49; iv. 408. *Cartulary of St Bartholomew's Hospital founded 1123: a calendar*, ed. N. J. M. Kerling, London 1973, no. 531.

71 *RHF* xviii. 361; 'Estoire de Eracles', in *Recueil des historiens des croisades*, ii. 321; Alberic of Trois-Fontaines, 'Chronicon', MGH SS xxiii. 905.

72 Matthew Paris, *Historia minor*, ii. 213; Y. Delaporte and E. Houvet, *Les Vitraux de la cathédrale de Chartres: histoire et description*, Chartres 1926, 230. I am grateful to Lindy Grant for her help with this reference.

was effectively ended. After Thomas's death, his uncle's tenure of the county only postponed the final extinction of the house of Rotrou and with it the independence of the Perche.

The Perche under the count-bishop, 1217–26

William was to be a valued counsellor of the kings of France for the next nine years. In his episcopal capacity he had been present in July 1216 at the celebrated arbitration of the succession to Champagne, the participants in which would henceforth be considered among the peers of France.[73] He was an acceptable surety for the homage of other great nobles, including that of his own cousin, Isabelle of Chartres, who inherited that county when the direct line of the counts of Blois failed in 1218. He was also to play a part in all the major events of French history for the best part of ten years. In 1223 he was to be placed first in the list of the peers of France with whom the king made the important *stabilimentum* concerning the Jews of the kingdom, while two letters from Pope Honorius III dated April 1219 indicate William's intention of participating in the crusade against the Albigensians. The expedition's costs may also account for William's sale of a rent in Châlons which Philip Augustus confirmed in January 1220.[74] A series of benefactions, made by William in May 1219 to fund his *anniversarium*, together with a general confirmation to the family foundation of Chêne Galon made at the same time, reveal William's own spiritual preparations for that crusade.[75] But, high as was William's personal standing with King Philip and King Louis, it was insufficient to protect his county.[76]

The king had already secured Count Thomas's acceptance of royal rights over the castle of Marchainville, which Bishop William had acknowledged in Thomas's lifetime. No sooner had Count Thomas died, however, than King Philip challenged the count of the Perche's rights to a further two castles. Concessions on comital control of Moulins and Bonsmoulins that belonged to the ducal demesne of Normandy, now held by the king himself, were clearly the price to be paid for Philip's confirmation of William's succession. When William came to Melun in June 1217 to make formal homage to the king for the county of the Perche, he was obliged to accept a royal inquiry into his right to hold the castles and, even if the inquiry found in his favour, he would only retain a life interest in them.[77] While the king made claims on

---

[73] *Recueil des actes de Philippe Auguste*, iii. nos 1436–7.

[74] Langmuir, 'Judei nostri', 203–39; *RHF* xix. 681–2; *CPA*, no. 1949.

[75] He gave £5 to the cathedral at Chartres: BN, MS lat. 10095 (Privilegia ecclesiae Carnotensis [cartulaire 28 bis]), fo. 65; 40s. each to Val Dieu (*La Trappe*, 73), to La Trappe (ibid. 19), and to Chêne Galon (BN, MS Duchesne 54, p. 459). For his confirmation to Chêne Galon see ibid. p. 461.

[76] GC ix. 885; *Diplomatic documents, 1101–1272*, no. 153, p. 105.

[77] AN, MS JJ31, quoted in De Romanet, *Géographie*, ii. 8.

large portions of William's inheritance, his officials, who had already made their presence felt in Bellême during the lifetime of Count Thomas, made further inroads on the business of running the Perche, sometimes with the connivance of the count-bishop himself. In June 1217, for example, shortly after his accession, William found it expedient to grant a regular money payment of £10 a year from the *prepositura* of Mortagne to Bartholomew Drogo, the king's bailiff in the Verneuil region, who presumably then took up some responsibilities within the Perche.[78]

The advance in royal influence was thus aided in some measure by the count-bishop's own actions, and it is clear that William attached far less importance to his claims in England than his ancestors had done. Although he went to England in December 1217 it was remarkably easy for his cousins, William Marshal and the earl of Salisbury, to buy out William's claims to the family's English lands, concerning which he made no further representations, tamely nominating William Marshal to act on his behalf in a lawsuit concerning family lands in 1220.[79] It is possible that the sheer size of William's episcopal revenues at Châlons meant that he had adequate resources and he was certainly able to lend other members of the French nobility substantial sums of money, as surviving details of his loans to Simon of Joinville, Henry count of Bar-le-Duc and Count Theobald of Champagne show.[80]

The extent of William's responsibilities as both bishop and count is indicated by the fact that he clearly spent much of his time away from the Perche. A *generalis procurator* for all the land of the count of Perche is mentioned in 1220 and William even anticipates his own absence in one of his acts by specifying that a render is to be made to himself, his successors or the baliff of his land if he is not in his land.[81] It is possible therefore that he was happy to leave much of the routine work of running the county to the king's bailiff of Verneuil and his son, who in 1225 gave his retainer to La Trappe.[82] William dealt with his dual responsibilities by allocating portions of time to the Perche, as is indicated by the 'bunching' of his acts in, for example, May 1219,[83] June/August 1221,[84] April 1222[85] and August/September 1225,[86] but

[78] *La Trappe*, 7–8. On Bartholomew see *RHF* xxiv/1, 124–6.

[79] For letters patent granting William a safe conduct to England see *Calendar of patent rolls Henry III, 1216–1225*, London 1901, 129. For subsequent events see *Book of fees*, iii. 1154; Carpenter, *Minority*, 92. For the lawsuit see *Curia regis rolls*, ix. 301.

[80] Arbois de Jubainville, *Histoire*, v. nos 1441, 1629, 2266.

[81] *CMPerche*, no. 211; 'nobis et nostris successoribus vel ballivo nostre terre, si in terra nostra non fuerimus quadam calcaria . . . pro omnibus serviciis . . . annuatim exinde persolvendo': ibid. no. 68.

[82] *La Trappe*, 9.

[83] *NDC* ii. 93; *La Trappe*, 73; BN, MS Duchesne 54, p. 461; *NDC* ii. 94 n. 1.

[84] *Clairets*, nos xvi, xvii; De Romanet, *Géographie*, ii. 8–9; *CMPerche*, no. 68.

[85] *Clairets*, no. xx; *NLR*, no. xci.

[86] *La Trappe*, 9; *Tiron*, no. ccclviii.

the problems associated with William's status as both a bishop and a secular ruler are suggested by a letter from Pope Honorius III in reply to a request from the bishop.[87] The death of this largely absentee count-bishop would therefore have had less impact in the Perche than that of any of his predecessors.

When William died in February 1226 on the eve of King Louis's expedition to the south, the question of the succession to the Perche was left unresolved and it remained unresolved for several years. Significantly, however, it was left to the king to settle the matter, for by the 1220s such was the increase in royal power that the king was expected to dispose of the succession. The remarkable revival in the authority of the French crown had been due in no small part to a surprising run of luck, characterised by the French historian, André Chédeville as 'l'élément humain', as lineage after lineage either failed or ran to disputed successions.[88] The Thibaudian counts of Champagne, for example, had been forced to make concessions to the king's power to secure his recognition, and many of King John's problems stemmed from his need for Philip's approval for his succession.[89] Bishop William seems to have succeeded his nephew, Count Thomas, without question in 1217, but the failure of the direct line of the Thibaudian counts of Blois/Chartres in 1218 raised the question of succession to a principality in the absence of a male heir. After the death of Count Theobald in 1218, his lands were partitioned, with Blois passing to his sister, Margaret, and Chartres to his other sister, Isabelle. A similar failure of a major lineage, that of the counts of Alençon, which took place at much the same time, however, was treated differently. For when the death of Robert count of Alençon in 1217 was soon followed by that of his infant heir, the property was divided among the descendants of Robert's sisters, but significantly, unlike Blois/Chartres, the title was not passed on.[90]

There were therefore several precedents in 1226 when the death of the count-bishop gave a further occasion for royal intervention, and it was the Alençon settlement which provided the pattern for the Perche. Comital authority was extinguished within the county, leaving only the demesne property to be distributed among his heirs. After some years the landed property of the comital family was divided into two portions and distributed among the collateral descendants of the house of Rotrou, but the comital title itself was not granted to any of the heirs and fell into abeyance. Part of the

---

[87] 'suppresso episcopi nomine Comitem te appellent ut sic possint ad loca remotiora trahere te in causam': *RHF* xix. 747.

[88] Chédeville, *Chartres*, 319.

[89] Bur, 'Rôle et place de la Champagne'.

[90] Robert of Alençon died on 8 September 1217: *Perseigne*, 17. When Robert's posthumous son died two years later the property was divided between Robert's sister, Ella of Almenêches, and their nephews, Aimeri of Châtellerault and Robert Malet: *Cartulaire normand de Philippe Auguste, Louis VIII, Saint Louis et Philippe le Hardi*, ed. L. Delisle (Mémoires de la Société des antiquaires de Normandie 2 sér. vi, 1852), nos 284, 1126.

property had already been appropriated by the king before the partition was made and was used by him to mollify the troublesome magnate, Peter of Dreux. Later the dower of Thomas's widow, Countess Helisende, was used to dower Queen Margaret, the wife of Louis IX, rather than being returned to the patrimony.[91]

Although the extinction of the line was postponed until 1226, the house of Rotrou effectively ended therefore at the battle of Lincoln on 20 May 1217 when Count Thomas fell to the English onslaught. He had chosen the path of wholehearted support for the Capetians as the best means to preserve the fortunes of the Perche. It is quite likely that, had he left an heir, the Rotrou lineage might have survived in the county of the Perche for some generations, as the counts of Blois were to continue into the thirteenth and fourteenth centuries. In the event the Perche became an apanage of the Capetian dynasty. Thomas's wholehearted support of Prince Louis's expedition to England was completely in the tradition of political action followed by his ancestors. In supporting Louis's claim to the English throne, Thomas was in effect attempting to repeat Count Rotrou II's successful duke-making activities of 1141, when he withdrew his support from the English King Stephen and accepted Geoffrey of Anjou's claims to rule in Normandy. Unfortunately, just as Rotrou II's enthusiastic support for Geoffrey of Anjou had led him to his death at the siege of Rouen in 1144, so Thomas's commitment to Prince Louis lost him his life at Lincoln. Thomas's youthful enthusiasm and over-confidence had catastrophic consequences for the dynasty. He was the only male heir of his grandfather's five sons and his death gave King Philip yet another opportunity to demonstrate Capetian power in northern France.

[91] Details of the collateral heirs and disposition of comital property are given in K. Thompson, 'The counts of the Perche, c. 1066–1217', unpubl. PhD diss, Sheffield 1995, ch. ii.

7

The Rotrou Counts and England, 1100–1226

For more than a hundred years from early in the twelfth century until 1210 the counts of the Perche held lands in England. Like many others these interests began in a small way, but were increased through access to royal favour, inheritance and marriage until, at the turn of the thirteenth century, the counts could rival all but the greatest magnates in England. The history of these English interests has never been adequately investigated, yet the richness of the material preserved in the records of English government adds to our understanding of the family's particular skills and talents, as well as to our knowledge of its material resources. In addition the acquisition of this property and its management casts light on several of the themes which have recently preoccupied historians of the Anglo-Norman and Plantagenet realms: the means by which land was accumulated and transferred within families;[1] the collapse of the cross-Channel *regnum* under King John;[2] and, in particular, the debate on the 'cross-Channel' estates and the effect of such estates on political society.[3] The Rotrous' English interests were assembled late and, unlike the magnates of the years immediately after the Norman Conquest, the Rotrous never put down roots in the English localities. The family's experience and its attempts to retain its position in the changed political circumstances of the early thirteenth century therefore adds a new element to the latter debate.

The foundations of power: Aldbourne and Wanborough

The Anglo-Norman historian, Orderic Vitalis, took the view that the foundations of the Rotrou family's territorial holdings in England were laid at the time of the Norman Conquest. He describes the 'great revenues and fiefs in England', received by Geoffrey, the son of Count Rotrou I of Mortagne, and

---

[1] J. C. Holt, 'Politics and property in the early Middle Ages', *Past & Present* lvii (1972), 3–52; 'Feudal society and the family in early medieval England, I: The revolution of 1066', *TRHS* 5th ser. xxxii (1982), 193–212; 'II: Notions of patrimony', xxxiii (1983), 193–220; 'III: Patronage and politics', xxxiv (1984), 1–25; 'IV: The heiress and the alien', xxxv (1985), 1–28.

[2] Gillingham, *The Angevin empire*, 70–4; Holt, 'The loss of Normandy and royal finances', 92–105.

[3] Le Patourel, *The Norman empire*, 191ff; J. Green, 'Unity and disunity in the Anglo-Norman state', *Historical Research* lxiii (1989), 128ff.

other companions of the Conqueror, and he indicates that King Henry I enhanced the position 'by greatly augmenting [the] estates and wealth' of Geoffrey's son, Count Rotrou II.[4] The participation of a neighbour of the Normans in the 1066 campaign was by no means unusual. The Bretons were clearly the largest contingent, but several of William the Conqueror's other continental neighbours joined his forces, including Count Eustace of Boulogne, and many of these men received rich rewards in England.[5] Generally speaking Orderic is a reliable source for the history of the house of Rotrou: his religious community was located near to the Perche and the Rotrous were counted among its patrons, yet on this matter it is possible to disprove one element of his statement, for there is no trace of that rich reward in the Domesday Book. It is, however, significant that such a well-placed commentator as Orderic stressed a long-standing and lucrative association between the Rotrou family and the kingdom of the English, for he is likely to have derived that impression from members of the Rotrou family, if not directly from Count Rotrou II, and Orderic's conviction is therefore an indication of the importance attached to the English connection by the count.

It is of course perfectly possible that Count Geoffrey was present at Hastings and gave up early during the settlement or perhaps had never intended to stay more than the length of the initial campaign.[6] The listing of a Matthew the Mortagnard among the landholders of Essex in 1086 does suggest that men from the Perche settled in England and that Geoffrey himself may have remained there for a little while before acquiring better prospects on the death of his elder brother.[7] The foundation of the Rotrou family honour in England lay, however, not in his reward, but in the property given to Count Rotrou II in the early twelfth century when he married Matilda, the illegitimate daughter of King Henry I. Orderic Vitalis is again the primary source, but he gives no indication of the nature or location of the property.[8] For that information it is necessary to turn to the records of the Cluniac priory of Lewes in Sussex, whose cartulary preserves the texts of two acts by Count Rotrou, one granting property at Aldbourne and the other at Wanborough.[9]

These two manors lay on the eastern borders of the county of Wiltshire on the downlands overlooking the Vale of the White Horse. Aldbourne had

---

[4] OV ii. 266; vi. 398.
[5] G. Beech, 'The participation of the Aquitanians in the conquest of England, 1066–1100', ANS ix (1986), 1–24; R. George, 'The contribution of Flanders to the conquest of England, 1065–86', Revue belge de philologie et d'histoire v (1926), 81–96; K. S. B. Keats-Rohan, 'Le Rôle des bretons dans la politique de colonisation normande à l'Angleterre', Mémoires de la Société d'histoire et d'archéologie de Bretagne lxxiv (1996), 181–215.
[6] OV ii. 220.
[7] DB ii. 91.
[8] OV vi. 398.
[9] BL, MS Cotton Vespasian F xv, fos 167v, 171v.

been royal demesne in 1086 while Wanborough had been in the hands of the bishop of Winchester, but significantly the Domesday record gives no 1066 lord for Wanborough, so it is possible that the bishop's hold on it was tenuous and it must have subsequently come into royal possession before being granted to Rotrou.[10] Together they represented a substantial dowry for an illegitimate daughter: Aldbourne was assessed at 40 hides in 1086 and paid £70 by weight, while Wanborough was 19 hides, worth £18. It is necessary therefore to place Henry's generosity to Matilda and his son-in-law in the context of his policy for promoting the security of his borders, which led him to marry illegitimate daughters to his neighbours.[11] The two Wiltshire manors gave Rotrou a stake in the Anglo-Norman realm and ensured his continuing support for Henry I's tenure of both England and Normandy. Rotrou thus received a cross-Channel interest similar to those held by Norman barons which would, in the words of John Le Patourel, 'inevitably tend to bind' together the two parts of the Anglo-Norman realm, but he could not be described as a cross-Channel magnate.[12] His holdings were not as extensive as the great Norman barons; he is not known to have made the frequent journeys across the Channel undertaken by, for example, Roger of Montgommery, and there is no record of settlement by Percherons on his Wiltshire estates.[13]

Rotrou's acquisitions were made in the second generation of the Conquest when the opportunities for making a family fortune in England were constrained by the patterns of lordship already in place and his response to the increase in his resources in terms of religious patronage was similarly a 'second-generation' response.[14] Instead of establishing a priory dependent on a family foundation on the French side of the Channel, as first generation settlers had done, Rotrou patronised the earliest English house of the Cluniac order to which his family had already looked for the reform of the family foundation of Saint-Denis of Nogent-le-Rotrou. The sum of 20s. from the returns of Aldbourne was paid annually to the Cluniac priory at Lewes and, at the request of the Countess Matilda, a hide of Wanborough's lands was given to the same priory.[15] Neither of these benefactions can be precisely dated, though the countess's request places the latter before her death in 1120. It may be, however, that they were made in the 1100s shortly after Rotrou received the manors, since he chose to favour the established Cluniac order, rather than his new foundation of Tiron which dates from around 1107.

---

[10] DB i. 65, 65b.
[11] Hollister, 'War and diplomacy', 82.
[12] Le Patourel, *Norman empire*, 191.
[13] K. Thompson, 'Cross-Channel estates of the Montgomery-Bellême family', unpubl. MA diss. Cardiff 1983, 226–8.
[14] M. Chibnall, 'Monastic foundations in England and Normandy, 1066–1189', in Bates and Curry, *England and Normandy in the Middle Ages*, 41.
[15] BL, MS Cotton Vespasian F xv, fos 167v, 171v.

Another portion of the Wanborough estate called Broom was also detached before 1120 in order to endow the Cluniac priory of Marcigny-sur-Loire.[16]

The subsequent history of the countess's two dowry manors reveals something of contemporary attitudes to women's interest in family property. The countess died in the wreck of the White Ship in 1120, but the two estates remained with the Rotrou family. Later, however, Aldbourne and Wanborough became the property of John, son of William Talvas, count of Ponthieu, who had married Beatrix, the granddaughter of Count Rotrou and Matilda, probably in the 1140s. John's interests in Wiltshire are revealed in the Wiltshire section of the 1156 pipe roll, which records his tax exemptions, and by a writ issued by King Henry II in or before 1158 ordering him to ensure that the prior of Lewes could hold in peace the hide of land there which the Countess Matilda had given in the time of the king's grandfather.[17] In a society where noblewomen were expected to bring a dowry, it was not unusual for property to descend in this manner through the female line, so that the lands which Countess Matilda had brought into the Rotrou lineage passed out of it as the dowry of Beatrix, and an undated act conceding land at Aldbourne to Odo, the son of Walter of Aldbourne, which was issued jointly by John and Beatrix, demonstrates Beatrix's connection with the estates.[18]

The Chaources connection: Toddington, Newbury and Berwick

In addition to Aldbourne and Wanborough, the Rotrou family also had other English interests. Count Rotrou III (1144–91) was able to grant half a silver mark from the mill of Berwick St James in Wiltshire to the Augustinian canons at Bradenstoke, while in the 1170s his brother, Geoffrey, had interests in two more English manors: Newbury (Berks) and Toddington (Beds).[19] The factor which unites all these properties is their tenure, at the time the Domesday book was compiled, by Ernulf de Hesdin, an important magnate with property in Wiltshire and twelve other counties worth over £270. Ernulf had been implicated in the 1095 uprising against King William II and, despite being cleared through trial by combat, left England to join the First Crusade. A large proportion of his lands then came into the possession of Patrick of Chaources and his wife, Matilda, who jointly gave the church of Toddington

---

[16] *Book of fees*, 738. A papal confirmation granted in 1120 gives an indication of date: *Cartulaire de Marcigny-sur-Loire*, no. 270.

[17] *The great roll of the pipe for the second, third and fourth years of the reign of King Henry the second, 1155–1158*, ed. J. Hunter, London 1844, 59; BL, MS Cotton Vespasian F xv, fo. 171v. The writ is witnessed by Warin fitzGerold who died in 1158, shortly after Henry visited Salisbury where it was issued. I was indebted to the late Professor T. Keefe for his advice in dating these documents.

[18] The descent of the property is discussed in Thompson, 'Dowry and inheritance patterns'. See also PRO, MS E 326/7482.

[19] *Cartulary of Bradenstoke*, no. 655; *PR 26 Henry II*, 46; *PR 29 Henry II*, 82.

Figure 5
The English connections of Countess Hawise

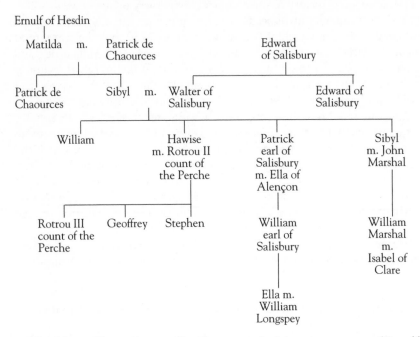

to the abbey of Saint-Pierre of La Couture in Le Mans in memory of Ernulf de Hesdin. Since joint acts of this nature by husband and wife often related to the wife's property, it is not unreasonable to infer that Ernulf's lands descended to his daughter or just possibly his widow.[20]

Patrick of Chaources and Matilda were the maternal grandparents of Rotrou II's second wife, Hawise of Salisbury and through Hawise the Rotrou lineage acquired claims on the estates of Ernulf of Hesdin. Those claims are indicated by the consent given by Count Rotrou at some point before his death in 1144 to Ernulf and Patrick de Chaources's grants from the manor of Kempsford (Glos.) to St Peter's abbey, Gloucester.[21] The nature of the Rotrous' claims on Ernulf's estates is unclear. Since Patrick and his wife Matilda were still alive in 1133 and their daughter, Sibyl and her husband, Walter of Salisbury, survived until at least 1139, it is possible that Hawise and Rotrou did not enjoy direct possession of any property, but had expectations of an inheritance.[22] Ernulf of Hesdin had not been among the mightiest beneficiaries of the Norman Conquest, but his holdings in 1086 were substantial

20 F. Barlow, *William Rufus*, London 1983, 358; *CDF*, no. 1033.
21 *Original acta of St Peter's Abbey*, no. 248.
22 For Patrick and Matilda see *Historia et cartularium monasterii S. Petri Gloucestriae*, ed. W. H. Hart (RS xxxiii, 1863–7), no. cccxxxiv; for Walter and Sibyl see *Cartulary of Bradenstoke*, no. 570.

and during the twelfth century his estates were used to improve the fortunes of three families: the Chaources, the earls of Salisbury and the Rotrous. Their distribution among those three families, however, demonstrates the point that from the first third of the twelfth century opportunities to make a fortune in England were usually confined 'within the existing structures of power and lordship' and dependent as much on royal favour as on hereditary right.[23]

The 1140s were a period of uncertainty for those who held lands in both England and Normandy, and these difficulties were compounded for the Rotrou family with the succession of Rotrou III as a minor. Other families with estates on both sides of the Channel divided responsibility among different members of the family, and a ready-made custodian for the Rotrous' Wiltshire estates was available in the person of Earl Patrick of Salisbury who was the brother of Countess Hawise of the Perche. For the Rotrous, however, the difficulties were probably solved by the assignment of Aldbourne and Wanborough as a marriage portion to Rotrou II's granddaughter by his first marriage, Beatrix. Earl Patrick might still have been retained as their guardian, however, for he was married to Beatrix's sister-in-law, Ella of Alençon. It was not then until the mid 1160s that the family was apparently offered another opportunity to establish itself in England.

The evidence for the restoration of the Rotrous' English land comes from the pipe roll of 1166/7, which indicates that Count Rotrou held a pardon by the king's writ against charges payable by the community of Aldbourne, and the pipe roll for the next year, which describes the count rendering account of 20s. for Wanborough.[24] The circumstances which led to this recovery of the first Countess Matilda's dowry are unknown. It is, of course, possible that some exchange, involving property on the borders of Normandy, had taken place between Count Rotrou III and his Norman in-laws, but it is perhaps significant that in the summer of 1166 King Henry II had taken action against troublesome subjects on the Manceau/Breton border, including Rotrou's nephew-in-law, John of Alençon. On the grounds of general misgovernment the king had deprived John's father, William Talvas, count of Ponthieu, and his heirs of the castles of Alençon and La Roche-Mabille, and he may also have seized their English lands at the same time. While he was taking this action against his over-mighty subjects, however, King Henry was also in negotiation with Rotrou's brother-in-law, Count Theobald of Blois, to whom he paid a subsidy of £500, and it would be a reasonable step for him to make a friendly gesture towards Rotrou by restoring to him the English property forfeited by his nephew-in-law.[25]

By 1169 Rotrou was in undisputed possession and an act preserved in the cartulary of Lewes Priory indicates that his brother, the otherwise unknown

[23] Bates, 'Normandy and England after 1066', 856.
[24] PR 13 Henry II (1166/7), 127; PR 14 Henry II (1167/8), 159.
[25] Robert of Torigni, Chronique i. 360; Materials for the history of Thomas Becket, ed. J. C. Robertson and J. B. Sheppard (RS lxvii, 1876), vi. 74.

Archdeacon Evrard, was acting as his agent in England.[26] This act is our first evidence for a new expedient in the Rotrous' management of their English property. Although Rotrou II was in England in 1126 and 1139, both visits are closely linked to political events and he probably made little direct contribution to the running of the estates, relying instead on the bailiffs whom he is known to have employed. The residence of the archdeacon in whose presence an act was made in 1169 suggests that the family was beginning to practise division of labour in the exploitation of its lands. Archdeacon Evrard did not perform that task for any length of time, however, for by the mid 1170s the property was in the hands of Count Rotrou's legitimate brother, Geoffrey of the Perche, who received a pardon of 53s. 4d. against charges payable for justice in Wiltshire in 1174/5.[27]

Geoffrey made a career at the court of Henry II, attesting royal acts from the mid 1170s, and his tenure of the Rotrou estates in Wiltshire suggests that a decision had been taken to endow a cadet member of the comital house with the family acquisitions in England.[28] Once established in Wiltshire Geoffrey must have used his access to royal favour to pursue family claims to the lands of Ernulf of Hesdin, which had been inherited through his mother, Hawise. Geoffrey's uncle, Earl Patrick of Salisbury, the brother of Countess Hawise, had already made good his claims to a share of the Hesdin inheritance. In his response to the inquiry into knight service made by King Henry II in the mid 1160s Earl Patrick declared that he held knights' fees from the marriage portion of his mother ('de matrimonio matris meae') and it was probably to this arrangement that Payn of Chaources alluded in the pipe roll of 1166/7 when he rendered £18 13s. 4d. for knight service at Newbury, but asserted that the money ought to be demanded of Earl Patrick who had the knights.[29] By the year of his own death (1179/80) Geoffrey had been successful in securing interests in Ernulf's lands at Newbury (Berks.) and Toddington (Beds.), although as late as 1171 Toddington had still been in the hands of Patrick of Chaources who leased 52 acres of demesne land there.[30]

Geoffrey's accumulation of property had been achieved largely through royal favour. The family had a claim to the two Wiltshire manors through Rotrou II, but arguably they should have passed to the descendants of Rotrou III and Geoffrey's elder half-sister. Possession of the Hesdin interests was probably the result of Geoffrey's own standing with King Henry II, which led to other signs of favour such as the payment to him of £56 recorded in the

---

26 BL, MS Cotton Vespasian F xv, fo. 159v.

27 *PR 21 Henry II (1174/5)*, 103.

28 Holt, 'Politics and property', 12.

29 *Red book of the exchequer*, ed. H. Hall (RS xcix, 1897), i. 298. The figure of 20 knights comes from the *carta* of Payn of Mondoubleau, but Earl Patrick admitted to only 16: *Red book*, i. 241.

30 *26 Henry II (1179/80)*, 46; *29 Henry II (1182/3)*, 82. For Patrick at Toddington see *Cartulary of Bradenstoke*, no. 195.

1180 Norman pipe roll.[31] Title to such acquired property was weaker than that to hereditary lands and when Geoffrey died during the course of the year 1179/80 his modest English property was seized by the crown.[32] It remained in the hands of the sheriff until the summer of 1183 when, probably in recognition of Count Rotrou's role in negotiating with the Young King during his final rebellion, Aldbourne and Wanborough were again restored to Count Rotrou.[33] The pipe rolls do not refer to the payment from Berwick, but that too must have been enjoyed by Rotrou since he granted it to Bradenstoke.

These properties remained the core of the Rotrous' honour in England until the end of the 1180s. As cross-Channel magnates they had not been conspicuously successful. They had missed the early period of opportunity directly after the Conquest, securing their interests only under Henry I. Unlike Henry's 'new men', however, who could devote themselves to his service and their own advancement, Count Rotrou II had other interests, in the Perche and in Spain.[34] The English lands following the female line of descent were assigned as dowry in the 1140s and 1150s, so there was no opportunity for the family to profit from the unsettled conditions of Stephen's reign. Geoffrey of the Perche had re-asserted claims to smallish portions of the Hesdin inheritance, but the Rotrous' English estates were to remain insignificant in the context of aristocratic landholding until 1189 when another royal marriage, this time to a legitimate member of the royal house, took place.

The countess's dowry: the honour of the constable and the lands of Henry of Essex

In July 1189 Geoffrey, eldest son and heir of Count Rotrou III, married Matilda, daughter of Duke Henry the Lion of Saxony and niece of King Richard I of England (1189–99). The marriage refashioned the family's English fortune, for new landed interests on a much grander scale were provided by Matilda's dowry. Such was the scale of these interests that the Rotrou family was lifted from the level of middling barons to a position rivalling that of all but the greatest magnates. As the new countess's marriage portion King Richard gave substantial holdings in Suffolk, Essex and Kent.[35] These lands were a ready-made honour, for they had formerly been the property of Henry of Essex, one of the leading figures at King Henry II's court until his disgrace in 1163, and they were to be used by King Richard to buy the support of the Rotrou lineage.

---

31 *Rotuli scaccarii Normanniae*, i. 39.
32 Holt, 'Politics and property', 19.
33 *PR 29 Henry II (1182/3)*, 128.
34 Cf. the local interests identified in Green, 'Unity and disunity', 131ff.
35 *Gesta*, ii. 73; *Curia regis rolls* xiii. no. 684.

Figure 6
The accumulation of Henry of Essex's lands

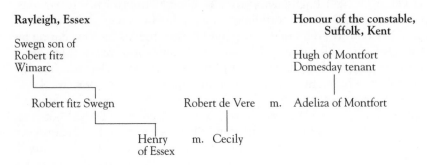

The lands of Henry of Essex which Richard assigned as his niece's dowry had been accumulated through inheritance and marriage over a period of more than one hundred years. The fortunes of Henry's family had been laid by Robert fitzWimarc, a Norman who had settled in England before the Norman Conquest. His son Swegn became the Domesday sheriff of Essex and in 1086 held land centred on Rayleigh in Essex and the manors of Polstead and Stoke-by-Nayland in Suffolk, valued at a total of more than £280.[36] In due course it was inherited by his son, Robert fitzSwegn, and grandson, Henry of Essex. To this property Henry of Essex had added further lands in Suffolk and Essex, together with extensive interests in Kent, as successor to Robert de Vere, who may have been the father of Henry's wife, Cecily. Robert de Vere had been Henry I's constable from around 1127 and continued in office under King Stephen until his death in the early 1150s. Henry inherited Robert de Vere's office and the lands which Robert had acquired through his own wife, Adeliza of Montfort, whom he had married shortly before 1130.[37] The Montfort lands, which thus descended to Henry and were passed on to Count Geoffrey of the Perche, were often known as the honour of the constable or the honour of Haughley from the large manor in Suffolk held by the constable.

The precise date of the grant to Count Geoffrey is unknown. The two components of the constable's property were accounted separately in the pipe rolls during the period when they had been in royal hands and in the last year of the old king Henry's reign Robert de Welles and William of Ashford rendered account of more than £250 for the Montfort lands, while Henry of Cornhill, the sheriff of Surrey, was responsible for receipts of more than £200

---

[36] DB ii. 42, 401; C. P. Lewis, 'The French in England before the Norman Conquest', *ANS* xvii (1994), 128.

[37] For Robert de Vere see J. Green, *The government of England under Henry I*, Cambridge 1986, 276–7. Henry of Essex described Hugh and Robert of Montfort, his predecessors in the honour of the constable, as his relatives 'parentes mei': J. R. Scott, 'Charters of Monks Horton priory', *Archaeologia Cantiana* x (1876), 269–81.

from the land of Henry of Essex.[38] The grant cannot have followed directly on the marriage between Geoffrey and Matilda which took place in July 1189, for these same royal agents accounted for the property when the pipe roll was compiled at Michaelmas of that year.[39]

On 11 October 1189 Henry of Cornhill still held the lands of Henry of Essex for he was confirmed by King Richard in all the offices he held of the crown, except for the bailliwick of London. Like his father, Gervase, before him, Henry of Cornhill had been a useful servant and Richard needed to retain his expertise.[40] Although Geoffrey of the Perche was present at the royal court at Westminster in mid November 1189, it is unlikely that the king chose to grant him the lands of Henry of Essex at that point because in December he issued a confirmation to Henry of Cornhill's ward, Robert fitzPhilip fitzRobert, covering all the lands held by his father and grandfather in Henry of Essex's honour of Rayleigh.[41] Henry of Cornhill had in fact proffered 200 marks for this confirmation and it included specific provision that if Robert were to die before attaining his majority, Henry would be able to retain Robert's lands until he had recovered the cost of the proffer, but its issue indicates that in December 1189 the lands of Henry of Essex were still at the king's disposal.

The grant must have been made during the course of the next few months, however, since King Richard, as he prepared to embark at Marseilles in August 1190, specifically confirmed to Henry of Cornhill a grant made by Geoffrey of the Perche and his wife Matilda, and there are indeed no accounts for Henry of Essex's lands at Michaelmas 1190, merely outstanding debts which the former agents owed.[42] Henry of Cornhill's accounts in the 1180s reveal that the proceeds of these lands had often been used for the expenses of the king's household. In 1183/4, for example, he had spent 16 marks on lengths of cloth and furs which were sent to the king at Limoges and in 1184/5 he disbursed sums on food and wine for the royal household, jewellery and clothing for the king of France's daughter, the Princess Alice. During the course of the year 1189/90 the new king decided that these revenues were better spent in the grand gesture of cultivating the counts of the Perche. It was a significant departure from the practice of his father. Where King Henry had retained Henry of Essex's lands and used their profits, Richard used the

---

38 PR 34 Henry II (1188/89), 16, 28–9.

39 PR 1 Richard 1 (1189), 14–15.

40 BL, MS Harleian charter 43.c.29, indexed as Acta of Henry II and Richard I, ed. J. C. Holt and R. Mortimer (List and Index Society s.s. xxi, 1986), no. 331. For the Cornhill family see S. Reynolds, 'The rulers of London in the twelfth century', History lvii (1972), 346, and J. H. Round, Geoffrey de Mandeville, London 1892, appendix K.

41 Acta of Henry II and Richard I, part two, no. 191, citing Winchester College muniments, MS 9019.

42 PRO, MS Duchy of Lancaster 10/43, calendared as L. Landon, The itinerary of King Richard I (PRS n.s. xiii, 1935), no. 337. I am indebted to Professor Nicholas Vincent for supplying a text of this act. See also PR 2 Richard (1190), 9, 103–112.

lands themselves as a means of securing the goodwill of the Rotrou lineage. Like the marriage of William Marshal to the great heiress Isabel of Clare, it was a great act of generosity by a king who chose to bind men to him in this way.[43]

The precise extent of the lands which passed to Geoffrey of the Perche is difficult to establish. The Domesday account indicates that, even by 1086, much of this property had been granted to subtenants, and the great manor of Clavering was still held in dower by Henry of Essex's step-mother in the 1180s.[44] The monastic foundations of Henry of Essex's forbears had also depleted the landed resources described in Domesday. Cluniac priories had been founded at Prittlewell in Essex and at Monk's Horton in Kent, while Thetford Priory had also profited from the generosity of Geoffrey's predecessors.[45] Further inroads on the lands had been made when they were in royal hands after the disgrace of Henry of Essex in 1163.[46] King Richard's favourite, Baldwin of Béthune, for example, held the former Montfort manor of Brabourne in Kent which he had probably received shortly before the grant to Geoffrey and Master Urricus, the siege engineer, was probably given the manor at Wickford in Essex at the same time.[47]

To form the most accurate picture of the honour of Perche at the turn of the thirteenth century, it is necessary to turn to a series of statements of account (*compotus*) which appear in the pipe rolls, when the Perche property was in the king's hand at various times between 1206 and 1212, and to the seventeen surviving acts, issued by Count Geoffrey before his death in April 1202. The records enrolled in the pipe rolls provide details of the tax assessments of the lands and they also on occasion preserve details of the revenues that the counts might expect from their property, which ranged from the customary payment from poultry-rearing through the proceeds from livestock and grain sales to the perquisites derived from dispensing local justice. The count's own acts register his religious benefactions and the property conveyances he guaranteed, and they survive from all the areas where he held property: Aldbourne (2) and Wanborough (3) in Wiltshire; Toddington (4) in Bedfordshire; Newbury (1) in Berkshire; Essex (4); Suffolk (2) and Kent (1).

The annual value of the property which he accumulated in England seems to have been between £400 and £500. Account is rendered for a grand total of £1,116 20½d. in a *compotus* covering the period Easter 1209 until 22 January 1210, which specifically excluded Aldbourne and Wanborough.[48] Such a figure is probably disproportionately high and reflects the ruthless

---

[43] For Richard's generosity see Gillingham, *Richard I*, 261–2.

[44] *Rotuli de dominabus et pueris et puellis de donatione regis in xii comitatibus 31 Henry II 1185*, ed. J. H. Round (PRS 1913), 77, 29, 76.

[45] *Monasticon*, v. 22–3; Scott, 'Charters of Monks Horton priory', no. i; *Monasticon*, v. 141.

[46] *PR 13 Henry II*, 63; *14 Henry II*, 92, *16 Henry II*, 132.

[47] Scott, 'Charters of Monks Horton priory', no. ix. For Urricus see *Red book*, ii. 596, and Powicke, *Loss of Normandy*, 224.

[48] *PR 12 John (1210)*, 204–5.

exploitation by the king's agent of every resource. The account for the following twelve months to 22 January 1211 shows the much less inflated figure of £266 13s. 4d. which included no pleas, no sales of cheese, wool or hides, and no 'gifts' such as that proffered the year previously by the prior of Wardon.[49] Taking this figure as a base it is possible to deduce an overall figure for the revenues of the count's English property by supplementing it to take account of the property he held at Aldbourne, Wanborough and Newbury. Although these last three were nowhere precisely accounted in the 1200s, Albourne and Wanborough had been accounted for more than £20 annually in 1194 and Newbury for £49 in 1179/80, suggesting an income of more than £400 annually from England.[50]

King Richard's generosity to his niece's husband had, then, established Geoffrey among the English magnates, but that did not necessarily mean that Geoffrey was established in England. Geoffrey's surviving English acts indicate that his English activities were confined to the leasing of property and the confirmation of previous conveyances for fees. There are, for example, four major property conveyances among the seven surviving acts relating to Matilda's dowry lands in Essex, Suffolk and Kent: two in the hundred of Rochford, Co. Essex to Lawrence fitz Jordan of Paglesham for rents of £8 and £6 annually, the third to Geoffrey Perdriz at Eastwood, Co. Essex and the fourth to Simon fitz Odin in Hadleigh, Co. Essex.[51] There is no indication that Geoffrey intended to settle the English lands or to behave as anything other than a rentier landlord. All Geoffrey's English acts involve the transfer of property to men whose interests lay in England, and the knights who paid scutage for fees in Geoffrey's honours are men who had been appearing in the pipe rolls for some time, rather than Percheron settlers. Robert de Scalis, for example, to whom before 1198 Geoffrey conceded the right to present to the church of Wetherden (Co. Suffolk), was a member of a long-established East Anglian family. His father, Roger de Scalis, of Middleton near Lynn had founded the nunnery of Blackborough in the mid twelfth century and his son, also Roger de Scalis, was to hold five fees of the honour of the Perche in 1206.[52] Reginald fitz Serlo who paid scutage as a Perche tenant in the 1206 list is recorded as holding property from the honour of Henry of Essex as early as 1180/1 and continued to do so in 1211/12.[53]

Some of Geoffrey's tenants were important figures in their own right. Philip of Columbières, for example, who held five fees of the honour of the

49 PR 13 John (1211), 82–3.
50 PR 6 Richard I (1194), 18; PR 25 Henry II (1179/80), 46.
51 Canterbury, Dean and Chapter archives, MSS carta antiqua R62, T27; BL, MS Harleian charter 54.g.26; PRO, MS E40/3873.
52 BL, MS Egerton 3137 (cartulary of Blackborough), fo. 101v; CP xi. 496ff.; PR 8 John 1206, 180.
53 PR 8 John (1206), 179; PR 27 Henry II (1180/1), 107; Red book, 596. Reginald witnessed two of Geoffrey's acts: Canterbury D&C, MS carta antiqua T27, and BL, MS Harleian charter 54.g.26.

constable, had inherited the Domesday interests of Robert of Chandos in East Anglia and was a substantial landholder in Somerset.[54] Reginald of Cornhill was a son of Gervase of Cornhill and brother of the Henry of Cornhill who had administered Henry of Essex's lands in the reign of Henry II. In the mid 1190s Reginald became sheriff of Kent and in 1206 held a knight's fee of the honour of the Perche.[55] Reginald witnessed an act in which land in Suffolk was conceded by Count Geoffrey in return for a twentieth part of a knight's fee to Osbert fitzHervey, the king's justice. Osbert, who served on the king's bench and in the exchequer under King Richard and King John, had begun his career under Henry of Essex and was for a time an under-sheriff. A memorable portrait of him is preserved in the 'Vision of Thurkill' by Ralph of Coggeshall. Osbert it seems was famous for his 'over-flowing eloquence and experience in the law', but was guilty of taking bribes from litigants and in hell he was forced to swallow burning coins and then regurgitate them.[56]

There are few indications that Geoffrey's Percheron subjects had interests in his English lands. It appears that Geoffrey (or his father) assigned a rent in Wanborough to Robert Quarel, probably a member of the prominent Percheron family from Pervenchères (Orne) but no further information is available and the only Percheron for whom it is possible to trace substantial English interests is Hugh of Tabarie.[57] All Count Geoffrey's English acts, with the exception of that confirming the church of Toddington to the abbey of La Couture in Le Mans, were witnessed by Hugh, and he is described as the count's seneschal in *curia regis* records of 1200.[58] Hugh first appears in an act by Count Rotrou III dated 17 April 1186 in favour of the cathedral of Le Mans and he probably originated from the area immediately to the north-west of Nogent-le-Rotrou, if he is identical with the Hugh of Thagaric mentioned in an act analysed by the nineteenth-century French antiquarian, Stanislaus Proust. In the act Hugh and his wife, Anne of Doncourt, gave half the patronage of the church of Préaux-du-Perche (Orne, cant. Nocé) to the Maison-Dieu in Nogent-le-Rotrou. Unfortunately this act can no longer be located in the archives of the hospital, but the identification is supported by a further link between Hugh and the hospital, since the churches of Aldbourne and Wanborough, where Hugh was tenant-in-chief by 1210/12, were given to the hospital by Count Rotrou III in 1190.[59]

Geoffrey's religious benefactions reveal something of this attitude too. He

---

[54] I. Sanders, *English baronies*, Oxford 1960, 67.

[55] *PR 8 Richard I (1196)*, 288; *PR 8 John 1206*, 179.

[56] For Geoffrey's grant to Osbert see PRO, MS E 210/1532. The vision of Thurkill is quoted in R. V. Turner, 'The reputation of royal judges under the Angevin kings', *Albion* xi (1979), 306, repr. in his *Judges, administrators and the common law in Angevin England*, London 1994, 108.

[57] BL, MS Stowe 666, fo. 79.

[58] *Curia regis rolls* i. 124.

[59] *Chart. cenom.*, no. dxxxv; *Inventaire sommaire des archives des hospices de Nogent-le-Rotrou*, 8; Bry, *Additions*, 75; *Red book*, ii. 482.

picked up the threads of the Chaources' lordship in Toddington, confirming their benefactions to Dunstable priory and the grant of its church to the abbey of Saint-Pierre of La Couture in Le Mans by his ancestors, Patrick and Matilda of Chaources. He also practised a conventional family piety when he conceded 8s. annual rent at Wanborough to the priory at Bradenstoke, where his great-grandparents, Walter of Salisbury and Sibyl of Chaources, were buried, but there is little to indicate commitment to the English properties.[60] When a new Premonstratensian house was founded by former Montfort tenants at St Radegund's in Bradsole, near Dover, Geoffrey and Matilda jointly conceded the endowment. Surprisingly, however, they granted no other confirmations to religious houses, such as Monk's Horton or Prittlewell, which their predecessors had founded, even though both houses were Cluniac foundations and the Rotrou family had close links with that order.[61] A grant of two virgates of land at Aldbourne to fund the supply of wine for the mass at the Augustinian priory of Southwick in Hampshire made by Geoffrey and Matilda between 1194 and 1199 appears to favour a house conveniently situated for a passage between northern France and the Wiltshire/Berkshire estates. The act is witnessed, however, by Master Reginald, the head of the hospital at Nogent-le-Rotrou, the Maison Dieu, and by Master Hugh, the physician, and this medical element suggests that it may have been a thank-offering, possibly by the countess, who, although she had no family interest in Aldbourne, is given a prominent place within the act and described as the niece of the illustrious king of the English and daughter of the duke of Bavarians and Saxons.[62]

Geoffrey had succeeded to a ready-made honour from which it was easy to take the profits, yet there are indications that the flow of wealth from England to the Perche was not always smooth. The terms of the treaty of Mantes, negotiated between King Philip of France and King Richard's Norman agents during Richard's captivity, are revealing.[63] They specify Philip's gains in his recent campaigns, but they also make a number of provisos concerning Philip's allies, among whom was Count Geoffrey of the Perche. Geoffrey's demands were that he should have full enjoyment of his rents in England and that there should be peace between the king of England's men and himself. The implication is therefore that Geoffrey's access to the profits of his English property had been impeded. Possibly the English authorities, in their eagerness to raise Richard's ransom, had prevented coin from being exported. The treaty refers specifically to rents in contrast to the land of other lords, such as the count of Meulan, which had

---

[60] BL, MS Harleian 1885 (cartulary of Dunstable), fo. 27v; *La Couture*, no. clxv; BL, MS Cotton Vitellius A xi, fo. 105.

[61] *Monasticon* vi. 941.

[62] *Cartularies of Southwick*, 87–8.

[63] Roger of Howden, *Chronica* iii. 217–20.

apparently been seized, and it may be that Geoffrey's preoccupation, as articulated to the French king, was with the rents rather than the lands.

When King Richard eventually returned from captivity in the spring of 1194 he found Count Geoffrey ranged amongst his enemies, and his irritation is made manifest in the pipe rolls. Just as the king had used lands in England to bind Geoffrey to him when he married Matilda, so the lands were used to convey his displeasure.[64] The pipe roll of 1194 shows that Geoffrey's property at Aldbourne, Wanborough, Toddington and an income of 37s. from the Berwick holding had been in the king's hand for three months.[65] The count was thus deprived of his English property, although King Richard pointedly did not touch the countess's dowry. The deprivation was not long-lasting however, for Richard needed to recover his position against the Capetian king and Geoffrey's goodwill was invaluable to him. By September of the next year all the property had been restored to the count and the only mention of the forfeiture to appear in the 1195 pipe roll is a reference to the sum of 24s. outstanding against the perquisites of Toddington for the previous half year.[66] At some point, therefore, in the year 1194/5 Richard and Geoffrey must have been reconciled and, as might be expected of Richard, new signs of favour followed.

In 1196 Geoffrey was granted exemption in Essex and Kent from the second scutage, which was levied to fund the king's campaigns in Normandy, and the debts of his uncle Geoffrey of the Perche, which had been contracted to the Jewish financier, Aaron of Lincoln, in the 1170s and were chargeable against the Wiltshire property, were allowed to run.[67] It was probably at this time too that Geoffrey received additional property in Newbury (Berks.) and Chelsfield (Kent). His ancestor, Ernulf of Hesdin, had held both manors at Domesday, when they rendered £24 and £35 respectively.[68] King Henry II had apparently recognised the family's claims by granting some of Newbury's proceeds to Geoffrey of the Perche but after Geoffrey's death it remained in the king's possession until at least the autumn of 1194.[69] Less is known of the history of Chelsfield between 1086 and its appearance in an account of the count of Perche's lands rendered in 1205, when it is linked with Newbury. It was, however, a particularly valuable holding in 1086 and for much of the twelfth century was held by one family which took its name as a toponymic.[70]

---

[64] On Richard's attitude to those 'who had let him down' see Gillingham, *Richard I*, 262.

[65] *PR 6 Richard 1 (1194)*, 18, 26, 199.

[66] *PR 7 Richard 1 (1195)*, 61.

[67] *PR 8 Richard 1 (1196)*, 120, 288, 6.

[68] DB i. 62b, 6b.

[69] For Ernulf's grant to Préaux see *Monasticon* vi. 1027. For Newbury in the hands of Pagan of Chaources see *PR 13 Henry II (1166–67)*, 6. See also *PR 26 Henry II (1179/30)*, 46; *PR 6 Richard I (1194)*, 254.

[70] *Textus roffensis*, ed. T. Hearne, Oxford 1720, 236; *Calendar of Kent feet of fines to the end of Henry III's reign*, ed. I. J. Churchill, R. Griffin and R. W. Hardman (Kent Records xv, 1956), 9–10; *Records of the Templars in England in the twelfth century: the inquest of 1185*, ed. B. A.

Patronage continued to flow from the English crown to the Rotrous, then, throughout the 1190s with only the one minor interruption in 1194 and culminating in the grant of the castles of Moulins and Bonsmoulins in Normandy. There is, however, some evidence that the family treated their English holdings in much the same way as King Richard treated his English kingdom – as a source of revenue rather than as a place of residence. There is only one conclusive piece of evidence for a visit by Count Geoffrey to England, which took place in the late autumn of 1189. Geoffrey's acts relating to English property are attested by men whose toponymics link them to England which suggests that the acts were given in England, but none is dated and they could all have been given during the visit of 1189 or given in the Perche and witnessed by representatives of the English tenants.

In the mid 1190s, at some point after the election of Herbert le Poer as bishop of Salisbury on 5 June 1194, Geoffrey and Matilda made their strongest commitment to their English property, using some of their recently acquired resources to found an Augustinian priory at Sandleford just outside Newbury, to which they committed the church and land of Sandleford, the wood of Brademore and thirteen marks of revenue from the mills of Newbury.[71] It was not a particularly generous endowment and the house struggled to survive for the rest of the Middle Ages, but it set the seal on Rotrou family possession of the town of Newbury, where their tenure was less secure. By the end of Richard's reign Count Geoffrey of the Perche was a significant English proprietor with an income little short of £450 a year. It was a remarkable advance in the family's fortunes and an indication of the value which Richard placed on the continued co-operation of the Perche.

To secure that co-operation Richard was prepared to offer not only a marriage alliance with a Plantagenet princess, but also property whose worth was far beyond anything previously held by the Rotrous in England. At first sight the magnitude of the inducement is surely an indication of the seriousness with which King Richard viewed the situation facing him in 1189 and suggests that his assessment of King Philip's calibre as an opponent was markedly higher than that of his father. Should Richard's generosity therefore be seen as the desperate act of a ruler whose realm was disintegrating under the attacks of a determined opponent? The more successful of Richard's ducal ancestors, William the Conqueror and Henry I, would certainly have been reluctant to alienate their castles in the way that Richard had disposed of Moulins and Bonsmoulins, but they would have recognised the need to reward loyalty and could be generous when the need arose. Richard was particularly skilled in the exercise of patronage and seems to have been a good judge of character.[72] Richard's favour to Count Geoffrey was more likely

---

Lees, London 1935, 24; *Reading Abbey cartularies*, ed. B. Kemp (Camden Society 4th ser. xxxi, xxxiii, 1986–7), nos 249, 251, 253a, 257, 248, 259, 260.

71 *Monasticon*, vi. 565. For subsequent history see VCH, *Berkshire*, ii. London 1907, 86–8.

72 J. Gillingham, 'The art of kingship: Richard I, 1189–99', *History Today* (April 1985),

a manifestation of a different kind of kingship than an act of desperation and it is certain that he exercised that patronage at times when his own fortune was high (1189/90, 1196/8).

Circumstances were perhaps rather different under King John, whose position as Richard's successor was by no means secure. While England clearly acknowledged the king's brother, Count John, as king, the continental lands wavered and Anjou, Maine and Touraine opted for Arthur of Brittany, the son of Count John's elder brother, Geoffrey. A divided succession was a possibility and the geographical position of the Perche between the two blocs made wholehearted support of either candidate difficult. Countess Matilda was left to maintain contacts with her uncle, Count John, whom she saw at Fontevraud in April 1199, and an exemption for the Essex property from the scutage assessed at two marks, which was issued shortly after John's coronation in May 1199, indicates that there was no threat of dispossession. Count Geoffrey seems to have remained uncommitted, however, during the months which followed until in September 1199 he appeared at King John's court at Le Mans and from then on he acknowledged John as Richard's successor.[73]

For John, however, the essential acknowledgement was that of the French king, Philip Augustus, and that acknowledgement was not forthcoming for more than a year after Richard's death. When it finally came in the treaty of Le Goulet on 22 May 1199 Count Geoffrey of the Perche had a major part to play, for he was one of King Philip's guarantors.[74] Two days later on 24 May 1199 'for his homage and service' John gave Geoffrey the sum of £1,000. He specified that it was to be taken from new enfeoffments on the lands of Henry of Essex, which the count was holding, and he made over the lands to the count, promising to compensate those to whom the enfeoffments had been made.[75] In addition the king conceded the revenues of the royal manor of Shrivenham in Wiltshire until land of an equal value could be found. Shrivenham had been assessed at 46 hides in 1086 when it was worth £45, but in 1202, when the sheriff of Berkshire accounted on Geoffrey's behalf, the figure involved was £52 and it is possible that Geoffrey was granted the royal rights from the whole hundred of which Shrivenham was the head.[76] The remainder of the £1,000 was to be delivered to the count through the English exchequer at Easter and Michaelmas until the king could make up the difference in lands from escheats.

The weakness of John's initial position made it necessary for him to cultivate Geoffrey who was able to re-establish contacts with the French king in a

17–18, repr. in his *Richard Coeur de Lion: kingship, chivalry and war in the twelfth century*, London 1994, 95–6. On the debate about Richard's kingship see R. V. Turner, 'Good or bad kingship? The case of Richard Lionheart', *Haskins Society Journal* viii (1996), 63–78.

[73] *CDF*, no. 1301; *PR 1 John* (1199), 180; *Rot. chart.*, 31.

[74] *Diplomatic documents*, no. 9.

[75] *Rot. chart.*, 64b. Geoffrey's own notification of the grant is also enrolled ibid. 96.

[76] DB i. 57b; *PR 4 John* (1202), 1, 2.

way that had never been necessary for his brother, King Richard, and the repercussions of John's favour to Geoffrey can be traced in the records dating from the early years of his reign. On 29 September 1201, for instance, the king authorised Geoffrey fitzPeter to give William of Bretteville cash for the value of his land at Rotherhithe, one of the new enfeoffments that had been given to Geoffrey, until land of equal value could be assigned to him.[77] William, however, was not prepared to accept this arrangement and in 1202 he undertook to pay 40 marks of silver for seisin of his lands, paying ten marks into the English exchequer and twenty into the king's treasury at Montfort by March 1202.[78] King John therefore ordered William's land and that of Hugh Neville at Waching, and Master Urricus to be restored, but was careful to indemnify Geoffrey against any loss.[79] As the new king's title became more secure, his favour towards his niece's husband none the less continued. A fine (prestitum) incurred on the Essex estates for infringement of royal forest rights was allowed to remain unpaid over a number of years and the debts of Count Geoffrey's uncle, Geoffrey of the Perche, continued to run. Exemptions were given against the scutage in 1201 and Geoffrey was able too to secure concessions related to his crusading intentions.[80]

Dispossession

The sudden death of Count Geoffrey in 1202 placed the responsibility for the Perche and for the English estates upon the countess who undertook the task with some competence. Within weeks of the death of her husband in early April she had made a deal to repay the 300 marks of silver which her husband had borrowed from his cousin, William Marshal.[81] On 8 September at Sainte-Suzanne in Maine the king gave a truce to 'his most beloved niece and her fee' and shortly thereafter at the Michaelmas exchequer the royal generosity continued with payments from Shrivenham, exemptions from scutage payments and continued acceptance of non-payment of debt.[82]

When King John's rule in Normandy began to collapse during the course of 1203 his favour towards his niece remained constant, and the 1203 pipe roll indicates the same payments, exemptions and indebtedness.[83] Yet by the end of the year even she was being pressed to provide more for the failing Norman war effort. By November some of her English property had already been seized by the justiciar, Geoffrey fitzPeter, and at the end of a year when

---

[77] Rotuli de liberate ac de misis de praestitis, 20.
[78] Rotuli de oblatis et finibus, 186; PR 4 John (1202), 271, 275, 186.
[79] Rot. de liberate ac de misis de praestitis, 28.
[80] PR 3 John (1201), 70, 76, 141, 172, 173; Rot. litt. pat., 7.
[81] Rot. litt. pat., 9b.
[82] Ibid. 18.
[83] PR 5 John (1203), 44, 97, 128.

nearly £15,000 was imported from England the countess was prevailed upon to deliver £100 annually to the king, to render scutage whenever it was required in England and to perform ten knights' service for the lands which the count of the Perche held of the duke of Normandy at Bellême.[84] In return the king ordered fitzPeter to restore the countess's property after he had taken the £100.[85]

On 5 December 1203 King John set sail from Normandy for England. He was never to return to the duchy as duke, leaving it to be overrun by the forces of King Philip of France in the course of 1204. At the time he may have thought it would be easier to mobilise his English resources within the kingdom, and his return to England was indeed followed by a tallage of the towns and a scutage raised on land held by military tenure. Countess Matilda's scutage for her lands in Kent and East Anglia was duly accounted at the exchequer at Michaelmas 1204 and the king's exemption from her tallage obligations is recorded both in the pipe roll and the Liberate roll, but the honour of the Perche was no longer completely protected by her royal status.[86] During the summer of 1204, as first Château Gaillard, then Caen and finally Rouen itself were taken by Philip Augustus, John began to chip away at the Rotrou family holdings.

Initially his targets were those parts of the family property whose tenure was owed to royal favour: Shrivenham, Newbury and Toddington.[87] The payments from the royal manor of Shrivenham ceased after March 1204, and by 3 June Simon of Pattishall, a trusted royal agent and justice of the king's bench, had custody of Newbury.[88] Some weeks later, on 24 July 1204, the king ordered Simon to hand over all the count's lands in his possession, with the exception of the manor of Shrivenham, to his own illegitimate son, Geoffrey, and on 13 September it was to this same individual that he ordered the sheriff of Kent to deliver the manor of Selling in Kent.[89] Toddington was assigned to John's financial adviser, Peter des Roches, who would shortly be elevated to the bishopric of Winchester.[90]

The factor which united the three manors of Shrivenham, Newbury and Toddington was a recent royal interest. Shrivenham had been a royal manor in 1066 and had remained so until its revenues had been assigned to Geoffrey in 1202. Newbury had been part of the royal demesne as recently as 1194 and

[84] Powicke, *Loss of Normandy*, 235 n. 157; *Rot. de liberate ac de misis de praestitis*, 74. The agreement was accounted in *PR 6 John (1204)*, 15.
[85] *Rot. de liberate ac de misis de praestitis*, 74.
[86] *PR 6 John (1204)*, 217, 242, 61; *Rot de liberate ac de misis de praestitis*, 92.
[87] *Rot. norm.*, 132, 137.
[88] *PR 6 John (1204)*, 56. For earlier payments from Shrivenham see *PR 4 John (1202)*, 1–2; *PR 5 John (1203)*, 44; *Rot. litt. claus.*, i. 1. For Simon see R. V. Turner, 'Simon of Pattishall', *Northamptonshire Past and Present* vi (1978), 5–14.
[89] *Rot. litt. claus.*, i. 3b, 8b.
[90] *Rot. norm.*, 131; N. Vincent, *Peter des Roches: an alien in English politics, 1205–1238*, Cambridge 1996, 57ff.

Toddington had been partitioned between King Henry II and Geoffrey of the Perche in the 1170s. As King John desperately looked for funds during the spring and early summer of 1204 these connections gave him his opportunity. Despite the repossessions, however, the king went to some lengths to preserve the Rotrou family association with the lands. He guaranteed two pensions which Count Geoffrey had granted from the revenues of Newbury, ordering that Simon of Pattishall was to be reimbursed for their continued payment, and he instructed Simon to honour Count Geoffrey's grant of a rent from the mill at Newbury to the canons of Sandleford.[91]

Confident in the agreement she had made with her uncle in the previous November, Matilda assigned ten marks from her manor of Haughley in Suffolk to her newly-founded nunnery at Les Clairets, near Nogent-le-Rotrou, in July 1204, and she met most of her tax obligations, but to no avail, for by April 1205 the king had seized the whole of the honour.[92] It was placed under the control of Peter of Stoke, whose seneschal, Gilbert of Stanford, gave a precise account for the scutage of all the Rotrou family lands in September 1205.[93] There were by Gilbert's own account ('ut ipse dicit') forty-six and a sixth knights' fees in the honour of Henry of Essex; fifty-three, one half, an eighth and a quarter knights' fees in the honour of Haughley, and ten and a half in Chelsfield, Aldbourne and Wanborough.[94] John's machinery of government was remarkably thorough for none of the Rotrou interests were overlooked. The king ordered the sheriff of Norfolk and Suffolk to seize any interests in the fee of the count of the Perche held by Hubert de Burgh and to add it to the property in Gilbert of Stanford's custody. Despite his valiant service in defending the castle of Chinon in the Loire valley against the forces of King Philip of France, Hubert de Burgh, the king's chamberlain, was under something of a shadow at the time and the king's instruction must refer to property which Hubert, an East Anglian by origin, had secured from the count of the Perche, rather than to any custody arrangement put in place by the king himself.[95]

The honour remained in royal hands for the best part of two years, first under the control of Peter of Stokes and then from August 1206 under that of Robert Deverell.[96] The reassignment was probably caused by the death of Peter of Stoke, who was certainly dead by 3 March 1207 when the king ordered that his estate should be credited with the costs of the property and livestock with which Peter had equipped the Rotrou family lands while he had held them on the king's behalf.[97] There is no indication, however, of the

91 Rot. litt. claus., i. 3b.
92 Clairets, no. iv; PR 6 John (1204), 217, 242.
93 Rott litt. claus., i. 51b; PR 7 John (1205), 174–5.
94 PR 7 John (1205), 175.
95 Rot. litt. claus., i. 51b; F. A. Cazel, 'Intertwined careers: Hubert de Burgh and Peter des Roches', Haskins Society Journal i (1989), 174–5.
96 Rot. litt. pat., 66b.
97 Rot. litt. claus., i. 79.

king's reason for withholding Newbury, Aldbourne and Wanborough from Robert Deverell's stewardship, but this division of the honour was not long-lasting, for during the course of the year 1206/7 Matilda negotiated with her uncle and offered 2,000 marks to have all the lands of her late husband, except Shrivenham, together with custody of her son.[98] Clearly the king could do little to prevent the countess's control of her son, but the size of the fine she was prepared to offer reveals her commitment to the English property, as well as the increasing rapacity of the king's demands. Her initial payment of 400 marks secured her wishes, and in early February 1207 Robert Deverell presented a *compotus* at the exchequer on surrendering the lands. Altogether nearly £200 had been raised in less than six months, of which £190 was paid into the king's chamber.[99] The keeper's statement is a long catalogue of livestock, produce and timber sold, and reveals that Toddington had been restored to the honour.

For the next few years the countess held the family property and there are signs that she made every attempt to stay on the right side of her royal uncle. Her seneschal, Robert Gulaur', was summoned for non-payment of twenty-nine and half marks outstanding from the fourth scutage taken in 1204 and although he did not attend the hearing, the sum of £10 3s. 9d. was paid into the treasury.[100] A long running debt for infringements of forest law dating from before the death of Count Geoffrey was settled and a further 400 marks were paid against the countess's debt.[101] At Michaelmas 1209 a sterling effort was made to pay off the fourth scutage debt and the knights account for their payments.[102] Despite these efforts to retain the good opinion of the king, however, when Countess Matilda died in January 1210 John had little time for family feeling. Disregarding the rights of his great-nephew, Count Thomas, the entire honour of the Perche was seized. From midsummer 1210 Aldbourne and Wanborough were assigned to John's Tourangeau favourite, Gerald of Athée. The rest of the property was placed in the custody of Fulk of Kantelou.[103]

In less than nine months Fulk squeezed £1085 1s. 9½d. from the honour of the Perche in a combination of rents, judicial perquisites, sales of livestock, produce and timber and the enforcement of feudal rights, such as fines for marriages, reliefs and custodies of under-age heirs. During the succeeding eighteen months to Michaelmas 1212 the rate of exploitation slowed with only £266 8s. paid into the treasury and £252 12s. 4½d. accounted at Michaelmas 1212. By then Toddington was separately accounted for, but Newbury may well have been added to the custody of Fulk of Kantelou for

---

98   *PR 9 John 1207*, 100.
99   *PR 9 John 1207*, 112–13. See *Rot. litt. claus.*, i. 80b for the receipt.
100 *Memoranda roll 10 John (1207/8)*, 59; *PR 10 John (1208)*, 5.
101 *Memoranda roll 10 John (1207/8)*, 59; *PR 10 John (1208)*, 5, 29.
102 *PR 11 John (1209)*, 42.
103 *PR 12 John (1210)*, 204–5; *PR 14 John (1212)*, 1–2.

Count Geoffrey's pension to Hamo le Bret, originally derived from the revenues of Newbury, was accounted by Fulk on the 1212 pipe roll.[104] Altogether it was a remarkable piece of asset-stripping and reveals much about the rapacity of John's regime.

In the closing years of King John's reign the property remained in royal hands and the *Red book of the exchequer* lists under 'Inquisitiones de honoribus eschaetis aliquo tempore' the honours of Perche, Rayleigh and Haughley.[105] From time to time the king drew on their resources: in 1214, for example, he ordered 40 marks of rent from the honour of the Perche to be assigned to two of Hugh of Boves's knights, and in 1216 he presented to the living of Hadleigh.[106] The honour of the Perche disappears from the last pipe roll of John''s reign, that of 1214, however, and Fulk of Kantelou accounts only for the lands which belonged to Henry of Essex, so John must have used the ancestral lands of the Rotrous in Wiltshire and the central English counties for other purposes.[107] An indication of those purposes is given by John's order in 1216 to his mercenary captain and leading henchman, Fawkes de Breauté, to deliver to Payn of Chaources possession of *Newchir*. As this must surely be a reference to Newbury, it is not unlikely that John had assigned the Perche patrimony to Fawkes sometime shortly before.

None the less John's reassignment of Newbury to Payn was made on condition that the legal right of the king's great-nephew, the son of the count of Perche, was preserved and that Payn was to act as keeper during the king's pleasure.[108] This formula suggests that, even as his rule was collapsing around him and under threat from an invasion by Prince Louis, the son of Philip Augustus, John was still reluctant to relinquish the notion that it might one day still be possible to hold lands in both France and England and that legal rights should not therefore be extinguished. Although no formal record has survived, it seems that John granted the honours of Rayleigh and Haughley to his justiciar, Hubert de Burgh, on precisely these terms 'during the king's pleasure' and in July 1217 these grants were renewed in the name of the young King Henry III.[109]

Reallocation

The battle of Lincoln in which Count Thomas of the Perche lost his life was a decisive victory for the forces of the young king of England, Henry III (1216–72), but the French troops under the command of Prince Louis still

---

104 John had guaranteed Hamo's pension: *Rot. litt. claus.*, i. 1.
105 *Book of fees*, 1154; *Red book* ii. 595–7, 621–2.
106 *Rot. litt. claus.*, i. 162b; *Rot. litt. pat.*, 199.
107 *PR 16 John (1215)*, 9.
108 *Rot litt. claus.*, i, 250b.
109 *Cal. pat. rolls, 1216–25*, 82.

remained in England and the rest of the summer was spent in negotiation before Louis finally retired to France in late September.[110] Despite these pressing concerns those who ruled England on young Henry's behalf still found time to dispose of Count Thomas's lands. On 21 June, a month after the death of Count Thomas, instructions were sent to the sheriffs of Wiltshire, Berkshire and Buckinghamshire that Aldbourne, Newbury and Toddington should be handed over to the king's uncle, William Longspey, earl of Salisbury. The instruction concerning Aldbourne specifically mentions that it was to be held on the same terms as Count Geoffrey held it on the day of his death and the instruction was repeated on 27 October when Aldbourne, Wanborough and Newbury were assigned to Salisbury.[111] One month after the first instruction on 24 July the two substantial additions to the Rotrou family interests, the constable's honour of Haughley and the honour of Rayleigh, the patrimony of Henry of Essex, were assigned, during the king's pleasure, to the justiciar Hubert de Burgh.

The distinction in the two grants, the one outright grant to Salisbury, the other to de Burgh during the king's pleasure, reflects the composition of the honour of the Perche. The property which was allocated to the earl of Salisbury was essentially the core of the honour of the Perche: the two Wiltshire manors acquired through the first marriage of Count Rotrou II and two properties associated with Ernulf de Hesdin, Newbury and Toddington, although there was no mention of the manor of Chelsfield, which had also been held by Ernulf.[112] It may well be that Salisbury represented himself as Thomas's nearest heir, for his wife, Ella, was the grand-daughter of Earl Patrick of Salisbury, brother of Countess Hawise of the Perche and uncle of Count Thomas's grandfather, Count Rotrou III.

The lands allocated to Hubert de Burgh, however, had come to the Rotrou family at the end of the twelfth century through Count Geoffrey's marriage to Matilda of Saxony. The earl of Salisbury would have a less defensible claim to those lands and, with the death of the countess's only son, Count Thomas, they might be considered to have reverted to the crown. The final element of Count Geoffrey III's interests in England, the former royal manor of Shrivenham, had already gone its own way. In February 1217 it had been granted during the king's pleasure to Henry of Trublevill and in November 1217 it was granted on the same terms to Robert of Dreux, a cousin of the French king. These arrangements are therefore understandable, but they were not long-standing, for within months of Count Thomas's death the Perche inheritance was to be taken in hand by the regent, William Marshal.[113]

From relatively modest beginnings as the second son of the second

---

110 J. B. Smith, 'The treaty of Lambeth, 1217', *EHR* xciv (1979), 562–79.
111 *Rot. litt. claus.*, i. 311b. *Red book* ii. 748, adds Wanborough to the other three properties.
112 *Rot. litt. claus.*, i. 333.
113 *Cal. pat. rolls, 1216–25*, 34; *Rot. litt. claus.*, i. 306b; *Cal. pat. rolls, 1216–25*, 119.

marriage of a small landed proprietor in Wiltshire, William Marshal had established a formidable reputation as a knight and came to move among the highest circles, serving in turn the Young King and King Henry II.[114] For his loyalty to the royal house he was rewarded by Richard I with the hand of one of the wealthiest heiresses of her day, Isabel of Clare, and William became earl of Pembroke. He continued to serve King John and was one of the few lords who managed to retain lands in England and France after 1204. On the death of King John he was persuaded to assume the title of rector of the kingdom as protector of the young king, Henry III.

William Marshal was also a cousin of the counts of the Perche, for his mother, Sibyl, was the sister of Earl Patrick of Salisbury and Countess Hawise of the Perche. The family connection can seldom be detected in contemporary sources, though it may well have influenced the relationship between the Rotrous and the English crown. Family links were maintained as the presence of Anselm Marshal, William's younger brother at the foundation ceremony for Val Dieu in 1170 demonstrates, and it cannot have been without significance that when in 1183 William left the court of the Young King under something of a shadow he did so by way of the Perche.[115] In the 1190s when relations between the counts of the Perche and the English crown were at their warmest William was enjoying a period of consistent royal favour and it was William who lent Count Geoffrey substantial sums to fund his crusading endeavours.[116]

In December of 1217 the new count of the Perche, Thomas's uncle, William, bishop of Châlons-en-Champagne, arrived in England.[117] The purpose of his visit is unclear. In the safe conduct for him enrolled in the patent rolls there is reference to the count-bishop dealing with the king about his business ('ad tractandum nobiscum de agendis suis'), but as the king was a young boy his business was most likely with the regent. There are no contemporary records of the outcome of the count-bishop's visit, but an inquiry preserved in the *Liber feodorum* indicates that William Marshal and the earl of Salisbury used the opportunity to buy off his rights.[118] Some years later in 1220 when he was summoned to an English court the count-bishop nominated William Marshal to take his place.[119] With the last heir of the Rotrou family suitably compensated William Marshal and the earl of Salisbury partitioned the Perche property. Salisbury took Aldbourne and Wanborough and the Marshal Newbury and Toddington.[120]

---

114 S. Painter, *William Marshal*, Baltimore 1933; G. Duby, *Guillaume le maréchal, ou le meilleur chevalier du monde*, Paris 1984; Crouch, *William Marshal*.
115 RCVD, fos. 1–2; *Histoire de Guillaume le maréchal*, lines 5838–40.
116 *Rot. litt. pat.*, 9b.
117 See *Cal. pat. rolls, 1216–25*, 129, for letters patent granting William a safe conduct to England.
118 'Emerunt ius suum': *Book of fees*, 1154.
119 *Curia regis rolls* ix. 301.
120 Carpenter, *Minority*, 92.

It was not the first time that William Marshal had apparently benefited from proximity to the Rotrous. At the turn of the thirteenth century he had secured Chambois in southern Normandy, which had been held by Stephen of the Perche, brother of Count Geoffrey III during the lifetime of King Richard, and he was permitted by King John to retain the profits of a Jew whom Stephen had settled there.[121] The appropriation of the English honour of the Perche was, however, an act of opportunism and it is in the words of the Marshal's distinguished biographer, Sidney Painter, 'impossible to justify William's part in this transaction. The honor of Perche belonged either to the bishop of Chalons or to the king as an escheat'.[122] It was none the less a successful manoeuvre and the two elder statesmen also secured possession of the royal manor of Shrivenham, despite the tenuousness of the Rotrou claim to it.

Although the honour of the Perche would survive as a convenient description used by royal clerks for much of the thirteenth century, it had effectively ceased to exist when the count-bishop William sold his rights to his cousins. It had begun as a relatively small holding, intended to secure the support of King Henry I's son-in-law and neighbour, Rotrou II of the Perche. Although only two manors were involved, their tenure gave Rotrou an interest in continuing his support for Henry as ruler of both England and Normandy. When the two parts of the Anglo-Norman realm had drifted apart under King Stephen it must have become difficult to administer the properties and the Rotrou family were content that they should slip from its control as a dowry for Rotrou II's granddaughter. King Henry II revived the policy of his grandfather however and rekindled an alliance with the Rotrou dynasty using English property as encouragement. The inducements he offered were by no means grand, and the change of scale in the next generation is remarkable and significant.

Richard I offered the count of the Perche a marriage alliance with a Plantagenet princess and widespread and lucrative property in England. In the debate about the revenues available to the Plantagenet and Capetian kings in the closing years of the twelfth century the consensus points in Philip Augustus' favour, but Richard clearly understood and ruthlessly used the resources of his English kingdom to great effect.[123] The seizure of the Rotrou lands in the months immediately after the loss of Normandy and the fate of those lands at the hands of King John's agents were an early indication of the rapacity that would eventually provoke the English barons into open revolt. None the less John's reluctance to abandon completely the legal rights of those, like the Rotrous, whose primary interests lay in France, demonstrates

---

[121] *Rot. norm.*, 39; *Rot. chart.*, 75b.

[122] Painter, *William Marshal*, 272.

[123] Gillingham, *The Angevin empire*, 70–4; Holt, 'The loss of Normandy and royal finances'; N. Barratt, 'The revenues of John and Philip Augustus revisited', in S. D. Church (ed.), *King John: new interpretations*, Woodbridge 1999, 75–99.

both the strength of his conviction that his French patrimony would be recovered and his appreciation of the worth of his baronage's cross-Channel interests.

When Count Thomas of the Perche took part in Prince Louis's invasion of England his motives may have been the pursuit of knightly reputation, but his confirmation of his parents' concession to the abbey of St Radegund at Bradsole suggests that he was also intent on the recovery of his English property. It was a quest which would take Thomas to his death at Lincoln, enable his cousins to enrich themselves and lead to the extinction of the Rotrou lineage, but it was also a powerful vindication of King Henry I's policy more than a century before. For the lord of such a small territory as the Perche the attraction of English revenues remained undimmed and the prospect of recovering the lucrative property held by his parents led Thomas to seek the reunification of the family's French and English lands under one master. That master, however, would have been a Capetian, and Thomas's unequivocal support for the Capetians, in contrast to the balancing acts of his forbears, demonstrates the changed political circumstances of the early thirteenth century, when the separation of the English realm and the Norman duchy precipitated the emergence of the distinct political units that would develop into the nation states of France and England.[124]

---

[124] Powicke, *Loss of Normandy*, 280–97.

Conclusion

At the end of the first millennium the county of the Perche did not exist. It was created by the Rotrou family during the eleventh and twelfth centuries, and the study of its formation offers an opportunity to observe power during the central Middle Ages, the period between the collapse of the Carolingian empire and the establishment of the centralised monarchies of western Europe. The picture which emerges is of a succession of able men and women who seized every opportunity to build on their situation. A new political unit appeared as a result of their efforts, but it was not a creation *ex nihilo*. The Rotrous accumulated lands and powers, developing a new powerbase within existing structures and manipulating those structures to their advantage.

In the years before 1000 the territory that would become the Perche lay at the borders of several units of power. Although our information is by no means comprehensive it is clear that a paraphernalia of power existed in the locality and was being exploited. The inhabitants recognised that certain individuals and institutions had rights to raise and provision troops; might make demands for payments, renders and labour services; could insist on the maintenance of bridges, roads and castles; and that a host of other obligations might be enforced. The names of the important aristocrats who served as the king's counts during the Carolingian period are known, but not those of the lieutenants and underlings who gave practical expression to their power by enforcing these obligations. The Rotrou lineage may have had its origins in any or indeed all of these groups. It is impossible to determine their genealogy with precision, but it is clear that that the Rotrous had long-standing associations with the Chartrain, the Dunois and the area that would become the Perche, and exercised power there.

Over a number of generations the family probably worked in association with whichever count was given responsibility for the area. The success of these counts and ultimately the power of kings depended on their ability to harness the support and power of local potentates such as the Rotrous. In the eighth, ninth and tenth centuries, however, we can seldom see these local men because their activities went unrecorded. As the monasteries began to recover after the disruption of the Viking period, however, the monks started to preserve accounts of their relations with these lords – a gift here, a lawsuit there. These accounts suddenly shed light on the local potentates and the picture is not always pleasing. These men are often cast as the villains because they have taken advantage of the monks, but these records do present an unprecedented opportunity to observe this layer of power at work.

The local potentates, whom we are now able to observe, were absolute

190

masters in their locality, and the castle which had proved so effective against the Vikings was a useful tool in maintaining their position. A local man who was able to develop a powerbase and attract support could accumulate power, establishing a new political unit.

> Your pier-glass or extensive surface of polished steel made to be rubbed by a housemaid, will be minutely and multitudinously scratched in all directions; but place now against it a lighted candle as a centre of illumination, and lo! the scratches will seem to arrange themselves in a fine series of concentric circles round that little sun.

George Eliot's description is 'a parable' to underline the egoism of a character in her novel *Middlemarch*, yet it is an appropriate image to describe the process at work during the eleventh century as the Rotrous, and others like them, carved out new political units. Through a judicious combination of their wealth, their military leadership, their monastic patronage and their prestige, successive members of the family were able to increase their power. They exploited the office of viscount of Châteaudun to give them access to the lucrative tolls on commerce in the Loir valley. They extended their power northwards towards Mortagne and found means to legitimise their tolls on the main road which ran across the southern reaches of Normandy towards Le Mans. They provided a forum for the settlement of disputes in their courts, and they demonstrated an ability to identify and exploit the latest religious developments. In each generation the Rotrous' capacity for lay leadership in religious matters enabled them to adjust adeptly and to provide a new focus for their followers' piety. Above all, however, they were mighty warriors and they participated in successful military expeditions such as the conquest of England in 1066 and the capture of Jerusalem in 1099. In all of these activities they set themselves up as centres of illumination and their neighbours arranged themselves accordingly.

Although the largely monastic sources are often critical of members of the family in their pursuit of these ambitions, it is clear that the Rotrous were not creating radically new institutions. Instead they adapted 'existing' or indeed defunct institutions. Thus they resurrected the power of a count of the Corbonnais which legitimated the power they held and gave them a decisive advantage over other families such as the L'Aigles, the Gouet or the lords of Châteauneuf-en-Thymerais. The use of the title gave them parity with the Thibaudian counts of Blois/Chartres whose agents the Rotrous had probably been in the tenth century. Such title inflation was by no means unusual: the elevation of the viscounts of Angers to become counts of Anjou is well-remarked by historians, but there are other examples. During the eleventh century the title of count proliferated in the Île de France and the areas to the east of Paris as similar local potentates enhanced their status.[1] For the

---

1 Lemarignier, *Le Gouvernement royal aux premiers temps capétiens*, 126–31.

Rotrous the title of viscount had been a useful stepping stone, but it implied subordination. Under Count Rotrou II in the twelfth century, some acknowledgement was paid to the Thibaudian counts – attendance at the comital court, for example, but Rotrou never took the trouble to obtain Thibaudian assent to his acts as his father had done to the donation of Nogent-le-Rotrou to the Cluniacs.

The particular act of genius of the Rotrou lineage was, however, to recognise the importance of the Norman conquest of England. The traditionally volatile conditions of the Norman marches would be more troublesome for the Rotrous' northern neighbours when Norman resources were stretched in holding down the English kingdom. Some of the new-found wealth of the Normans therefore found its way to the Rotrous in the form of subsidies in the late 1070s and Count Rotrou I entered into a client relationship with his northern neighbour which his successors were to exploit to varying degrees throughout the rest of the history of the Perche as an separate polity. This new relationship in which the Norman ruler formed a powerful 'centre of illumination' had the effect of distancing the Rotrous from the counts of Blois/Chartres and opened up new perspectives for them as English landholders.

As the twelfth century progressed the political environment of western France changed. Rulers consolidated their power through more systematic processes of government and there was less opportunity for the formation of new units. Inheritance and marriage still offered some scope for the greater princes, however, and the accumulation of power by King Henry II of England (1154–89) threatened to eclipse the Capetian monarchy entirely. The study of the Rotrou counts in this period is important for the light that it sheds on the power struggles of the Plantagenets and Capetians. Just as the eleventh-century power blocs of Normandy, Anjou and Blois were replaced in the twelfth by the broader alignments of Plantagenet and Capetian, so the stakes for which the Rotrous played were also raised. Where Henry I had given a couple of manors in Wiltshire and an illegitimate daughter to secure the support of the count of the Perche, Richard I was to offer an entire English honour and a Plantagenet princess to his grandson. The relationship between the kings of England and the counts of the Perche can thus be used as an index of each king's confidence in his position. In the early years of his reign Henry II had sought to hold his diverse lands together by military means and his own restless energy. By the mid 1170s his improving relations with his Percheron neighbours suggest that he was resorting to new tactics which owed something to those of his grandfather, Henry I, and great-grandfather, William the Conqueror, who had both cultivated the counts of the Perche. The enormous inducements offered by Richard and John for the support of the Rotrou counts suggest that they took a more pessimistic view than their father about their relations with the king of France.

In the early thirteenth century the great increase in family wealth coupled with crusading prestige and a network of marriage ties raised the Rotrous to a position among the territorial princes of western Europe which was out of all proportion to the size and resources of the Perche. The role of those territorial princes in France was, however, challenged by the growing power of King Philip II (Augustus) (1180–1223). The means available to the king from the royal demesne had been increasing in the second half of the twelfth century and were being more carefully managed, while Philip himself was learning to enforce his royal rights. The factors that had contributed to the rise of the counts of the Perche can also be found in the recovery of Capetian power. The king had wealth to reward those who were attracted to his court and to pay for those who enforced his will and he had prestige through participation in military campaigns such as the Third Crusade, but above all he made use of the law. From 1202 the rulers of the Perche were faced with an overlord who was able to reassert royal authority, enforcing his rights to determine succession, operating his courts and developing new partnerships with the lords of the localities. The Rotrou lineage had a recognised position among the peers of France, but recognition came at the price of accepting the power of the king. When the last count of the Perche died in 1226, the true extent of Philip Augustus' achievement can be gauged. The count-bishop William left no direct heir and the natural expectation was that the succession would be left for King Louis VIII to determine.

The powers of the Merovingian and Carolingian kings were those of barbarian war-leaders grafted on to the surviving apparatus of the Roman state in France. When the great expeditions of conquest ended in the ninth century and the Carolingian empire moved from the offensive to the defensive, the warrior-elite was forced to look exclusively within the empire for its maintenance. The Viking raids enforced a local dimension and within a couple of generations the men who controlled the localities realised that they need not always co-operate with their immediate superiors, the counts, nor their ultimate overlord, the king. During the tenth and eleventh century this testing of the conventional frameworks of power led to the emergence of new political entities such as the Perche and to the dislocation of royal and local power which lasted until King Philip Augustus was able to reassert his kingship. The Rotrou counts of the Perche took advantage of these opportunities, but their rise does not conform to a model which stresses the importance of the year 1000. They retained an association with the counts of Blois/Chartres into the twelfth century and arguably their position among the peers of France was only achieved as a result of the role which the sons of King Henry II sought to assign them at the turn of the thirteenth century. With the collapse of the Plantagenet empire the position of the Perche was fatally compromised. When Count Thomas of the Perche took part in Prince Louis's invasion of England he no doubt saw it as an opportunity to recover the English lands of his family. Those English lands had been a reward for the Rotrous' adroit manipulation of the rivalry of the French and English kings, but by the beginning of the thirteenth century such manipulation was no longer possible.

Partnership with and service to the French crown were becoming the only options available to the territorial princes, and Thomas sought to recover the English lands as agent of the Capetians. The experiment in the localisation of power in the Perche was at an end.

The Ancestry of Viscount Geoffrey

The descent of Viscount Geoffrey has provoked considerable scholarly discussion. Two options need to be considered. First that the Rotrou lineage ran to an heiress. This is the thesis of the nineteenth-century historian of the Perche, the vicomte de Romanet, who declared that Milesindis, the daughter of Rotrou of Nogent-le-Rotrou, married the viscount of Châteaudun, Geoffrey, and so the lordship of Nogent passed to another family.[1]

Figure 7
The ancestry of Viscount Geoffrey: De Romanet's reconstruction

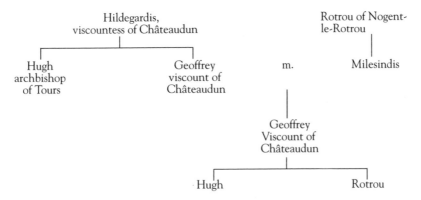

De Romanet based his reconstruction on the information given about the family in the records of the family foundation of Saint-Denis of Nogent-le-Rotrou and on the evidence of a bequest made before 1023 to the abbey of Saint-Père of Chartres by Hildegarde, viscountess of Châteaudun.[2] Hildegarde's act was made with the approval of her son, Hugh archbishop of Tours, and was witnessed by the archbishop and his nephew, Geoffrey. This nephew Geoffrey has been identified with the Viscount Geoffrey who exercised power at Nogent and Châteaudun, and Geoffrey's use of the archbishop's name, Hugh, for his eldest son supports the identification, suggesting that it was a link he wished to emphasise.

The alternative hypotheses is, of course, that the Châteaudun family

---

1 De Romanet, *Géographie*, i. 44–5.
2 *SPC*, 117–18.

ended with an heiress. Milesindis may have been married to the lord of Nogent-le-Rotrou and, when her family's male heirs failed, her son, Geoffrey, named perhaps after her illustrious ancestors, took over as the agents of the counts of Blois/Chartres in Châteaudun. Milesindis's husband may have been the Rotrou who was associated with the counts of Blois/Chartres in the late tenth century, which could account for the naming of Viscount Geoffrey's second son, Rotrou. On balance this reconstruction of events is preferable. Milesindis is known to have held dower land at Cossonville (Eure-et-Loir, cant. Auneau), some 20 kilometres east of Chartres, which supports the picture of her husband as a follower of the counts of Chartres who had been given property near the city. She also held dower land close to Nogent, which indicates that it was her husband's family rather than her own which controlled Nogent.[3]

Figure 8
The ancestry of Viscount Geoffrey: hypothesis 2

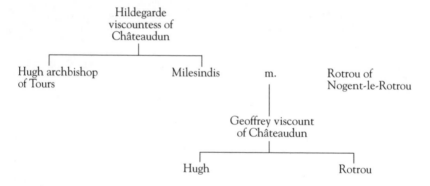

APPENDIX 2

The Ancestry of Count Rotrou II and the Countess Adeliza

The vicomte de Romanet deduced a pedigree for Count Rotrou I of Mortagne which accounted for the northwards shift in the family's interests in the second half of the eleventh century. He proposed that Count Rotrou's mother, Helviza, the wife of Viscount Geoffrey was the descendant of a line of counts of Mortagne that had died out with her father, Count Fulcuich. The thesis is based on information given in Count Rotrou's act in favour of the abbey of Saint-Vincent of Le Mans in which he mentions his grandfather – or possibly ancestor (*avus*), Count Fulcuich, his uncle (strictly speaking maternal uncle – *avunculus*), Hugh, and his father, Viscount Geoffrey. It is assumed that, because Rotrou's father Geoffrey is described with the title of viscount and his grandfather, Fulcuich, with that of count, Fulcuich must have been his maternal grandfather. His *avunculus*, Hugh, would thus be Fulcuich's son who had died without heirs, leaving his sister's son (Rotrou) to inherit the title of count.

Figure 9
The ancestry of Count Rotrou I: De Romanet's reconstruction

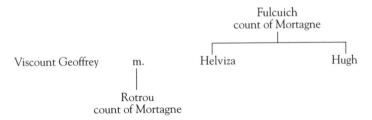

It has to be said, however, that there is nothing to link Fulcuich with Mortagne, for the act gives him no toponymic and the thesis rests on the assumption that Fulcuich was count of Mortagne for two slender reasons: because Rotrou's comital title was associated with that town and because record of another count of Mortagne, Hervey, who was alive in 954, has also survived.[1]

It is not, however, the only genealogical reconstruction which can account for Rotrou's assumption of comital title, and it is worthwhile glancing briefly at the alternative, which relates to Rotrou's wife. Adeliza was the daughter of

1   *SPC*, 198–9.

197

Warin of Domfront, a member of the powerful clan which we have already encountered at their stronghold of Bellême in the mid tenth century. Descendants of the Ivo of Bellême who founded the church dedicated to Notre Dame, the Bellême lineage had accumulated property along the southern marches of the duchy of Normandy, stretching from Domfront in the west through Alençon and Sées to Bellême itself.[2] Adeliza is mentioned only once among surviving references concerning Rotrou and so it is all the more significant that she appears in Rotrou's act in favour of Saint-Vincent of Le Mans, the very document which gives details of Count Fulcuich, Uncle Hugh and Rotrou's father, the Viscount Geoffrey.

In his agreement with the abbot of Saint-Vincent Rotrou was scrupulous to associate his wife and their children with the concession of property at Saint-Longis (Sarthe, cant. Mamers) which had come to them by hereditary right ('qui nobis attinebat jure patrimonii'). This stress on the hereditary nature of the property, which lay some distance from the historic core of Rotrou's family holdings at Nogent, together with the adaptation of the conventional diploma language to include Adeliza ('notum fieri volumus, ego Rotrochus, comes Mauritaniae et mea uxor Adeliz et filii nostri Rotrochus et ceteri nostri infantes . . . concederemus') suggests that Rotrou may here have been acting on behalf of his wife and her heirs, their children.[3]

Figure 10
The ancestry of Count Rotrou I: hypothesis 2

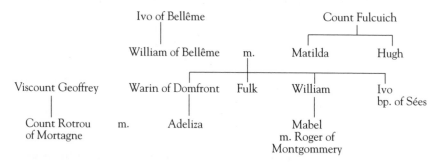

Rotrou's comital title may therefore have been derived from his wife's ancestors, and a further indication that she had a forebear named Fulk can be found in her family's naming stock. Adeliza's father, Warin of Domfront, one of the six sons of William of Bellême, had a brother called Fulk, who appears to have been one of the two eldest, if not the eldest of his brothers. It is

---

[2] On Adeliza's family see J. Boussard, 'La Seigneurie de Bellême aux Xe et XIe siècles', in *Mélanges d'histoire dediés à la mémoire de Louis Halphen*, 43–54.
[3] VLM, no. 609. On the changing nature of the legal relationship between man and wife see Duby, *The knight, the lady and the priest*, 99ff.

known that the name, Fulk, did not come from her paternal grandfather's family since Adeliza's paternal grandfather was named William and her great-grandfather, Ivo. It is a reasonable assumption, therefore, that the name Fulk was derived from the family of her paternal grandmother, Matilda.[4] The uncle Hugh, referred to in the Le Mans charter, might therefore be Matilda's brother.

4 On the sons of William of Bellême see interpolations by Orderic Vitalis in *Gesta normannorum ducum*, ii. 50. Fulk appears first among the witnesses of his father's act of foundation for Lonlay: *Monasticon*, vi. 1095–6.

Bibliography

Unpublished primary sources

ENGLAND

Canterbury, Dean and Chapter archives
Carta antiqua R62, T27

Hereford, Dean and Chapter archives
MS 798

London, British Library
MS Cotton Caligula A xiii Registrum chartarum abbatiae de Pipewell
MS Cotton Vespasian F xv Cartulary of Lewes priory
MS Cotton Vitellius A xi Cartulary of Bradenstoke priory
MS Egerton 3137 Cartulary of Blackborough priory
MS Harleian 1885 Cartulary of Dunstable priory
MSS Harleian charters 43.c.29, 54.g.26
MS Stowe 666

London, Public Record Office
DL 25/3387, DL 25/3394(2)
MSS E 40/3873, E 210/1532, E 326/7482

Winchester, Hampshire Record Office
1M54/1–3 Cartulary of Southwick priory

FRANCE

Alençon, Bibliothèque municipale
MS 108 Cartulaire de la Chartreuse du Val Dieu
MS 112 Recueil sur la Chartreuse du Val Dieu

Calvados, Archives départementales (Caen)
Abbey of Saint-André-en-Gouffern
MSS H6511/4, H6511/6, H6511/8

Eure, Archives départementales (Evreux)
Cathedral chapter of Evreux
MS G122 Premier cartulaire du chapitre

Priory of La Chaise-Dieu du Theil
MSS H1419, 1437, 1438 Muniments of La Chaise-Dieu du Theil

Priory of Notre-Dame du Désert
MS G165 Cartulaire de Notre-Dame du Désert

Eure-et-Loir, Archives départementales (Chartres)
MS H1438 Inventaire du Prieuré de Chaise-Dieu Cartulaire de Laigle

Abbey of Bonneval
MS H619

Abbey of Saint-Avit de Châteaudun
MS H4611

Abbey of Saint-Père of Chartres
MS H533

Abbey of Saint-Vincent-aux-Bois
MS H3906 Inventaire des titres et papiers de l'abbaye de Saint-Vincent-aux-Bois
MS H3907 Registre de Saint-Vincent-aux-Bois
MS H3932

Abbey of Tiron
MSS H1412, H1419, H1420, H1579, H1737, H1956

Cathedral chapter of Chartres
MSS G131, G134, G135 Inventaires des titres du chapitre de Notre-Dame de
   Chartres
MS G1459

College of Saint-Jean de Nogent-le-Rotrou
MS G3479 Inventaire des titres des rentes appartenant au chapitre de Saint-Jean
   de Nogent-le-Rotrou
MS G3480 Repertoire des actes passés par les notaires de Nogent-le-Rotrou
MS G3485 Nécrologe de Saint-Jean de Nogent-le-Rotrou

Priory of Belhomert
MSS H5132, H5207, H5211,

Priory of Saint-Denis of Nogent-le-Rotrou
MS H2601 Cartulaire de Saint-Denis de Nogent-le-Rotrou
MSS H2602, H2650

Le Mans, Médiathèque Louis Aragon (formerly Bibliothèque municipale)
MS 23 Missale ad usum monasterii S. Dyonisii de Nouigento

Loir-et-Cher, Archives départementales (Blois)
Abbey of Pontlevoy
MS 17 H55

Abbey of Saint-Laumer de Blois
MS 11 H27/1
MS 11 H128 Cartulaire de l'abbaye royalle de Saint-Laumer de Blois

Loiret, Archives départementales (Orléans)

Abbey of Saint-Benoît-sur-Loire
MS H22 Cartulaire de Saint-Benoît-sur-Loire

College of Orléans
MS D668 Cartulaire de Saint-Sulpice-sur-Risle

Nogent-le-Rotrou, Bibliothèque municipale

MS 11 Cartulaire de Sainte-Gauburge (s. xix copy of AN, LL1158)
MS 14 Copies des chartres diverses

Nogent-le-Rotrou, Château Saint-Jean

Archives de l'hôpital
MSS A/1, A/6, A/7, C/108, C/112

Orne, Archives départementales (Alençon)

Abbey of La Trappe
MSS H725, H1846, H1847, H1858, H1864, H1865

Abbey of Saint-Évroul
MS H553 Fragment of Saint-Évroul inventory
MSS H702, H721, H722

Charterhouse of Val Dieu
MSS H2621, H2622, H2730

College of Toussaints, Mortagne
MS IG 1071/30 Inventaire des pièces justicatives . . . de l'église collegiale et
  royalle de Toussaints de la ville de Mortagne au Perche

Priory of Bellême
MSS H2153, H2154, H2156, H2158, H2160, H2163, H2164, H2165, H2170,
  H2519, H2520

Priory of Chêne Galon
MSS H1951

Priory of the Madeleine, Chartrage
MSS H5438, H5441

Paris, Archives nationales

MS J399
MSS KK894, KK895 Cartulaires des comtes de Blois
MS LL1158 Livre blanc de l'abbaye de Saint-Denis
MS S2238 Titres de propriété de l'abbaye de Saint-Denis
MS S4983 Titres de la Commanderie de Villedieu en Dreugesin
MS S4999A Titres de la Commanderie de Sours

Paris, Bibliothèque nationale

MS Baluze, fos 231–2

MS de Bourgogne 78, item 144
MS Duchesne 20, fos 217–30; 22, fos 172–4, 276–98; 54, pp. 433–61; 68, fos 26–37
MS Dupuy. 222, p. 127
MS Moreau 84, fo. 85

Fonds francais

MS franc. 20691, fos 553–62 Extraits du cartulaire du comté de Chartres
MS franc. 24133, pp. 301–14 Guillaume Laisne, prieur de Mondonville, mémoires généalogiques, t. x

Fonds latins

MSS lat. 5417, 5474, 5480, 5993A, 9220
MS lat. 10089 Cartulaire de Saint-Euverte d'Orléans (1775)
MS lat. 10094 Privilegia ecclesiae Carnotensis (Cartulaire 28)
MS lat. 10095 Privilegia ecclesiae Carnotensis (Cartulaire 28 bis)
MS lat. 11055
MS lat. 11056 Cartulaire de Saint-Evroul
MS lat. 11060 Cartulaire de Notre-Dame de La Trappe
MS lat. 17139 Extraits relatifs à Bonneval par Gaignières
MS lat. 17140 Cartulaire de l'abbaye de Notre-Dame des Clairets
MS lat. nouvelle acquisition 1498 Cartulaire de Cluny B
MS lat. nouvelle acquisition 2309, no. 38

Sarthe, Archives départementales (Le Mans)
Abbey of Perseigne
MSS H927, H930.

Abbey of Saint-Vincent du Mans
MSS H92, H93, H97, H250

Priory of Bersay
MS H1113

Priory of Gué de Launay
MSS H84, H85
MS H1991 Inventaire des titres de l'abbaye du Gué de Launay (1737)

Priory of Torcé
MS H375

Sées, Bibliothèque de l'évêché
MS Livre Blanc de Saint-Martin de Sées
MS Livre Rouge du chapitre de Sées

Printed primary sources

Abbaye royale de Notre Dame des Clairets: histoire et cartulaire, 1202–1790, ed. le vicomte de Souancé, Nogent-le-Rotrou 1894

L'Abbaye Toussaint d'Angers des origines à 1330: étude historique et cartulaire, ed. F. Comte, Angers 1985

Acta of Henry II and Richard I, ed. J. C. Holt and R. Mortimer (List and Index Society s.s. xxi, 1986)

Acta of Henry II and Richard I, part two, ed. N. Vincent (List and Index Society s.s. xxvii, 1992)

Actus pontificum cenomannis in urbe degentium, ed. G. Busson and A. Ledru, Le Mans 1901

Adam of Eynsham, *Life of St Hugh of Lincoln*, ed. D. L. Douie and H. Farmer, London 1961–2

Adam of Perseigne, *Lettres*, Paris 1960

Alberic of Trois-Fontaines, 'Chronicon', MGH SS xxiii. 631–950

Albert of Aachen, 'Historia Hierosolymitana', in *Recueil des historiens des croisades*, iv. 265–713

Ambroise, 'L'Estoire de la guerre sainte', trans. by M. J. Hubert and J. La Monte, as *The crusade of Richard Lionheart*, New York 1941

Annales monastici, ed. H. R. Luard (RS xxxvi, 1864–9)

'Annals of Montecassino', MGH SS xix. 310

Annals of St-Bertin: ninth century histories, i, trans. J. L. Nelson, Manchester 1991

Arnulf of Lisieux, *Letters*, ed. F. Barlow (Camden 3rd ser. lxi, 1939)

Bernard, *Opera*, viii, ed. J. Leclerq and H. Rochais, Rome 1977

Book of fees, London 1921–31

Calendar of documents preserved in France, ed. J. H. Round, London 1899

Calendar of Kent feet of fines to the end of Henry III's reign, ed. I. J. Churchill, R. Griffin and R. W. Hardman (Kent Records xv, 1956)

Calendar of patent rolls Henry III, 1216–1225, London 1901

Cartae antique rolls 1–10, ed. L. Landon (PRS n.s. xvii, 1939)

Cartulaire de l'abbaye cistercienne de Perseigne, ed. G. Fleury, Mamers 1880

Cartulaire de l'abbaye de Notre-Dame de Ourscamp, ed. M. Peigné-Delacourt, Amiens 1865

Cartulaire de l'abbaye de Notre-Dame de la Trappe, ed. H. de Charencey, Alençon 1889

Cartulaire de l'abbaye de Saint-Aubin d'Angers, ed. A. Bertrand de Broussillon, Paris 1903

Cartulaire de l'abbaye de la Sainte-Trinité de Tiron, ed. L. Merlet, Chartres 1883

Cartulaire de la leproserie du Grand-Beaulieu et du prieuré de Notre-Dame de la Bourdinière, ed. R. Merlet and M. Jusselin, Chartres 1909

Cartulaire de Marcigny-sur-Loire (1045–1144): essai de reconstruction d'un manuscrit disparu, ed. J. Richard, Dijon 1957

Cartulaire de Marmoutier pour le Dunois, ed. E. Mabille, Châteaudun 1874

Cartulaire de Marmoutier pour le Perche, ed. P. Barret, Mortagne 1894

Cartulaire de Notre-Dame de Chartres, ed. E. de Lépinois and L. Merlet, Chartres 1865

Cartulaire de Saint-Jean en Vallée de Chartres, ed. R. Merlet, Chartres 1906

Cartulaire de Saint-Père de Chartres, ed. B. Guérard, Paris 1840

Cartulaire de Saint-Vincent du Mans, ed. R. Charles and S. Menjot d'Elbenne, Le Mans 1886

Cartulaire des abbayes de S. Pierre de la Couture et de S. Pierre de Solesmes, Le Mans 1881

Cartulaire Manceau de Marmoutier, ed. E. Laurain, Laval 1911–45

Cartulaire normand de Philippe Auguste, Louis VIII, Saint Louis et Philippe le Hardi, ed. L. Delisle (Mémoires de la Société des antiquaires de Normandie 2 sér. vi, 1852)

Cartularies of Southwick priory, ed. K. A. Hanna, Winchester 1988

Cartulary of Bradenstoke priory, ed. V. C. London (Wiltshire Record Society xxxv, 1979)

Cartulary of St Bartholomew's Hospital founded 1123: a calendar, ed. N. J. M. Kerling, London 1973

Catalogue des actes d'Henri Ier roi de France (1031–1060), ed. F. Soehnée, Paris 1907

Catalogue des actes de Philippe Auguste, ed. L. Delisle, Paris 1856

Chanson d'Antioche, ed. S. Duparc-Quioc, Paris 1977–8

Charters of the honour of Mowbray, 1107–1191, ed. D. E. Greenway, London 1972

Chartes de l'abbaye de Jumièges, ed. J.-J. Vernier, Rouen 1916

Chartes du Bourbonnais, 918–1522, ed. J. Monicat and B. de Fournaux, Moulins 1952

Chartes de Saint-Julien de Tours, 1002–1227, ed. L.-J. Denis (Archives historiques du Maine xii, 1912)

Chartularium insignis ecclesiae cenomannensis quod dicitur liber albus capituli, ed. A. Cauvin, Le Mans 1869

'Chronica de gestis consulum Andegavorum', in *Chroniques d'Anjou*, 34–157

'Chronicae Sancti Albini Andegavensis', in *Chroniques des églises d'Anjou*, 19–126

'Chronicle of Morigny', in *RHF* xii. 68–88

'Chronicle of St Maxient of Poitiers', in *Chroniques des églises d'Anjou*, 351–433

'Chronicle of Saint-Wandrille', in *RHF* vii. 40–3

Chronicles and memorials of Richard I, ed. W. Stubbs (RS xxxviii, 1864–5)

'Chronique d'un anonyme de Béthune' (excerpt), in *RHF* xxiv/2, 771

Chroniques d'Anjou, ed. P. Marchegay and A. Salmon, Paris 1856

Chroniques des églises d'Anjou, ed. P. Marchegay and E. Mabille, Paris 1869

Colección diplomática de Irache, i, ed. J. M. Lacarra, Zaragoza 1965

Colección diplomática medieval de la Rioja: documentos, ed. Ildefonso Rodrìgues de Lama, Logroño 1976–9

La Conquête de Jérusalem, ed. C. Hippeau, Paris 1868

Curia regis rolls, London 1923–

Diplomatic documents preserved in the Public Record Office, I: 1101–1272, ed. P. Chaplais, London 1964

Documentos para el estudio de la reconquista y repoblación de Valle del Ebro, ed. J. M. Lacarra, Zaragoza 1982–5

Documents relatifs au comté de Champagne et de Brie, 1172–1363, ed. A. Longnon, i, Paris 1901

Dugdale, W., *Monasticon anglicanum*, ed. J. Stevens, London 1817, repr. 1846

Earldom of Gloucester charters, ed. R. Patterson, Oxford 1973

'Estoire de Eracles empereur et la conqueste de la terre d'Outremer', in *Recueil des historiens des croisades*, ii. 1–481

Flodoard, *Annales*, ed. P. Lauer, Paris 1906

Foedera, ed. T. Rymer, 2nd edn, London 1816

Fulbert of Chartres, *Letters and poems*, ed. F. Behrends, Oxford 1976

Geoffrey Grossus, 'Vita Beati Bernardi Tironiensis', PL clxxii. 1367–446

———— 'Vita Beati Bernardi Tironiensis', in B. Beck, *Saint Bernard de Tiron, l'ermite, le moine et le monde*, Caen 1998, 303–461

Geoffrey of Vigeois, 'Chronicon lemovicense', in *RHF* xii. 421–51; xviii. 211–23

Geoffroi de Villehardouin, *La Conquête de Constantinople*, ed. and trans. E. Faral, 2nd edn, Paris 1961

Gesta normannorum ducum of William of Jumièges, Orderic Vitalis and Robert of Torigni, ed. E. M. C. van Houts, Oxford 1992–5

Gesta regis Henrici secundi, ed. W. Stubbs (RS xlix, 1867)

Great roll of the pipe for the first year of the reign of Richard I, ed. J. Hunter, London 1844

Great rolls of the pipe for the second, third and fourth years of the reign of King Henry the second, 1155–1158, ed. J. Hunter, London 1844

Gregory of Tours, 'Libri octo miraculorum, viii: liber in gloria confessorum', MGH Scriptores rerum merovingicarum i. 744–820

Guibert of Nogent, *Self and society in medieval France*, ed. J. F. Benton, New York 1972

Herman of Laon, 'De miraculis S. Mariae Laudunensis', PL clvi. 961–1018

Hildebert of Le Mans, ep. xviii to Serlo, bishop of Sées, PL clxxi. 225–8

Histoire des ducs de Normandie et des rois d'Angleterre, ed. F. Michel, Paris 1840

Histoire de Guillaume le Maréchal, ed. P. Meyer (Société de l'histoire de France, 1891–1901)

Historia et cartularium monasterii S. Petri Gloucestriae, ed. W. H. Hart (RS xxxiii, 1863–7)

HMC, *Report on manuscripts in various collections*, London 1901–14

Hugh de Cleeris, 'De majoratu et senescalcia', in *Chroniques d'Anjou*, 387–94

Hugh Falcandus, *La historia o liber de regno Sicilie*, ed. G. B. Siragusa, Rome 1897

Ivo of Chartres, 'Letters', PL clxii

Layettes de trésor de chartes, ed. A. Teulet, H.-F. Delaborde and E. Berger, Paris 1863–1909

Liber censualis, seu Domesday Book, London 1783–1816

Magni rotuli scaccarii Normanniae sub regibus Angliae, ed. T. Stapleton, London 1840–4

Magnus rotulus scaccarii de anno 31 Henrici I, ed. J. Hunter, London 1833

Materials for the history of Thomas Becket, ed. J. C. Robertson and J. B. Sheppard (RS lxvii, 1876)

Matthew Paris, *Historia minor*, ed. F. Madden (RS xliv, 1866–9)

Memoranda roll 1 John, 1199–1200 (PRS n.s. xxi)

Monumenta Germaniae historica legum sectio II: Capitularia regum francorum, ed. A. Boretius and V. Krause, ii, Hanover 1897

Necrologio de Liber Confratrum di S. Matteo de Salerno, ed. C. A. Crombi, Rome 1922

Obituaires de la province de Sens, ii, ed. A. Molinier and A. Longnon, Paris 1906

Odo of Deuil, *De profectione Ludovici VII in orientem*, ed. and trans. V. G. Berry, Morningside Heights, NY 1948

Orderic Vitalis, *Ecclesiastical history*, ed. M. Chibnall, Oxford 1969–80

Original acta of St Peter's abbey, Gloucester, c. 1122 to 1263, ed. R. B. Patterson (Gloucestershire Record Ser. li, 1998)

Peter of Vaux de Cernay, *The history of the Albigensian crusade*, trans. W. A. Sibly and M. D. Sibly, Woodbridge 1998

Pièces detachées pour servir à l'histoire du diocèse de Chartres, ed. C. Métais, Chartres 1899–1904

The political songs of England, ed. T. Wright (Camden Society, 1839)

Polyptique de l'abbaye de Saint-Germain-des-Prés, ed. A. Longnon, Paris 1895

Le Premier Budget de la monarchie française: le compte générale de 1202–1203, ed. F. Lot and R. Fawtier, Paris 1932

'Querimoniae normannorum', in *RHF* xxiv/1, 1–73 (second pagination sequence)

Ralph of Diceto, *Opera historica*, ed. W. Stubbs (RS lxviii, 1876)

Ralph Glaber, *The five books of the histories*, ed. and trans. J. France, Oxford 1989

Reading abbey cartularies, ed. B. Kemp (Camden 4th ser. xxxi, xxxiii, 1986–7)

Records of the Templars in England in the twelfth century: the inquest of 1185, ed. B. A. Lees, London 1935

Recueil des actes de Charles II le chauve, roi de France, ed. G. Tessier, Paris 1948–55

Recueil des actes des ducs de Normandie, 911–1066, ed. M. Fauroux (Mémoires de la Société des antiquaires de Normandie xxxvi, 1961)

Recueil des actes de Henri II roi d'Angleterre et duc de Normandie concernant les provinces françaises et les affaires de France, ed. L. Delisle and E. Berger, Paris 1906–27

Recueil des actes de Philippe Ier, roi de France, ed. M. Prou, Paris 1908

Recueil des actes de Philippe Auguste, ed. H. F. Delaborde and others, Paris 1916–79

Recueil des chartes de l'abbaye de Cluny, ed. A. Bernard and A. Bruel, Paris 1876–1903

Recueil des chartes de l'abbaye de Saint-Benoît-sur-Loire, ed. M. Prou and A. Vidier, Paris 1900–7

Recueil des historiens des croisades: historiens occidentaux, Paris 1844–95

Recueil des historiens des Gaules et de la France, ed. M. Bouquet and others, Paris 1869–1904

Red book of the exchequer, ed. H. Hall (RS xcix, 1897)

Regesta regum anglo-normannorum, ii, ed. C. Johnson and H. A. Cronne, Oxford 1956

Regesta regum anglo-normannorum, iii, ed. H. A. Cronne and R. H. C. Davis, Oxford 1968–9

Registres de Philippe Auguste, ed. J. W. Baldwin, Paris 1992–

Rigord, 'Gesta Philippi Augusti', in *Oeuvres de Rigord et de Guillaume le Breton*, ed. H. F. Delaborde, Paris 1882–5

Robert of Torigni, *Chronique*, ed. L. Delisle, Rouen 1872

Roger of Howden, *Chronica*, ed. W. Stubbs (RS li, 1868–71)

Roger of Wendover, *Chronica*, ed. H. G. Hewlett (RS lxxxiv, 1886–9)

Rotuli chartarum in turri Londinensi asservati, 1199–1216, ed. T. D. Hardy, London 1837

Rotuli de dominabus et pueris et puellis de donatione regis in xii comitatibus 31 Henry II 1185, ed. J. H. Round (PRS 1913)

Rotuli de liberate ac de misis de praestitis regnanate Johanne, ed. T. D. Hardy (Record Commission xxx, 1844)

Rotuli de oblatis et finibus in turri Londinensi asservati tempore regis Johannis, ed. T. D. Hardy, London 1837

Rotuli litterarum clausarum in turri Londinensi asservati, ed. T. D. Hardy, London 1833–44

Rotuli litterarum patentium in turri Londinensi asservati, 1201–1216, ed. T. D. Hardy, London 1834

Rotuli Normanniae in turri Londinensi asservati, 1200–1205, ed. T. Hardy, London 1835

Rouleaux des morts de IXe au XVe siècle, ed. L. Delisle, Paris 1866

Saint-Denis de Nogent-Le-Rotrou, 1031–1789, ed. Charles Métais, Vannes 1894

Sammarthanus D., *Gallia Christiana in provincias ecclesiasticas distributa*, ed. P. Piolin, Paris 1870–7

Scott, J. R., 'Charters of Monks Horton priory', *Archaeologia Cantiana* x (1876), 269–81

'Scripta de feodis', in *RHF* xxiii. 605–723

Suger, *The deeds of Louis the Fat*, ed. R. C. Cusimano and J. Moorhead, Washington, DC 1992

Templiers en Eure-et-Loir: histoire et cartulaire, ed. C. Métais, Chartres 1902

Textus roffensis, ed. T. Hearne, Oxford 1720

'Translatio Sancti Launomari', in *RHF* vii. 365

William of Malmesbury, *De gestis regum* (RS xc, 1887–9)

William of Tyre, *Chronique*, ed. R. B. C. Huygens, Turnholt 1986

William the Breton, 'Gesta', in *Oeuvres de Rigord et de Guillaume le breton*, ed. H.-F. Delaborde, Paris 1882–5

Secondary sources

Adigard de Gautries, J., 'Étude onomastique ornaise, II: Les toponymes anciens formés à l'aide de l'appellatif *court*', *Bulletin de la Société historique et archéologique de l'Orne* lxxviii (1960), 3–17

Aniel, J.-P., *Les Maisons de Chartreux des origines à la Chartreuse de Pavie*, Geneva 1983

d'Arbois de Jubainville, H., *Histoire des ducs et des comtes de Champagne*, Paris 1859–66

Bachrach, B., 'Enforcement of the *forma fidelitatis*: the techniques used by Fulk Nerra, count of the Angevins (987–1040)', *Speculum* lix (1984), 796–819

Baldwin, J. W., *The government of Philip Augustus: foundations of French royal power in the Middle Ages*, Berkeley, CA 1986

Barber, M., 'The order of St Lazarus and the crusades', *Catholic Historical Review* lxxx (1994), 439–56

Barlow, F., *William Rufus*, London 1983

——— *Thomas Becket*, London 1986

Barratt, N., 'The revenues of John and Philip Augustus revisited', in S. D. Church (ed.), *King John: new interpretations*, Woodbridge 1999, 75–99

Bart des Boulais, L., *Recueil des antiquitéz du Perche, comtes et seigneurs de la dicte province ensemble les fondations, bâtiments des monastères et choses notables du dict païs*, ed. H. Tournouer, Mortagne 1890

Barthélemy, D., 'La Mutation féodale a-t-elle eu lieu? (Note critique)', *Annales* xlvii (1992), 767–77

—— *La Société dans le comté de Vendôme de l'an mil au xive siècle*, Paris 1993

—— 'Encore le débat sur l'an mil', *Revue historique du droit* lxxiii (1995), 353–4

Bascher, J. de, 'La *Vita* de saint Bernard d'Abbeville, abbé de Saint-Cyprien de Poitiers et de Tiron', *Revue Mabillon* lix (1976/80), 411–50

Bates, D., *Normandy before 1066*, London 1982

—— 'Normandy and England after 1066', *EHR* civ (1989), 851–80

—— and A. Curry (eds), *England and Normandy in the Middle Ages*, London 1994

Bautier, R.-H., 'Les Foires de Champagne: recherches sur une évolution historique', *Recueils de la Société Jean Bodin* v (1953), 97–147

—— (ed.), *La France de Philippe Auguste: temps des mutations*, Paris 1982

Beck, B., 'Bernard de Tiron ou l'impossible sainteté d'après la *Vita Beati Bernardi* de Geoffroy le Gros', in P. Bouet and F. Neveux (eds), *Les Saints dans la Normandie médiévale: colloque Cérisy-la-Salle (26–29 septembre 1996)*, Caen 2000, 285–301

—— *Saint Bernard de Tiron, l'ermite, le moine et le monde*, Caen 1998

Beech, G., 'The participation of the Aquitanians in the conquest of England 1066–1100', *ANS* ix (1986), 1–24

Benjamin, R., 'A forty years war: Toulouse and the Plantagenets, 1156–96', *Historical Research* lxi (1988), 270–85

Bisson, T. N., *Conservation of coinage: monetary exploitation and its restraint in France, Catalonia and Aragon (c. AD 1000–c. 1225)*, Oxford 1979

—— 'The "feudal revolution" ', *Past & Present* clii (1994), 6–42

—— 'Reply: debate: the "feudal revolution" ', *Past & Present* clv (1997), 209–25

Blanchet A. and A. Dieudonné, *Manuel de numismatique française*, IV: *Monnaies féodales françaises*, Paris 1936

Bloch, M., *Feudal society*, 2nd edn, London 1962, trans. by L. Manion of *La Société féodale*, Paris 1939–40

Bonnassie, P., *La Catalogne du milieu du xe à la fin du xie siècle: croissance et mutation d'une société*, Toulouse 1975–6

Boussard, J., 'La Seigneurie de Bellême aux Xe et XIe siècles', in *Mélanges d'histoire dédiés à la mémoire de Louis Halphen*, 43–54

—— *Le Gouvernement d'Henri II Plantagenêt*, Paris 1956

—— 'L'Origine des familles seigneuriales dans la région de la Loire moyenne', *CCM* v (1962), 303–22

—— 'L'Éviction des tenants de Thibaut de Blois par Geoffroy Martel, comte d'Anjou en 1044', *Le Moyen Âge* lxix (1963), 141–9

—— 'Les Destinées de la Neustrie du IXe au XIe siècle', *CCM* xi (1968), 15–28

Bradbury, J., *Philip Augustus, king of France, 1180–1223*, London 1998

Brooke, C., *Monasteries of the world: the rise and development of the monastic tradition*, London 1974

Brundage, J. A., 'An errant crusader: Stephen of Blois', *Traditio* xvi (1960), 380–95

Brunterc'h, J., 'Le Duché du Maine et la marche de Bretagne', in H. Atsma (ed.), *La Neustrie: les pays au nord de la Loire de 65–850* (Beihefte der *Francia* xvi, 1989), i. 29–12

Bry de la Clergerie, G., *Histoire des pays et comté du Perche et duché d'Alençon*, Paris 1620, rev. P. Siguret, Paris 1970

—— *Additions aux recherches d'Alençon et du Perche*, Paris 1621

Bull, M., *Knightly piety and the lay response to the First Crusade: the Limousin and Gascony, c. 970–c. 1130*, Oxford 1993

—— 'The Capetian monarch and the early crusade movement: Hugh of Vermandois and Louis VII', *Nottingham Medieval Studies* xl (1996), 25–46

Bur, M., *La Formation du comté de Champagne v. 950–v. 1150*, Nancy 1977

—— 'Rôle et place de la Champagne dans le royaume de France au temps de Philippe-Auguste', in Bautier, *La France de Philippe Auguste*, 237–54

Burns, R. I., 'The significance of the frontier in the Middle Ages', in R. Bartlett and A. Mackay (eds), *Medieval frontier societies*, Oxford 1989, 307–30

Caille, J., *Hospitaux et charité publique à Narbonne au moyen âge*, Paris 1978

Carpenter, D., *The minority of Henry III*, Berkeley, CA 1990

Cazel, F. A., 'Intertwined careers: Hubert de Burgh and Peter des Roches', *Haskins Society Journal* i (1989), 174–5

Charles, L., *Histoire de la Ferté-Bernard*, Mamers 1877

'Chateaux forts et guerres au moyen âge', *Cahiers percherons* lviii (1978), 1–47

Chédeville, A., *Chartres et ses campagnes (XIe–XIIIe s.)*, Paris 1973

——'La Rôle de la monnaie et l'apparition du crédit dans le pays de l'ouest de la France xie–xiiie siècles', *CCM* xvii (1974), 305–25

Cheyette, F., 'Suum cuique tribuere', *French Historical Studies* vi (1970), 287–99

Chibnall, M., *The Empress Matilda: queen consort, queen mother and lady of the English*, Oxford 1991

—— 'Monastic foundations in England and Normandy, 1066–1189', in Bates and Curry, *England and Normandy in the Middle Ages*, 37–49

—— *The debate on the Norman Conquest*, Manchester 1999

Church, S., 'The rewards of service in the household of King John: a dissenting opinion', *EHR* cx (1995), 277–302

Colin A. and H. Capitant, *Traité de droit civil*, ed. L. Julliot de la Morandière, i, Paris 1957

Complete peerage of England, Scotland, Ireland, Great Britain and the United Kingdom, ed. G. E. Cokayne, London 1910–59

Corner, D., 'The *Gesta regis Henrici secundi* and the *Chronica* of Roger, parson of Howden', *Bulletin of the Institute of Historical Research* lvi (1983), 126–45

Coulson, C. H., 'Rendability and castellation in medieval France', in *Château-Gaillard*, VI: *Actes du colloque internationale tenu à Venlo . . .*, Caen 1973, 59–67

Cowdrey, H. E. J., *The Cluniacs and the Gregorian reform*, Oxford 1970

Crouch, D., 'Oddities in the early history of the marcher lordship of Gower, 1107–1166', *Bulletin of the Board of Celtic Studies* xxxi (1984), 133–41

—— *The Beaumont twins*, Cambridge 1986

—— *William Marshal: court, career and chivalry in the Angevin empire, 1147–1219*, London 1990

—— 'The administration of the Norman earldom', in A. T. Thacker (ed.), *The earldom of Chester and its charters: a tribute to Geoffrey Barraclough. Journal of the Chester Archaeological Society* lxxi (1991), 69–95

—— 'The local influence of the earls of Warwick, 1088–1242: a study in decline and resourcefulness', *Midland History* xxi (1996), 1–22

Cuissard, C., 'Chronologie des vicomtes de Châteaudun, 960–1395', *Bulletin de la Société dunoise* viii (1894/6), 25–120

Dauzat, A., *Dictionnaire étymologique des noms de famille et prénoms de France*, 3rd edn, Paris 1951

Davies, R. R., *Domination and conquest: the experience of Ireland, Scotland and Wales, 1100–1300*, Cambridge 1990

Davis, R. H. C., *The medieval warhorse: origin, development and redevelopment*, London 1989

—— *King Stephen*, 3rd edn, London 1990

Decaëns, J., 'La Motte de Rivray, chronique des fouilles médiévales', *Archéologie médiévale* xxii (1992), 489–9

—— 'Les Châteaux de la vallée de l'Huisne dans le Perche (R. Allen Brown Memorial lecture, 1994)', *ANS* xvii (1994), 1–20

Defourneaux, M., *Les Français en Espagne aux xie et xiie siècles*, Paris 1949

Delaporte Y. and E. Houvet, *Les Vitraux de la cathédrale de Chartres: histoire et description*, Chartres 1926

Delisle, L., *Le Cabinet des manuscrits de la Bibliothèque impériale*, Paris 1868–81

Delort, R. (ed.), *La France de l'an mil*, Paris 1990

Devailly, G., *Le Berry du Xe siècle au milieu du XIIIe siècle*, Paris 1973

Devroey, J., 'Un Monastère dans l'économie d'échanges: les services de transport à l'abbaye de Saint-Germain des Prés au IXe siècle', *Annales* xxxix (1984), 570–89

Dhondt, J., *Études sur la naissance des principautés territoriales en France (IXe–Xe siècle)*, Bruges 1948

Douët-d'Arcq, L.-C., *Collection des sceaux*, i, Paris 1863

Douglas, D. C., *William the Conqueror*, London 1964

Dubois, H., 'Le Commerce et les foires au temps de Philippe-Auguste', in Bautier, *La France de Philippe Auguste*, 689–711

Duby, G., 'Recherches sur l'evolution des institutions judiciaires pendant le xe et le xie siècle dans le sud de la Bourgogne', *Le Moyen Âge* 4th ser. i (1946), 149–94; ii (1948), 15–38, trans. as 'The evolution of judicial institutions', in his *The chivalrous society*, ed. C. Postan, London 1977, 15–58.

—— 'Le Budget de l'abbaye de Cluny entre 1080 et 1155', *Annales* vii (1952), 155–71

—— *La Société aux xie et xiie siècles dans la région mâconnaise*, Paris 1953

—— *L'Économie rurale et la vie des campagnes dans l'occident médiévale*, trans. as *Rural economy and country life in the medieval west*, London 1968

—— *Le Chevalier, la femme et le prêtre*, Paris 1981, trans. by B. Bray as *The knight, the lady and the priest*, London 1984

—— *Guillaume le maréchal, ou le meilleur chevalier du monde*, Paris 1984

Duchesne, A., *Histoire généalogique des maisons de Guines, d'Ardres, de Gand et de Coucy*, Paris 1621

Dumas, F., 'Les Monnaies normandes (xe–xiie siècles)', *Revue numismatique* 6e sér. xxi (1979), 84–140

——— 'La Monnaie dans le royaume au temps de Philippe-Auguste', in Bautier, *La France de Philippe-Auguste*, 541–72

Dunbabin, J., *France in the making, 843–1180*, 2nd edn, Oxford 2000

English, B., *The lords of Holderness, 1086–1260: a study in feudal society*, Oxford 1979

Estournet, G., 'Les Chartes de Franchard, prieuré de l'ordre de Saint-Augustin près Fontainebleau', *Annales de la Société historique et archéologique du Gâtinais* (1913), 275–369

Evergates, T., *Feudal society in the baillage of Troyes under the counts of Champagne, 1152–1284*, Baltimore 1975

Farmer, S., *Communities of St Martin: legend and ritual in medieval Tours*, Ithaca, NY 1991

Ferrante, J. M., 'Women's role in Latin letters from the fourth to the early twelfth century', in J. H. McCash (ed.), *The cultural patronage of medieval women*, Athens, GA 1996, 73–104

Ferreiro, A., 'The siege of Barbastro, 1064–5: a reassessment', *Journal of Medieval History* ix (1983), 129–44

Fletcher, R. A., 'Reconquest and crusade in Spain, c. 1050–1150', *TRHS* 5th ser. xxxvii (1987), 31–47

Fossier, R., 'La Naissance du village', in Delort, *La France de l'an mil*, 162–8

François, J. J., 'Les Domaines de l'abbaye de Saint-Germain au IXe siècle', *Mémoires de la Société archéologique d'Eure-et-Loir* xxvii (1974/7), 41–77

Gazeau, R., 'Glanfeuil', in *Dictionnaire d'histoire et de géographie écclesiastique*, xxi, ed. R. Aubert, Paris 1986, 142

Geary, P., 'Vivre en conflit dans une France sans état: typologie des mécanismes de règlement des conflits (1050–1200)', *Annales* xli (1986), 1107–33

George, R., 'The contribution of Flanders to the conquest of England, 1065–86', *Revue belge de philologie et d'histoire* v (1926), 81–96

Gillingham, J., *The Angevin empire*, London 1984

——— 'The art of kingship: Richard I, 1189–99', *History Today* (April 1985), 17–25, repr. in his *Richard Coeur de Lion: kingship, chivalry and war in the twelfth century*, London 1994, 95–103

——— *Richard I*, New Haven–London 1999

——— and J. C. Holt (eds), *War and government in the Middle Ages: essays in honour of J. O. Prestwich*, Woodbridge 1984

Giry, A., *Manuel de diplomatique*, Paris 1894

Gouverneur, A., *Essais historiques sur le Perche*, Nogent-le-Rotrou 1882

Grant, L., 'Suger and the Anglo-Norman world', *ANS* xix (1996), 51–68

——— *Abbot Suger of Saint-Denis: Church and State in early twelfth-century France*, London 1998

Green, J. A., 'Lords of the Norman Vexin', in Gillingham and Holt, *War and government*, 47–61

——— *The government of England under Henry I*, Cambridge 1986

——— 'Unity and disunity in the Anglo-Norman state', *Historical Research* lxiii (1989), 115–34

Grierson P. and M. Blackburn, *Medieval European coinage with a catalogue of the coins in the Fitzwilliam Museum Cambridge*, I: *Early Middle Ages (5th–10th centuries)*, Cambridge 1986

Griffiths, Q.,'The Capetian kings and Saint-Martin of Tours', *Studies in Medieval and Renaissance History* ix (1987), 83–134

Guenée, B., 'Les Généalogies entre l'histoire et la politique: la fierté d'être capétien en France au moyen âge', *Annales* xxx (1978), 450–74

Hallam, E., 'Henry II, Richard I and the order of Grandmont', *Journal of Medieval History* i (1975), 165–85

——— *Capetian France*, London 1980

Halphen, L., *Le Comté d'Anjou au XIe siècle*, Paris 1906

Haskins, C. H., 'The introduction of Arabic science into England', in his *Studies in the history of mediaeval science*, New York 1924, 113–29

Head, T., *Hagiography and the cult of saints: the diocese of Orléans, 800–1200*, Cambridge 1990

——— and R. Lander (eds), *The peace of God: social violence and religious response in France around the year 1000*, Ithaca, NY 1992

Heliot, P., 'Sur les résidences princières bâties en France du Xe–XIIe siècle', *Le Moyen Âge* lxi (1955), 27–61, 291–317

Hill, J. W. F., *Medieval Lincoln*, Cambridge 1948

Hollister, C. W., 'The Anglo-Norman succession debate of 1126', *Journal of Medieval History* i (1975), 19–39, repr. in his *Monarchy, magnates and institutions*, 145–69

——— 'Normandy, France and the Anglo-Norman *regnum*', *Speculum* li (1976), 202–42

——— 'The origins of the English treasury', *English Historical Review* xciii (1978), 262–75, repr. in his *Monarchy, magnates and institutions*, 209–22

——— 'War and diplomacy in the Anglo-Norman world: the reign of Henry I', *ANS* vi (1983), 72–88, repr. in his *Monarchy, magnates and institutions*, 273–90

——— *Monarchy, magnates and institutions in the Anglo-Norman world*, London 1986

Holt, J. C., 'Politics and property in the early Middle Ages', *Past & Present* lvii (1972), 3–52

——— 'The end of the Anglo-Norman realm', *Proceedings of the British Academy* lxi (1973), 3–45, repr. in his *Magna Carta and medieval government*, London 1985, 23–66

——— 'Feudal society and the family in early medieval England, I: The revolution of 1066', *TRHS* 5th ser. xxxii (1982), 193–212; 'II: Notions of patrimony', xxxiii (1983), 193–220; 'III: Patronage and politics', xxxiv (1984), 1–25; 'IV: The heiress and the alien', xxxv (1985), 1–28

——— 'The loss of Normandy and royal finance', in Gillingham and Holt, *War and government*, 92–105

Hunt, N., *Cluny under St Hugh, 1049–1109*, London 1967

James, E., *The origins of France: from Clovis to the Capetians, 500–1000*, London 1982

Jeanne, D., 'Quelles Problématiques pour la mort du lépreux? Sondages archéologiques du cimitière de Saint-Nicholas de la Chesnaie-Bayeux', *Annales de Normandie* xlvii (1997), 69–90

Jordan, K., *Henry the Lion*, Oxford 1986

Keats-Rohan, K. S. B., 'Le Rôle des bretons dans la politique de colonisation normande à l'Angleterre', *Mémoires de la Société d'histoire et d'archéologie de Bretagne* lxxiv (1996), 181–215

Keefe, T. K., 'Proffers for heirs and heiresses in the pipe rolls: some observations on indebtedness in the years before the Magna Carta', *Haskins Society Journal* v (1993), 99–109

King, E. J., 'Mountsorrell and its region in King Stephen's reign', *Huntington Library Quarterly* xliv (1980), 1–10

Lacarra, J. M., 'La conquista de Zaragoza por Alfonso I', *Al-Andalus* xii (1947), 65–96

Laliena Corbera, C., '*Larga stipendia et optima praedia*: les nobles *francos* en Aragon au service d'Alphonse le batailleur', *Annales du midi* cxii (2000), 149–69

Landon, L., *The itinerary of King Richard I* (PRS n.s. xiii, 1935)

Langmuir, G., '*Judei nostri* and the beginning of Capetian legislation', *Traditio* xvi (1960), 203–39

Lemarignier, J.-F., 'La Dislocation du *pagus* et le problème des *consuetudines*', in *Mélanges d'histoire dédiés à la mémoire de Louis Halphen*, 401–10

———— 'Le Domaine de Villeberfol et le patrimoine de Marmoutier (XIe siècle)', in *Études d'histoire du droit privé offertes à Pierre Petot*, Paris 1959, 347–62

———— *Le Gouvernment royal aux premiers temps capétiens (987–1108)*, Paris 1965

Lemoine, A., 'Chennebrun: un bourg castral au coeur des conflits franco-normands du xiie siècle', *Annales de Normandie* xlviii (1998), 525–44

Le Patourel, J., *The Norman empire*, Oxford 1976

Le Roy Ladurie E. and Z. Zysberg, 'Géographie des hagiotoponyms en France', *Annales* xxxviii (1983), 1304–35

Lewis, A. W., '*Royal succession in Capetian France: studies in family order and the state*, Boston 1981

———— '14 charters of Robert I of Dreux (1152–1188)', *Traditio* xli (1985), 145–80

Lewis, C. P., 'The French in England before the Norman Conquest', *ANS* xvii (1994), 123–44

Leyser, H. *Hermits and the new monasticism*, London 1984

Lifshitz, F., 'The migration of Neustrian relics in the Viking Age: the myth of voluntary exodus, the reality of coercion and theft', *Early Medieval Europe* iv (1995), 175–92

Lo Prete, K., 'The Anglo-Norman card of Adela of Blois', *Albion* xxii (1990), 569–89

———— 'Adela of Blois and Ivo of Chartres: piety, politics and the peace in the diocese of Chartres', *ANS* xiv (1991), 131–53.

Lot, F., 'La *Vicaria* et le *vicarius*', *Nouvelle Revue historique de droit français et étranger* xvii (1893), 281–301

Louise, G., 'La Seigneurie de Bellême xe–xiie siècles: dévolution des pouvoirs territoriaux et construction d'une seigneurie de frontière aux confins de la Normandie et du Maine à la charnière de l'an mil', *Le Pays bas-normand*, nos cxcix–cc (1990), 1–429; cci–ccii (1991), 1–349

Lourie, E., 'The will of Alfonso I, "el batallador", king of Aragon and Navarre: a reassessment', *Speculum* l (1975), 635–51

Lowenfeld, S., 'Documents relatifs à la croisade de Guillaume comte de Ponthieu', *Archives de l'orient latin*, Paris 1881–4, ii. 251–5

Luchaire, A., *Études sur les actes de Louis VII*, Paris 1885

McCrank, L. J., 'Norman crusaders in the Catalan reconquest: Robert Burdet and the principality of Tarragona', *Journal of Medieval History* vii (1981), 67–82

Maier, C. T., 'Crisis, liturgy and the crusade in the twelfth and thirteenth centuries', *Journal of Ecclesiastical History* xlviii (1997), 628–57

Mars, N., *Histoire du royale monastère de Sainct-Lomer de Blois . . . 1646*, ed. A. Dupré, Blois 1869

Martindale, J., 'The French aristocracy in the early Middle Ages: a reappraisal', *Past & Present* lxxv (1977), 5–45

Mélanges d'histoire du moyen âge, dédiés à la mémoire de Louis Halphen, Paris 1951

de la Motte-Callas, M., 'Les Possessions territoriales de l'abbaye de Saint-Germain des Prés du début du IXe au début du XIIe siècle', in *Mémorial du XIVe centenaire de l'abbaye de Saint-Germain-des-Prés*, Paris 1957, 49–80

des Murs, M. O., *Histoire des comtes du Perche de la famille des Rotrou de 943 à 1231*, Nogent-le-Rotrou 1856

Musset, R., 'Le Perche – nom du pays', *Annales de géographie* xxviii (1919), 342–59

———— 'Le Relief du Perche', *Annales de géographie* xxix (1920), 99–126

Myers, G. R., 'The manuscripts of the old French crusade cycle', in J. A. Nelson and E. J. Mickel (eds), *The old French crusade cycle*, i, Birmingham, AL 1977, pp. xiii–lxxxviii

Nelson, J., *Charles the Bald*, London 1992

Nelson, L., 'Rotrou of Perche and the Aragonese reconquest', *Traditio* xxvi (1970), 113–33

Norgate, K., *England under the Angevin kings*, London 1887

O'Callaghan, J. F., *A history of medieval Spain*, Ithaca, NY 1975

Pacaut, M., *Louis VII et les élections épiscopales dans le royaume de France*, Paris 1957

Painter, S., *William Marshal*, Baltimore 1933

Pelatan, J., 'Les Chemins finéraux: leur rôle dans le maintien des structures rurales: l'exemple des confins bocage-openfield dans l'ouest du bassin parisien', *Revue géographique de l'est* xxiii (1983), 359–67

Phillips, J., *Defenders of the Holy Land: relations between the Latin east and the west, 1119–1187*, Oxford 1996

Poey d'Avant, F., *Monnaies féodales de France*, Paris 1858–61

Poly, J.-P., *Le Provence et la société féodale, 879–1166*, Paris 1976

Poncelet, A., 'Les Saints de Micy', *Analecta Bollandiana* xxiv (1905), 5–104

Powicke, F. M., *The loss of Normandy*, 2nd edn, Manchester 1960

Proust, S., *Inventaire sommaire des archives des hospices de Nogent-le-Rotrou depuis leur fondation jusqu'à 1790*, Nogent-le-Rotrou 1869

Queller, D., *The Fourth Crusade: the conquest of Constantinople, 1201–4*, Leicester 1978

Randsborg, K., *The first millennium AD in Europe and the mediterranean: an archaeological essay*, Cambridge 1991

Renoux, A., 'Les Fortifications de terre en Europe occidentale du Xe au XIIe siècles: rapport', *Archéologie médiévale* xi (1981), 31–2

Reynolds, S., 'The rulers of London in the twelfth century', *History* lvii (1972), 337–57

———— *Fiefs and vassals: the medieval evidence reinterpreted*, Oxford 1994

Richard, A., *Histoire des comtes de Poitou (778–1204)*, Paris 1903

Riley-Smith, J., *The first crusaders (1095–1131)*, Cambridge 1997

de Romanet, O., *Géographie du Perche et chronologie de ses comtes suivies de pièces justificatives formant le cartulaire de cette province*, Mortagne 1890–1902

Round, J. H., *Geoffrey de Mandeville*, London 1892

Sanders, I., *English baronies*, Oxford 1960

Siguret, P., 'Recherches sur la formation du comté du Perche', *Bulletin de la Société historique et archéologique de l'Orne* lxxix (1961), 17–39; lxxx (1962), 3–42

Smith, J. B., 'The treaty of Lambeth, 1217', *EHR* xciv (1979), 562–79

Southern, R. W., *The making of the Middle Ages*, London 1953

Spufford, P., *Money and its use in medieval Europe*, Cambridge 1988

Stafford, P., *Queens, concubines and dowagers: the king's wife in the early Middle Ages*, Leicester 1998

Sumberg, L. A. M., *La Chanson d'Antioche: étude historique et littéraire*, Paris 1968

Tabuteau, E. Z., 'The family of Moulins-la-Marche in the eleventh century', *Medieval Prosopography* xiii (1992), 29–65

Thompson, K., 'Family and influence to the south of Normandy in the eleventh century: the lordship of Bellême', *Journal of Medieval History* xi (1985), 215–26

—— 'Robert of Bellême reconsidered', *ANS* xiii (1990), 263–86

—— 'William Talvas, count of Ponthieu, and the politics of the Anglo-Norman realm', in Bates and Curry, *England and Normandy*, 169–84

—— 'The lords of Laigle: ambition and insecurity on the borders of Normandy', *ANS* xviii (1995), 177–99.

—— 'Dowry and inheritance patterns: some examples from the descendants of King Henry I of England', *Medieval Prosopography* xvii/2 (1996), 45–61

—— 'The formation of the county of Perche: the rise and fall of the house of Gouet', in K. S. B. Keats-Rohan (ed.), *Family trees and the roots of politics: the prosopography of Britain and France from the tenth to the twelfth century*, Woodbridge 1997, 299–314

—— 'Family tradition and the crusading impulse', *Medieval Prosopography* xix (1998), 1–33

Tout, T. F., 'The fair of Lincoln and the "Histoire de Guillaume la maréchal" ', *EHR* xviii (1903), 240–67

Turner, R. V., 'Simon of Pattishall', *Northamptonshire Past and Present* vi (1978), 5–14

—— 'The reputation of royal judges under the Angevin kings', *Albion* xi (1979), 301–16, repr. in his *Judges, administrators and the common law in Angevin England*, London 1994, 103–18

—— *King John*, London 1994

—— 'Good or bad kingship? The case of Richard Lionheart', *Haskins Society Journal* viii (1996), 63–78

de Vajay, S., 'Ramire II le moine roi d'Aragon et Agnès de Poitou dans l'histoire et dans la légende', in P. Gallais and Y.-J. Riou (eds), *Mélanges offertes à René Crozet*, Poitiers 1966, 727–50

VCH, *Berkshire*, ii, London 1907

Vincent, N., *Peter des Roches: an alien in English politics, 1205–1238*, Cambridge 1996

von Walter, J., 'Bernard de Thiron', *Bulletin de la Commission historique et archéologique de la Mayenne* 2nd sér xxiv (1908), 385–410

Warren, W. L., *King John*, London 1961
——— *Henry II*, London 1973
Werner, K. F., 'Untersuchungen zur Frühzeit des französischen Furstentums (9.–10. Jahrhundert)', *Welt als Geschichte* xviii (1958), 256–89; xix (1959), 146–93; xx (1960), 87–119
——— 'L'Acquisition par la maison de Blois des comtes de Chartres et de Châteaudun', in *Mélanges de numismatique, d'archéologie et d'histoire offerts à Jean Lafaurie*, Paris 1980, 265–74
White, S. D., *'Pactum legem vincit et amor judicium*: the settlement of disputes by compromise in eleventh-century France', *American Journal of Legal History* xxii (1978), 281–308
——— 'Inheritances and legal arguments in western France, 1050–1150', *Traditio* xliii (1987), 55–103
Wickham, C., 'European forests in the early Middle Ages: landscape and land clearance', in *L'ambiente vegetale nell'alto medioevo* (Settimane di studio del Centro Italiano di Studi sull'alto Medioevo xxxvii, 1990), 523–8
Williams, A., *The English and the Norman Conquest*, Woodbridge 1995
Yver, J., *Égalité entre héritiers et exclusion des enfants dotés: essai de géographie coutumière*, Paris 1966

Unpublished dissertations

Stevenson, W., 'England and Normandy, 1204–1259', PhD diss. Leeds 1974
Thompson, K., 'Cross-Channel estates of the Montgomery-Bellême family', MA diss. Cardiff 1983
——— 'The counts of the Perche, c. 1066–1217', PhD diss. Sheffield 1995

Index

219